Liberating Language

Sites of Rhetorical Education in Nineteenth-Century Black America

Shirley Wilson Logan

Southern Illinois University Press • Carbondale

11 10 09 08   4 3 2 1

Library of Congress Cataloging-in-Publication Data
Logan, Shirley W. (Shirley Wilson), date.
  Liberating language : sites of rhetorical education in nine-
teenth-century black America / Shirley Wilson Logan.
     p. cm.
  Includes bibliographical references and index.
  ISBN-13: 978-0-8093-2872-7 (alk. paper)
  ISBN-10: 0-8093-2872-0 (alk. paper)
  1. English language—Rhetoric—Study and teaching—
United States—History—19th century. 2. African Ameri-
cans—Education—United States—History—19th century.
3. Literacy—Social aspects—United States—History—
19th century. 4. Rhetoric—Study and teaching—United
States—History—19th century. 5. Persuasion (Rhetoric)—
History—19th century. I.Title.
  PE1405.U6L64 2008
  808'.042071—dc22   2008004009

I dedicate this work to my mother, father, and stepmother—
Azzie Lee Ellis Wilson, John Theodore Wilson, and
Nelsie T. Wilson Johnson

Could we trace the record of every human heart, the aspirations of every immortal soul, perhaps we would find no man so imbruted and degraded that we could not trace the word liberty either written in living characters upon the soul or hidden away in some nook or corner of the heart.

—Frances Harper, 1857

Contents

Acknowledgments

First, I have been blessed with a loving, supportive family for whom I am constantly thankful—John, Enid, Malcolm, Youlanda, Monica, Chandler Elise, and an amazing host of others. I also appreciate colleagues who suggested sites of rhetorical education and pointed me in the right direction. I benefited greatly from the advice of two persistent anonymous reviewers. There are few services to the profession more valuable than a close critical reading of a work in progress, and I thank them. My work on this project was supported by the Department of English and the College of Arts and Humanities at the University of Maryland, as well as by fellowships from the American Association of University Women and the National Endowment for the Humanities. I also thank the editorial staff at SIU Press for guiding me through this process again.

Liberating Language

Introduction

"By the Way, Where Did You Learn to Speak?"

For centuries, curious observers have asked black speakers and writers, "Where did you learn to use the English language so effectively?" Determined to answer this question, eighteen of Boston's leading citizens put Phillis Wheatley through an extensive oral examination and pronounced her, even though "brought an uncultivated Barbarian from Africa," sufficiently "qualified to write" her 1773 *Poems on Various Subjects*.[1] The resulting papers of authentication, as one introduction to Wheatley suggests, "helped establish a convention, a kind of interracial literary etiquette, that white readers soon came to expect when encountering an African American author."[2]

Although no records suggest that Lucy Terry Prince was ever called before an examining board, a certain amount of skepticism is associated with accounts of her rhetorical acumen and the situations in which it was demonstrated. Prince, author of "Bars Fight" (1746), considered to be the first extant poem by an African American, was taken from Africa in 1730 and sold to a Deerfield, Massachusetts, innkeeper. She married Abijah Prince and purchased her freedom in 1756; they moved in 1780 to Guilford, Vermont, with their six children and settled on 100 acres of newly acquired land. Her obituary includes the claim that "the fluency of her speech captivated all around her" and that she "was not destitute of instruction and education."[3] According to some accounts, Prince used her rhetorical abilities to argue against the denial of admission of her son into Williams College "in a '3-hour speech' before the trustees, quoting abundantly text after text from the scriptures to support her claims for his reception." David Proper explores several problems in trying to authenticate this event, including the fact that candidates for admission to Williams were required to know Latin and Greek, or French, knowledge the school in Guilford would have been unable to provide Prince's son, although he could have been privately schooled.[4] A second rhetorical performance attributed to Prince is that she argued to protect their Vermont land claim before Supreme Court justice Samuel Chase of Maryland in 1796. Chase is reported to have given Prince the compliment that she "made a better argument than he had ever heard from a lawyer in Vermont." In her article "Women Advocates before the Supreme Court," Claire Cushman places Prince at the front of a long line of women Supreme Court advocates. Cushman concludes that Prince probably argued before Justice Chase when he was riding circuit in Vermont in 1796, during a period when Supreme Court justices also presided over circuit courts—still a remarkable accomplishment.[5] The questions surrounding Prince have had more to do with the occasions of her rhetorical performances than with her rhetorical skills.

The authenticating documents attached to slave narratives attesting to an author's literacy represent later attempts to answer this question.[6] In his preface to Frederick Douglass's *Narrative,* William Lloyd Garrison wrote that Douglass had written it "in his own style, and according to the best of his ability," and that it was "entirely his own production."[7] These same kinds of supporting documents, white-authored texts, like Garrison's letter attesting to Douglass's character and, just as important, to his literacy, surround the narratives of Harriet Jacobs and others for whom their readers needed the authentication of white society. In 2002, literacy questions swirled around authorship of the recently discovered manuscript "The Bondwoman's Narrative By Hannah Crafts A Fugitive Slave Recently Escaped from North Carolina." The central literacy question then was that if the manuscript is indeed autobiographical, how did the author develop the rhetorical skills to write her story? Most of the essays in the collection *In Search of Hannah Crafts: Critical Essays on "The Bondwoman's Narrative"* attempt in some way to answer this literacy-based question.

A twentieth-century fictional version of this question appears in Ralph Ellison's *Invisible Man* (1947) when the protagonist, having incited a riot by addressing a crowd at the scene of a Harlem eviction, flees the scene followed by Brother Jack, a member of the Brotherhood. When Brother Jack catches up with him, he puzzles, "You know, I haven't heard such an effective piece of eloquence since the days when I was in—well, in a long time. You aroused them so quickly to action, I don't understand how you managed it. If only some of *our* speakers could have listened!" He goes on finally to ask, "By the way, where did you learn to speak?" When the invisible man answers, "Nowhere," the man responds, "Then you're very talented. You are a natural. It's hard to believe."[8] It is this curiosity, especially of white inquirers, that fuels questions about rhetorical ability, leading one insightful graduate student to ask, following the presentation of an early paper on this project, "Why spend time answering a 'white' question?" I replied that it was not solely a white question; it was a question whose answer could broaden our approaches to contemporary rhetorical education and thereby help to further participation in democracy. Around the time that I was drafting this introduction, Senator Joe Biden was trying to interpret his comments that, among other attributes, Senator Barack Obama was "articulate." While some claimed not to understand the objections raised to this apparent compliment, I—and I suspect most other African Americans of a certain age—understood very well the impact of this, as Anna Perez, former communications counselor to Condoleezza Rice, called the attribution in this context a form of "soft bigotry."[9] So, I want to make it clear that my question about rhetorical education is not an interrogation of the "articulate" black person. I have written elsewhere about the freighted use of this expression several years ago, so it's not a new issue.[10] I interrogate here how African Americans, especially in the century that finally recognized their right to themselves, acquired and developed the rhetorical astuteness to negotiate a hostile environment and at the same time established a common language employed both to interact with and to challenge and change this environment, shared among one another in the variety of rhetorical situations explored here.

I use the term "rhetorical education" to mean various combinations of experiences influencing how people understand and practice effective communication. Rhetorical theorist Kenneth Burke describes rhetoric functionally as "the use of language as a means of inducing cooperation in beings that by nature respond to symbols."[11] Rhetorical education occurs at the intersection of symbol use and symbol reception. It informs both rhetorical production and rhetorical response. Sites of rhetorical education are located in those spaces where people and language and a need to communicate come together to create what Lloyd Bitzer calls a rhetorical situation; this situation becomes a site of rhetorical education when learning about rhetoric occurs. This rhetorical education for nineteenth-century African Americans rarely included explicit training in rhetorical theory or direct instruction in rhetorical performance, but the application of theoretical principles occurred nonetheless. Aristotle writes in his introduction to the *Rhetoric* that "ordinary people" make use of rhetoric, "either at random or through practice and from acquired habit," adding that it is "possible to inquire the reason why some speakers succeed through practice and others spontaneously."[12] It follows, then, that people develop and apply rhetorical skills in a variety of ways. Literacy education and rhetorical education are closely associated terms, frequently used synonymously. While literacy has been linked historically to writing, the term also offers a way to conceptualize "underlying language abilities that may be common to both reading and writing."[13] Literacy is the broader term, the ground upon which rhetorical education develops. Some manifestation of literacy, then, is implicated in one's rhetorical abilities. With this definition of literacy and rhetorical education, we can admit the experiences of such rhetors as Sojourner Truth into consideration, though conventional definitions would classify her as illiterate.[14] Jacqueline Jones Royster in *Traces of a Stream: Literacy and Social Change among African American Women* offers a definition of literacy that takes into account the combined abilities it demonstrates; it intersects comfortably with my own. She defines it as the "ability to gain access to information and to use this information variously to articulate lives and experiences and also to identify, think through, refine, and solve problems, sometimes complex problems, over time."[15] While Royster's definition of literacy is more action-oriented than the definition of the kinds of rhetorical abilities I identify in these sites, these abilities often did lead to action. I am primarily interested in development of these abilities; Royster, as the title of her book indicates, targets literacy as a critical component of social change.

I define a site of rhetorical education as involving the act of communicating or receiving information through writing, speaking, reading, or listening. Clearly the classrooms of nineteenth- and early-twentieth-century historically black college and universities (HBCUs) were important structured sites of such activities. A careful study of rhetorical education in these sites is beyond the scope of this volume, which focuses primarily on non-school settings. A good deal of important research has begun to highlight HBCU rhetorical education at the end of the nineteenth century and the beginning of the twentieth. In their article on African Americans in the history of composition studies, "History in the Spaces Left," Royster and Jean C. Williams emphasize the role played by HBCUs and black professional groups, like the College Language Association, in the rhetorical education of black students. These authors call for more attention to the rhetorical activities of historically marginalized students classified as other than "basic writers," with the term's attendant assumptions with respect to limitations, deficiencies, and racially marked identities. Some who have responded to this call to reconstruct histories of rhetorical education in HBCUs include Susan C. Jarratt, Scott Zaluda, and David Gold. Jarratt's work on classical training at Fisk and Atlanta universities demonstrates the extent to which black institutions sustained a more clearly articulated link between classical training and public discourse than other universities where the study of literature was separated from the civic discourse of the community. Jarratt draws on the views of W. E. B. Du Bois, who was affiliated with both institutions. Gold's work on Melvin Tolson and rhetorical education at Wiley College, a black liberal arts school in northeast Texas, highlights the complexities of employing the techniques of classical rhetoric in subversive teaching. Zaluda looks at the writing assignments at Howard University between 1919 and 1931, concluding that while most held the students to strict, conservative, "good English" requirements with respect to style and arrangement, the writing prompts frequently—and in my view, not surprisingly—encouraged topics that critiqued heavily racialized external constructions of reality.[16] Although many of the rhetors I consider received a solid rhetorical education in black colleges and normal schools, I am more interested in the ways they augmented that formal training outside of school or in college-based literary clubs.

The edited collection by Cheryl Glenn, Margaret M. Lyday, and Wendy B. Sharer, *Rhetorical Education in America,* brings together a range of perspectives on this topic of teaching rhetoric, reminding us, as Glenn points out in the introduction, that "the relationship of rhetoric to education and the ways that rhetorical awareness is developed in educational institutions still remains to be clearly and fully articulated."[17] We don't yet fully understand the distinction between the rhetoric of teaching and the teaching of rhetoric.

Several scholars are also considering black sites of rhetorical education in the twentieth century. In her study of literacy training in the Citizenship School Program between 1957 and 1970, Susan Kates points out that while civil rights scholars have written about the citizenship schools as a significant part of American history, education historians rarely consider what this history might tell us about teaching literacy skills in the twenty-first century. Stephen Schneider's article "Freedom Schooling: Stokely Carmichael and Critical Rhetorical Education" explores further the relationship between the political and pedagogical aims in Stokely Carmichael's pedagogy.[18]

This study also does not separately address questions of how African Americans learn to read and write the English language, which I refer to as basic literacy skills. Studies like James D. Anderson's 1988 book *The Education of Blacks in the South, 1860–1935* and articles in the *Journal of Negro Education* have made deep inroads into that history. Carter G. Woodson's *The Mis-Education of the Negro* offers a historical critique of many assumptions informing how blacks of all ages have been educated. Vincent P. Franklin and James D. Anderson's collection of essays *New Perspectives on Black Educational History* records histories of structured attempts to provide educational opportunities for African Americans, for example, in settings like the Institute for Colored Youth in Philadelphia, Hampton Institute in Virginia, Ware High School in Augusta, the Michigan Avenue YMCA in Buffalo, and the Meharry Medical College in Tennessee. These studies tend to consider large-scale acquisition of education. I am more interested in specific instances of rhetorical education that support what has already been generally established with concrete examples and that add new sites, not yet fully analyzed. For example, Dorothy Porter's seminal article "The Organized Educational Activities of Negro Literary Societies, 1828–1846" carefully documents the establishment of literary and benevolent societies in antebellum America, providing dates, locations, and key organizers. Elizabeth McHenry's important volume *Forgotten Readers* extends the work of Porter by considering specific instances of literary society activity, especially in antebellum Philadelphia, Boston, and New York, examining literary activities in the pages of the *Woman's Era* and the activities of the Saturday Nighters in the 1920s, and concluding with an assessment of current book club activities. In chapter 3 of this volume, I look at what tended to happen in gatherings of those groups, with an emphasis on the participants' rhetorical activities and how their participation enhanced their ability to influence public discourse.

To return, then, to a paraphrased version of Brother Jack's question: "Where *did* they learn to speak?" What were some sites of black rhetorical instruction, particularly in the nineteenth century? To answer these questions, I discuss manifestations of rhetorical training in the following sites: free-floating scenes of literacy; self-education in oratory and elocution; literary societies, broadly understood as collective social efforts to improve communicative skills; and the black press.

Chapter 1 takes its title, "Free-Floating Literacy: Early African American Rhetorical Traditions," from Ralph Ellison, who, in commenting on Henry Gates's recovery of Harriet Wilson's 1859 novel *Our Nig*—at that time thought to be the first novel ever written in English by a black woman—said, "Professor Gates' discovery confirms my suspicion that there was more 'free-floating' literacy available to Negroes than has been assumed."[19] The term captures the spirit of settings in which various levels of literacy and their attendant rhetorical skills were acquired and developed. They include white-sponsored slave missions and initiatives emerging from within communities of the enslaved. These sites of literacy frequently developed independently but were more often interdependent in the ways they shaped early rhetorical education. I also discuss some of the rhetorical activities that took place among the black Union regiments during the Civil War. It turns out that in many campsites, black soldiers were learning to read and write; others were corresponding with the editors of black newspapers and editing their own camp-based papers; and some formed literary associations. I consider one site following on the heels of emancipation, the activities of the Republican Loyal League, and the ways in which its efforts to transform newly enfranchised black men into political agents also advanced their rhetorical skills. I close this chapter with a coda on rhetorical education in cigar factories at the end of the nineteenth century, where, in some locations, black and white Cuban émigrés worked together while lectors read novels, newspapers, and other material chosen by the workers. The issues these readings raised generally stimulated heated discussion and thus opportunity to hone argumentative skills.

In chapter 2, "Private Learners: Self-Education in Rhetoric," portions of the diaries of Charlotte Forten Grimké, Frances Rollin, Mary Virginia Montgomery, Laura Hamilton Murray, Ida B. Wells, and Charles W. Chesnutt provide valuable insights into the motivations for their reading and writing practices, as well as their responses to oral performances. Their entries also describe the aspirations that their developing literacies supported. I make the point that these diarists understood rhetorical education as a means of race advancement. But while the desire to engage and counter the effects of slavery and racism motivated much of their push to develop rhetorical acumen, their quests should not be understood in racial terms alone. Their pursuits also brought them much pleasure. I close this chapter by looking at a few of the many advice manuals, including *The College of Life,* republished as *The Afro-American Home Manual and Practical Self-Educator,* popular during this period among individuals engaged in self-improvement.

As would be expected, literary societies provided the most clearly defined examples of rhetorical education, since they were generally formed to support a variety of "literary" activities in the nineteenth-century sense of the term, that is, involving the full gamut of rhetorical arts—reading, writing, speaking, listening—rather than in the contemporary sense of book clubs, with all members reading and then coming together to discuss the same book. The nineteenth-century associations supported elocutionary activities, debates, dramatic performances, public meetings, subscription libraries, schools, and various kinds of publications. In chapter 3, "Mental Feasts: Literary and Educational Societies and Lyceums," I consider selected gatherings of African Americans for any combination of these kinds of activities from the late 1820s to the end of the nineteenth century, primarily in Philadelphia and New York, both single sex and mixed, church-affiliated, school-affiliated, and community-based. I consider implicit and explicit rhetorical principles in five addresses to literary societies: William Hamilton's 1809 address to the New York African Society for Mutual Relief, William Whipper's 1828 address to the Colored Reading Society of Philadelphia for Mental Improvement, William G. Allen's 1852 address to the Dialexian Society at Central College, Charles Chesnutt's 1881 postbellum address at a meeting of the Normal Literary Society of Fayetteville, and Frances Harper's 1892 address to the Brooklyn Literary Union. This chapter demonstrates the central role literary societies played in African

American rhetorical education, overlapping with and connecting self-education and rhetorical education in the black press.

The pages of black periodicals are filled with references to lectures, rhetorical exercises, speeches, and eloquence in general. In chapter 4, "Organs of Propaganda: Rhetorical Education and the Black Press," I argue that this institution functioned as a site of rhetorical education in at least three ways: through the rhetorical training that the production of these periodicals provided, through direct subscriber instruction in rhetorical principles, and through critiques of rhetorical performances. After discussing the reflections of newspaper editors Frederick Douglass and Ida B. Wells on their publishing experiences, I consider first rhetorical education as disseminated through direct instruction in or promotion of the principles of rhetoric, such as in essays on elocution or eloquence. I then look at examples of rhetorical education indirectly enacted through sermons; through abolitionist and proslavery treatises; through lecturers at events sponsored by literary societies; and through the critique of speakers as diverse as Louis Kossuth, William J. Watkins, William Lloyd Garrison, and Frances Harper. Digitized versions of the antebellum and midcentury papers *Freedom's Journal*, the *North Star, Frederick Douglass' Paper*, the *Provincial Freeman*, and the *Christian Recorder* facilitated searches of these publications. I also draw examples from late-century newspapers including the *Indianapolis Freeman*, the *New York Freeman (Age)*, the *AME Church Review*, and the *Woman's Era*.

Moral improvement, broad knowledge, diligent and consistent effort, imitation of good models, and consistent practice—the five means of improving eloquence that Hugh Blair outlines in Lecture 34 of his *Lectures on Rhetoric and Belles Lettres*—frame my examination of these publications. As the editors of the 2005 edition of his *Lectures* point out, "Blair's is not an emancipatory rhetoric but one complicit with dominant ideologies."[20] I chose to apply his rhetorical principles to these texts because of the broad influence of his *Lectures* on African American and white rhetors. *Lectures* was a standard text across the nineteenth century in schools but also in literary societies and in homes. *The Columbian Orator,* to which Frederick Douglass attributes much of his early rhetorical training, contains two pieces by Blair. In remarks to the American Moral Reform Society in 1837, John Francis Cook, a black Washington, D.C., educator and Presbyterian minister, quotes from Blair's definition of charity.[21] Toward the end of the century, Blair's influence continued. In the late 1870s, Charles Chesnutt copied pages from Blair's lectures and discussed them in his journal. He also refers to Blair's advice on speech preparation in his 1881 address to the Normal Literary Society of Fayetteville. Commentary on the divisions of style from Blair is included in the popular 1895 conduct book *The College of Life or Practical Self-Educator: A Manual of Self-Improvement for the Colored*

Race, discussed in chapter 2. David Holmes observes that when contemporary rhetoric and composition scholars read Blair, we "should be able to recognize his participation in racialized discourses of his time and to understand more clearly the connections between rhetorical theory and the racist ideologies of the eighteenth century."[22] I suspect that nineteenth-century African American writers and speakers took from such texts, most not written with them in mind, what they could use to claim their own right to participate in various discourses.

Across all chapters, I draw on the experiences of various black rhetors of the era, including Frederick Douglass, Frances Harper, Fanny Coppin, Charles Chesnutt, and Ida Wells, but also on the experiences of extraordinary but less well-known rhetors like Oberlin-educated Mary Virginia Montgomery of Davis Bend, Mississippi; "Uncle Jack," a Virginia slave preacher; Elizabeth Johnson Harris of Augusta, Georgia; and "Mrs. Lee," a former slave from Florida, making some cautious generalizations from their experiences to a wider population. They were preachers, journalists, authors, teachers, antislavery lecturers, and school administrators. Paying attention to specific practices helps us understand how individual learners acquired various categories of literacy and rhetorical education. Not that we could or should attempt to replicate these bygone sites, but understanding them might help us to imagine rhetorical education in ways appropriate to current instruction. Students who have been historically marginalized need to be better prepared to understand and respond to the ways in which language is used to control and deceive as well as to inform and persuade. In their article on the usefulness of classical rhetoric in first-year college writing courses, Jeanne Fahnestock and Marie Secor remind us that "[w]e teach rhetoric to give people power against rhetoric. . . . We teach rhetoric to give people power against social and material differences. This is not to say that such education has been equally accessible to all throughout history; it has been monopolized by the powerful. But the response to that imperfect condition—that exigence—may be to make rhetorical competence more available to more people."[23] This study will expand our understanding of the various ways in which African Americans, faced with the consequences of enslavement and oppressive color prejudice, acquired rhetorical competence during the late eighteenth century and across the nineteenth century.

1

Free-Floating Literacy
Early African American Rhetorical Traditions

There was much more free-floating literacy among the slave community than any of us ever dreamed.

—Ralph Ellison, 1984

Learning English, learning to speak the alien tongue, was one way enslaved Africans began to reclaim their personal power within a context of domination. Possessing a shared language, black folks could find again a way to make community, and a means to create the political solidarity necessary to resist.

—bell hooks, 1994

In considering the ways in which the first African Americans acquired various forms of rhetorical education, we must remember that this obtained literacy was a literacy in the English language. While this might seem to be an obvious point, I state it here to distinguish lack of literacy in a particular language from lack of intelligence, a distinction often lost in much of the discourse regarding slave literacy. William D. Piersen observes that slaves "were not speaking English like idiots, but like Africans," adding that Africans who matured speaking another language were often considered less intelligent than those who were born in English-speaking countries. Many who spoke broken English also spoke other European languages—Portuguese, French, Spanish—they had acquired during their travels, along with their languages of origin. Even descriptions of runaways often included an assessment of their English skills.[1] As bell hooks points out, enslaved Africans soon recognized the need to master the language of their new surroundings in order to communicate with one another and "to reclaim their personal power within a context of domination."² Many of these early encounters with English literacy were surreptitious and were often facilitated by missionaries and slaveholders, primarily for evangelical purposes, especially prior to Nat Turner's 1831 Virginia slave rebellion. Led by a slave who could both read and write in English, the rebellion resulted in more rigid laws against slave literacy. For example, in Norfolk, Virginia, the early education of William G. Allen, who would later become the first African American professor of rhetoric, was disrupted when his all-black school was closed in the wake of the rebellion, and he subsequently devised other means of acquiring it.³ In this chapter, I consider sites of what Ralph Ellison, in response to the recovery of Harriet E. Wilson's 1859 autobiographical novel *Our Nig,* called "free-floating literacy."⁴ I apply the term generously to include both externally sponsored literacy initiatives and initiatives emerging from within communities of the enslaved, communities where slavery existed, or communities emerging in its aftermath.⁵ Also referenced here are what scholars like Shirley Brice Heath and Beverly J. Moss refer to as "literacy events," or sites in which printed texts are produced or interpreted, especially in the case of African American religious practices.⁶ I rely primarily upon records left by the learners themselves or, where silent, by those who worked among them, to develop a sense of these internal activities, and upon histories of plantation missions, for information on externally sponsored activities. Although these sites of literacy frequently developed independently, they were often interdependent in the ways they shaped early African American rhetorical education. I discuss four types of free-floating literacies—plantation literacies, pulpit literacies, battlefield literacies, and political literacies associated with the Reconstruction union leagues. I conclude the chapter with a reference to one end-of-the-century workplace site of rhetorical education, the cigar factories in south Florida, and the practices of the hired lector, who read to the workers.

Plantation Literacies

African Americans who found themselves in environments that limited their ability to develop English literacy created their own opportunities to do so, although the pursuit of other liberties was frequently their primary concern. In her memoirs, Elizabeth Johnson Harris, born in 1867 of parents who had been enslaved, recalls the religious gatherings or the "old-time Bush meetings," held in "Large Bush Harbors [that] were built out in an open field—during the summer season" near Augusta, Georgia.⁷ Harris is describing a post-emancipation event that had its origins in slavery. In the antebellum South, by law in some states, blacks were forbidden to assemble in groups of more than five, providing added incentive for these "hush harbor," "bush harbor," or "brush harbor" meetings.⁸

Melva Wilson Costen, scholar of African American religious practices, notes that these secret gatherings for religious as well as social and political purposes later became known as the "Invisible Institutions," sites where slaves functioned as independent agents, and describes a variety of religious practices that also enabled the development of rhetorical abilities, including catechetical instruction, preaching, praying, and singing songs of worship with lyrics that often served the political purpose of communicating plans for escape.[9]

Rhetoric scholar Vorris L. Nunley refers to the discourse produced in such sites as "hush harbor rhetoric" and calls for more attention to the function of material and discursive space in considerations of rhetorical situations. Nunley, advancing a more inclusive definition of hush harbors, includes the spaces of "woods, plantation borders, churches, burial societies, beauty shops, slave frolics, barbershops, and kitchens," where participants "loosed their words and their rhetorics."[10] Nunley's construction of these safe harbors enables us to consider their function as sites of resistance as well as of education. The discourse generated in such sites allowed a "loosening" of expression as much as an opportunity for developing expression. It offered participants the chance to "hear" one another and themselves in a space where their ideas could be formed in the act of expression, giving truth to the saying "I don't know what I mean until I hear what I say." These gatherings also provided the slaves an opportunity to worship in their own fashion, away from the gaze of missionaries and slaveholders. Albert J. Raboteau writes that one former slave, Kalvin Woods, recalled meeting in heavily vegetated or secluded woods, "huddled behind quilts and rags, which had been thoroughly wetted 'to keep the sound of their voices from penetrating the air' and then hung up 'in the form of a little room,' or tabernacle."[11] During these frequently daylong gatherings, attended by hundreds, there were many opportunities for exhorting, testifying, preaching, and other forms of oral expression.

Harris, later in her narrative, recalls the tales her grandfather told her, invoking the storytelling tradition that helped to transmit and preserve black folklore. She wrote, "Grandpa would sit and tell me of wonderful and terrible happenings during the days of slavery, including Ghost Stories, which he said all were true and many experienced by himself," although "in writing these I call them stories." Appended to her narrative, along with several poems, are some of these tales. "The Calf and the Ghost" is the story of a slave who fell asleep before completing the chore of bringing in a calf who had been put out to graze. When a companion wakes him, he hurries to the calf, accompanied along the way by a ghost, the sound of thunder, and a flash of lightning. After the mission is accomplished, "some mischievous person" exclaimed from the porch step, "Run, little Devil, Big Devil will catch You." Harris relates another story of her grandmother who, while her "mistress in the days of slavery" was attending church, dressed up in her clothes. Admiring herself in front of a mirror, she heard a noise in the room and ran downstairs, only to discover that the noise was her friend pretending to be a ghost. With an undercurrent of supernatural elements, these moralistic fables and others she relates all convey lessons about such forbidden activities as neglect of duties, hunting on Sunday, and speaking ill of the dead, partially rooted in an African tradition of storytelling. Charles Joyner makes the useful point that slaves drew on their African heritage as well as on their experiences of enslavement in America to fashion their tales. These stories could well borrow from European or Asian storytelling traditions, but what is more important than tracing precise origins is recognizing the extent to which these stories served the rhetorical purpose of teaching survival skills in memorable ways.[12] Further, this site of rhetorical practice, as with the hush harbor site, functioned to amuse, educate, and preserve the memories of a people denied conventional means of recording them.

Of particular interest is the role of slave missions in developing literacy and thereby rhetorical education in the antebellum South. White colonists were initially reluctant to convert slaves to Christianity, fearing that such conversions would nurture insubordination and the desire for emancipation or that slaves would not benefit from it. Costen observes that this desire to decouple religious rites, such as baptism, from liberation led some missionaries in the early eighteenth century to require slave candidates to agree that their acceptance of certain sacraments in no way implied freedom from bondage.[13] Agreeing to such declarations allowed many slaves to receive literacy education within the confines of slavery. Still, there were few explicit attempts to convert the enslaved to Christianity with its attendant forms of literacy until the Great Awakening of the 1740s. Subsequent to this series of religious revivals, missionaries began to devise systematic approaches to proselytizing. In the 1830s, Charles Colcock Jones, Georgia missionary and Presbyterian clergyman, spearheaded the plantation or slave mission movement. But Jones and other proponents recognized the difficulty of importing a reform movement into a slave society and proposed a local approach to missions, one that represented no threat to the existing institution of slavery. This was also the time when David Walker's revolutionary *Appeal, In Four Articles: Together With A Preamble To The Coloured Citizens Of The World, But In Particular, And Very Expressly, To Those Of The United States Of America* (1829) was circulating and arousing a great deal of concern among slaveholders after they learned that it had been distributed in the South. Further, this discussion was taking place amid the growing abolitionist movement, though Jones argued that his interest was only in the religious rather than the civil condition of the enslaved. Janet Duitsman Cornelius suggests that the plantation missions emerged as a result of the efforts of both black and white missionaries and survived to the extent that enslaved African Americans decided whether to receive the Christian message and to shape it to their own purposes. These purposes often included creating sites of resistance to oppression, incorporating the "ritual and language of the Christian religion: spoken, sung, invoked, and presented in the imagery and reasoning of the sacred word, the Bible," to improve leadership and literacy skills.[14]

Jones developed a style of delivery that enabled him to preach a message of salvation and predestined enslavement at the same time. Cornelius draws examples of this technique from Jones's 1842 book, *Religious Instruction of Negroes:* "He took care to adopt a 'grave, solemn, dignified, ardent and animated' manner, using perfect English without lapsing into familiarity or slang. . . . He also believed that his mission worshipers appreciated the thorough preparation and study he put into his sermons. . . . Jones worked hard on communication techniques and tried to use concrete examples, animated gestures, and clear and simple language to highlight precepts and parables."[15] When the mission school teacher could not be present, he often designated men and women whom he deemed trustworthy and who could read to teach the catechism in his absence. Through this process, many of these "assistants" received their first training as preachers and public speakers. Such rhetorical performances served liberatory as well as religious ends.

Various church denominations, in their effort to spread the gospel, developed mission schools to evangelize slaves, but few were prepared to condemn slavery. Thus, to gain access to slaves for conversion, they had to assure slaveholders that their instruction was not a threat to the institution. One of the principles developed to this end was that, in some instances, to avoid violating anti-literacy laws, slaves were taught through the oral method, wherein the missionary teacher asked and answered questions, catechistically, and then had the students do the same in order to memorize them. Some missionaries argued that mission school education would actually make them more manageable slaves, invoking what James Sidbury calls one of the "scriptural staples of proslavery thought": "Servants, obey in all things your masters."[16] For those enslaved, however, the mission schools provided a way to develop critical literacy skills for their own purposes. Consider, for example, that the recorded histories of the slave revolts of Gabriel, Denmark Vesey, and Nat Turner show that "literate slaves who were recognized by their peers to have spiritual insight could and did use the Bible to find a place for themselves and for their people in a sacred universe," and, in their cases, the "process . . . inspire[d] radical activism."[17]

Cornelius, quoting anthropologist Walter Pitt, writes that the missionary teachers "'instilled standard but biblical English in the black vernacular' of the nineteenth century, a form of speaking which still exists today in black church-es."[18] There is much truth in this sweeping claim. Clearly, the sermons of many black ministers are rich with syntactical and stylistic features and images from the King James Version of the Bible. The extent to which these features prevail in other linguistic contexts is less clear. Still, an acknowledgment of the influence of the King James Bible on black expression as a result of slave mission school training is germane to this discussion of sites of rhetorical education, although the extent of this linguistic influence is beyond the scope of this project.

Pulpit Literacies

That the rhetorical power of many African Americans originated in the mis-sion schools and the early religious sites is hardly contested. Those who heard ex-slave preachers shortly after the Civil War frequently commented on their rhetorical power. Their ability to read or write was often less important than their ability to memorize. In many instances, the oral instruction method employed in many of the plantation missions allowed for and promoted the development of memory. Hearing passages read repeatedly, especially in the slave missions, and reciting responses to catechism questions sharpened this skill.[19] As one missionary reported: "To those who are ignorant of letters, *their memory is their book. . . .* In a recent examination of one of the schools, I was forcibly struck with their remembrance of *passages of Scripture.* Those questions which turned upon and called for passages of Scripture, the scholars answered more readily than any other."[20] Given the frequency of such reports of indi-viduals having memorized long passages from the Bible, it is not difficult to imagine how these abilities also had an impact on preaching. One speaker was said to have held out his hand as if he were reading from a book and delivered a sermon filled with biblical phrases, repetition, parallelism, and other rhetori-cal devices.[21] Of course, the seamless delivery of a sermon interwoven with memorized passages of scripture increases its appeal. Even in secular contexts, a frequently mentioned attribute of orators is that they speak without notes, a required practice for those who cannot read and an effective tactic for all who wish to reach a wide range of auditors.[22]

Frederick Douglass's experiences as a class leader, exhorter, and licensed preacher in New Bedford's African Methodist Episcopal Zion (AMEZ) Church may have been the greatest influence on his polished oratory, in spite of frequent references to his possession of Caleb Bingham's popular rhetoric textbook *The Columbian Orator.* To become an exhorter or lay preacher, Douglass had to pass an examination and deliver a mini-sermon or exhortation in the presence of the congregation and various church officials. He had to perform. He was first licensed as an exhorter in 1839, two years before he became an antislavery lecturer, and the license had to be renewed annually. Although we do not know how often Douglass exhorted the congregation, church guidelines required that exhorters be allowed to speak frequently.[23] William L. Andrews makes the important observation that while we tend to assume that Douglass acquired his first speaking experience on the abolitionist circuit, more attention needs to be given to his time spent exhorting to AMEZ congregations. To support his point, Andrews includes in his article "Frederick Douglass, Preacher" a long passage from a letter Douglass wrote over fifty years later, in 1894, in response to an inquiry about his early affiliation with the denomination: "As early as 1839, I obtained a license from the Quarterly Conference as a local preacher [exhorter], and often occupied the pulpit by request of the preacher in charge. No doubt that the exercise of my gifts in this vocation, and my association with the excellent men to whom I have referred, helped to prepare me for the wider sphere of usefulness which I have since occupied. It was from this Zion church that I went forth to the work of delivering my brethren from bondage, and this new vocation, which separated me from New Bedford and finally so enlarged my views of duty, separated me also from the calling of a local preacher."[24]

These regular required performances contributed to the rhetorical education of many young men like Frederick Douglass; however, during the antebellum period, in the Bethel AME Church of Baltimore, and no doubt in many others, even though women outnumbered men more than two to one, women never held the position of class leader, exhorter, or minister.[25] Such a distinction leads to questions about whether the experiences of black women religious speakers provided them with different understandings of rhetorical training. The spiritual narratives of women evangelists like Jarena Lee (*Religious Experience and Journal of Mrs. Jarena Lee, a Coloured Lady,* 1836), Zilpha Elaw (*Memoirs of the Life, Religious Experience, Ministerial Travels, and Labours of Mrs. Zilpha Elaw, an American Female of Colour,* 1846), and Julia Foote (*A Brand Plucked from the Fire. An Autobiographical Sketch,* 1879) offer some answers. However, Amanda Berry Smith's narrative, *An Autobiography: The Story of the Lord's Dealings with Mrs. Amanda Smith, the Colored Evangelist* (1893), while sharing characteristics with those of earlier black women preachers, also contains an interesting analysis of her own response to rhetorical persuasion.

Smith was born into slavery in 1837 in Long Green, Maryland, some twenty miles from Baltimore. After her father, Samuel Berry, purchased himself and subsequently his family, they moved to Columbia, Pennsylvania. With considerable difficulty, Smith received the equivalent of only about three months' formal schooling and acquired most of her literacy skills from her parents, who were both readers. In the context of the Second Great Awakening, Smith attended a revival meeting when she was thirteen and was subsequently converted. Over the next sixty years, she went on to become an evangelist who preached in the United States, England, India, and West Africa. It was during this early post-conversion period that she was sensitized to the persuasive force of what she called "pernicious reading," which was so powerful that she began to question the existence of God and engaged her aunt in an argument on the subject.[26] Smith recalled her initial response to a persuasive piece that led to her doubt:

> While living at Black's hotel, in Columbia, I remember reading a book. I forget the title of it, but it was an argument between an infidel and a Christian minister. As I went on reading I became very much interested. "Oh," I thought to myself, "I know the Christian minister will win." It starts with the infidel asking a question. The minister's answer took two pages, while the question asked only took one page and a half. As they went on the minister gained three pages with his answer; and the infidel seemed to lose. And then it went on, and by and by the minister began to lose, and the infidel gained. So it went on till the infidel seemed to gain all the ground. His questions and argument were so pretty and put in such a way that before I knew it I was captured; and by the time I had got through the book I had the whole of the infidel's article stamped on my memory and spirit, and the Christian's argument was lost. . . . And I would say to my readers, "Beware how you read books tainted with error."[27]

In a similar passage, Douglass relates his early response to a piece of persuasive discourse, "Dialogue Between a Master and Slave," reprinted in *The Columbian Orator.*[28]

> I was now about twelve years old, and the thought of being A SLAVE FOR LIFE began to bear heavily upon my heart. Just about this time, I got hold of a book entitled "The Columbian Orator." Every opportunity I got, I used to read this book. Among much of other interesting matter, I found in it a dialogue between a master and his slave. The slave was represented as having run away from his master three times. The dialogue represented the conversation which took place between them, when the slave was retaken the third time. In this dialogue, the whole argument in behalf of slavery was brought forward by the master, all of which was disposed of by the slave. The slave was made to say some very smart as well as impressive things in reply to his master—things which had the desired though unexpected effect; for the conversation resulted in the voluntary emancipation of the slave on the part of the master.[29]

Both Smith and Douglass were between twelve and fourteen years old when these encounters with persuasion occurred, but their experiences made a deep impression. The difference between Smith's response to persuasion and Douglass's, however, has much to do with their engagement with the argument. Smith was persuaded by the argument itself, leading her to question her faith. Douglass needed no argument to persuade him that slavery was wrong. He was not persuaded by the argument but rather by the power of argument in that particular instance. Douglass understood that in the dialogue, the slave argues with the master and is able to persuade him to release him, although the slave does not convince the master of the wrong of slavery. He does gain his freedom through his rhetorical skills in that he persuades the master of his determination to escape. The slaveholder, recognizing the slave's determination, knows that he can gain his approval only by releasing him. Smith understood argument as having the potential for both good and evil, evil that for her took the form of religious doubt. These two developing rhetors learned different lessons about rhetoric's persuasive power.

Battlefield Literacies

When Congress passed the Militia Act in July 1862, making legal the employment of blacks in the military, it also inadvertently created a fertile site for rhetorical education, bringing together men with a broad range of backgrounds. Current statistics indicate that by the end of the Civil War, approximately 179,000 black soldiers, or 10 percent of the Union troops, served in the U.S. Army, and another 19,000 served in the navy.[30] One contemporaneous history of the conflict, *The Black Phalanx*, lists 138 infantry regiments alone.[31] Military service offered these men new educational opportunities, "both formal and experiential," as Vincent Carretta observes in speaking of Olaudah Equiano's time in the Royal Navy.[32] In addition to carrying out their military duties, the unlettered members of this newly formed community took advantage of the situation to develop their literacy skills. Those who were already fully literate corresponded with their families, sent letters to the press and to the government, formed debating societies, maintained diaries, and published newspapers.

Joseph T. Wilson dedicates his book on black soldiers to the white officers who led the black Civil War units in the face of derision and prejudice. He recognizes especially their role in supporting the soldiers' literacy efforts. As one general recalled concerning his service in Tennessee, "While at Chattanooga, I organized two other regiments, the 42nd and the 44th United States Colored Infantry. In addition to the ordinary instruction in the duties required of the soldier, we established in every company a regular school, teaching men to read and write. . . . The men who went on picket or guard duty, took their books as quite as indispensable as their coffee pots."[33] These soldiers spent a good portion of their free time learning to read, and every camp had someone assigned to instruct them. Often female teachers would visit the barracks and campgrounds. The soldiers themselves also used portions of their pay to hire teachers for themselves and to support the schools established in the army's wake. One army colonel observed that "when the truce was sounded after a day or night's hard fighting, many of these men renewed their courage by studying and reading in the 'New England Speller' . . . and upon more than one occasion have these soldiers been found in the trenches with the speller in hand, muttering, bla, ble."[34]

Orderly Sergeant Milton Harris of the Twenty-fifth Regiment at Fort Redout, Florida, refers to the establishment of a school in a letter to the *Christian Recorder:* "They are going to have a school for us in the Fort. Capt. Wm. A. Prickett, of Co. G, has lately returned from New Orleans, with a considerable number of books, for the benefit of our men, in the way of educating them. He has been furnishing them with books, so that a great many of them could learn to read and write."[35]

Many of the soldiers, of course, came into the army with fully developed rhetorical skills, especially those who had not been previously enslaved. Some could read and write as well as or better than most white soldiers; some had public school educations; some were college trained. The Fifty-fourth Massachusetts Regiment, for example, was made up primarily of free African Americans, including two of Frederick Douglass's sons, Charles and Lewis, and AME bishop Daniel Payne's nephew Charles Holloway. Medal of Honor recipient Christian Fleetwood of Baltimore was an 1860 graduate of Ashmun Institute in Pennsylvania and one of the editors of the *Baltimore Lyceum Observer* before joining the Fourth Regiment of the Colored Volunteer Infantry in 1863. He maintained a diary for all of 1864, providing a record of his daily routine in the unit. The chief rhetorical activity Fleetwood documents is writing—official reports, personal letters, letters to the newspapers, and letters for officers and other soldiers. In one entry, he also refers to reading the *Atlantic Monthly* and *Ballou's Monthly* and to having completed "Fantine," the first section of Victor Hugo's *Les Misérables,* on the same day.[36]

Literary and debating societies were often a part of camp life. The Douglass and Garnet Young Men's Literary Association was organized in 1864 by the son-in-law of the *Weekly Anglo-African* editor Robert Hamilton and the soldiers of the Twenty-ninth Connecticut Regiment to promote educational and communal activities.[37] The February 21, 1865, meeting of the Soldiers' Literary and Debating Association of the Twenty-second U. S. Colored Troops, a regiment recruited in Philadelphia, celebrated the fall of Charleston and the U.S. Congress's submission of the Thirteenth Amendment outlawing slavery to the states for ratification. The agenda featured speeches by regiment chaplain

Christopher Burroughs and Thomas Morris Chester, a black Civil War correspondent from Harrisburg, Pennsylvania. [38] Chester, an interesting Civil War rhetor in his own right, had written numerous articles during the war as the only black journalist assigned to cover the conflict for a major daily newspaper, the *Philadelphia Press*. Reporting from the James River front, Chester came from an activist Harrisburg family, where his father owned a restaurant and served as a correspondent to William Lloyd Garrison's *Liberator*. Chester was trained at the Allegheny Institute (later Avery College) and at Thetford Academy in Vermont, where he apparently excelled in debating. Chester spent some time in Liberia working with the American Colonization Society, returned to the United States, recruited black soldiers, raised money for the Freedmen's Bureau, and helped to organize the Colored Men's Equal Rights League of Richmond. Chester had a reputation for being an eloquent speaker and a compelling writer who never missed an opportunity in his submissions to the *Philadelphia Press* to highlight the accomplishments of black soldiers or the courage of the newly emancipated. [39]

Soldiers read and corresponded frequently with two black newspapers in particular, the *Weekly Anglo-African*, edited by Robert Hamilton, [40] and the *Christian Recorder*, organ of the AME Church, edited by Elisha Weaver, who assumed the position in 1861 and continued as editor through the war. These papers provided forums for debates on African American participation in the war, salary inequities, and emancipation. With the help of black correspondents like Thomas Chester, subscription agents, and family members, black soldiers were kept informed about events in other parts of the country and were able to participate in these discussions among themselves, through intercamp communications and written correspondence. In the January 16, 1864, issue of the *Christian Recorder*, a letter signed by Christian Fleetwood and other soldiers stationed at Yorktown expressed appreciation to the Baltimore women who had sent them a box of "delicacies of the rarest kind." In a December 19, 1863, letter, Orderly Sergeant J. H. Welch of the Fifty-fifth Regiment thanked "Brother Weaver" for issues of the *Christian Recorder*: "I receive my paper very regularly indeed, and you should receive the thanks of every soldier in the army of color, for your services in the preparation and publication of this truly valuable paper, and I certainly feel indebted to my father for sending it." A year later, Henry McNeal Turner, then chaplain of the First Regiment of U.S. Colored Troops, was more specific as to how these papers inspired readers at all levels:

> The *Recorder* is looked for weekly, as a precious visitor, in this part of our noble army. It is dearly prized by many of our gallant soldiers who, I am happy to say, are trying to prepare for whatever position the future may offer them: likely nothing could have inspired a more eager ambition into

the men of my regiment, for literary attainments, than the vast number of *Recorders* and *Anglos,* which weekly find their way into our different companies. One very ordinary looking fellow takes up the paper, and begins to lay open its columns, and to throw a glare of interest, where, to the uneducated all seems to be darkness and gloom, and a more stalwart and finer-looking fellow listens awhile, and becoming jealous at the idea, starts off in search of a spelling-book, saying to himself (as he fancies his superior abilities,) "I won't listen to him. I am going to do my own reading," and away he wends himself from tent to tent, and from one place to another, until a spelling-book is procured, regardless of price.—All that is then necessary, is to watch him a few months, and you will see him blundering through a newspaper like a child learning to walk. You had as well loose him, and let him go then, for you may be sure he is gone.[41]

Open letters to black newspapers served a recruiting function, especially at the onset of black participation in the war. Many were reluctant to join a cause that at first had refused their assistance and then could not guarantee them equity or protection if captured. Sattie Douglas, the wife of H. Ford Douglas, who was serving at the time with the Ninety-fifth Illinois Regiment, argued in her letter to Hamilton that the strife offered black soldiers their only opportunity "during the present generation" to actively fight against slavery and prejudice and that by refusing to come forward they prove themselves "unworthy of those rights which they have so long withheld from us." She supported her claims with the adage that those possessions most treasured are those "most dearly bought." Arguing from the position of one whose spouse had already entered the fight, she urged others to follow.[42] Letter writing was "a powerful avenue of redress, an empowering pastime," especially for soldiers who wanted to register complaints about pay inequity and treatment by officers.[43] The *Weekly Anglo-African* published letters from black soldiers regularly. In a January 10, 1864, letter to the paper, an anonymous black seaman, who had been serving in the navy since June 1862, used this outlet in an effort to reach government officials on the question of protection of black prisoners of war. The U.S. gunboat *South Carolina* sailor recounted two incidents in which three black "free men from the North" were captured. No information was ever provided on the first two men, and the third was hanged. Although the letter was signed merely "Rhode Island," the writer was careful to recognize the efforts of John Dahlgren, commander of the navy's South Atlantic Blockading Squadron, and to assure readers of the good health of the black soldiers on Morris Island.[44]

Nonmilitary black citizens aired their war grievances in communications to the black press as well, enabling them, at the same time, to show their support for the soldiers. In the June 25, 1864, *Christian Recorder,* a letter submitted by

"Pearl" concisely outlines these grievances: the "colored soldiers" are not paid the thirteen dollars per month they were promised; the soldiers are placed in front on the battlefield to bear the brunt of injuries; and the soldiers are not recognized or promoted for their military accomplishments, with the result that the Union "takes a part of its sons, and makes them sweat, and toil, and fight for nothing." In the same issue, one prolific writer whose letters appeared frequently in the *Christian Recorder* was Orderly Sergeant John H. W. N. Collins of Company H, Fifty-fourth Massachusetts Infantry. In one letter, interspersed with poetry and dated June 15, 1864, Collins praises the courage of the "over 100,000 colored soldiers" in the face of discrimination and inadequate pay. A month later, he wrote again from Block Island, South Carolina, including the Fifty-fifth "sister" regiment in his praise and continuing to develop arguments against the unequal pay that many soldiers in the Fifty-fourth and Fifty-fifth refused to accept.[45] Almost a year later, on April 30, 1865, Collins composed a letter from Georgetown, South Carolina, which must have been at least six handwritten pages. He describes a disagreement between two soldiers, resulting in the murder of one; some of the last battles of the infantry; and the bravery and the loss of life. Collins closes this letter with the promise that his next would "tell more of the condition of the poor slaves through the State of South Carolina" and with the hope that peace would come soon.[46]

Union troops frequently commandeered presses from captured Confederate printing establishments and used them to publish papers on campsites. It may have been by this means that this same orderly sergeant was able to edit the *Swamp Angel,* one of a few newspapers produced for the black troops. The paper was named after the 16,500-pound rifled cannon used to shell the fort at Charleston in 1863. The first issue, dated May 19, 1864, when the Fifty-fourth Regiment was attached to the 104th Pennsylvania Volunteers, was ostensibly published by its commander, Colonel William Davis. Yet as Keith P. Wilson notes in his book on Civil War black soldiers, "the real catalyst behind the regimental paper was its editor, an intelligent and politically active noncommissioned officer, Orderly Sgt. John H. W. Collins."[47]

In addition, the Fourteenth Regiment Rhode Island Heavy Artillery for a brief time in 1864 published the *Black Warrior* out of Camp Parapet, Louisiana. A printing press and necessary materials were provided by the Third Battalion to issue a semi-monthly paper, edited by Quartermaster-Sergeant George W. Hamblin, who prior to enlistment had been active in black Rhode Island politics. As part of its purpose, the *Black Warrior,* first issued on May 17, 1864, aimed "to raise the status of colored troops by proving their capability of appreciating, preserving, and defending the principles of Liberty either by pen or sword." The first issue closed with the notice, "This paper is owned, printed, and edited by the black warriors of the 14th R.I.H.A." This regiment was also the site of a required evening school for noncommissioned officers not on guard duty, with Sergeant Hamblin as one of the teachers.[48] The emphasis on improvement, so prevalent in African American discourse across the nineteenth century, as well as pride in the rhetorical accomplishment of publishing a newspaper are both apparent in this battlefield site.

In a July 12, 1863, correspondence to her newspaper, the *St. Cloud (Minn.) Democrat,* Jane Grey Swisshelm writes of her experiences as a Union nurse, just nine days after the battle of Gettysburg. Swisshelm had edited three antislavery newspapers before the outbreak of the Civil War when she volunteered to care for the wounded being brought to hospitals in Washington and Virginia. After recalling the chaos and jubilation surrounding General George Meade's defeat of General Robert E. Lee, the misappropriation of supplies, and the low morale of Southern sympathizers, she describes a scene near Georgetown that demonstrates the urgency with which black soldiers pursued facility with language: "Large bodies of troops are stationed here and a whole brigade of cavalry passed from the northward a few days ago going in the direction of Bull Run.—A regiment of colored troops are camped on the opposite side of the Potomac near Georgetown. Their officers appear to have been very carefully chosen and are men who are anxious they should succeed. In addition to military tactics they are learning to read and may be seen, in the intervals between their drills, in little groups with primers and spelling books conning over their lessons. People here are becoming accustomed to see them in the United States uniform, and they are more frequently hailed with signs of approbation than with sneers of scorn."[49] In this passage, Swisshelm also recognizes the work of the officers who arranged for and perhaps assisted in these sessions.

Thus, the admission of African American soldiers into the Union army brought together in regiments black men who, although from different social classes, with wide-ranging educational levels, some recently enslaved, some never enslaved, were all motivated by the struggle for freedom and human dignity that would affect them all. The rhetorical skills developed during their military service—reading, writing, debating, keeping diaries, gathering in associations, editing newspapers—trained these black soldiers for leadership during Reconstruction and beyond. Further research into the various types of communal and intra- and interracial rhetorical education and exchange occurring in this fertile site is a project for future historians of rhetorical practice.

I close this section, not on the battlefield, but at the scene of an oratorical reading at the Sansom Street Concert Hall in Philadelphia on Friday, January 27, 1865. In contrast to the backdrop of a falling Confederacy and General William T. Sherman marching through the South, this scene unfolds at the elocutionary performances of two recent graduates of the Institute for Colored Youth, established in 1837 by the Religious Society of Friends. It was reestablished in 1849 with a shift in emphasis from manual training to a curriculum that included "literary subjects," meaning such subjects as philosophy, elocution, logic, and composition, at the prompting of the black tradesmen, who apprenticed the students during the day. By 1865, the institute had developed an unequaled reputation for excellence in educating black youth under the leadership of Charles Reason and Ebenezer Bassett, who would be followed in the fall of that same year by Fanny Jackson (Coppin).[50] The *Christian Recorder* article praises the "superior talents" of graduate Caroline R. Le Count, demonstrated in her reading of Henry Wadsworth Longfellow's "Launch of the Ship," John Greenleaf Whittier's "Prisoner for Debt," and other literary compositions. The article also applauds the elocutionary skill displayed in John H. Smith's recitations of "Antony's Oration over Caesar's Dead Body" and two Civil War poems, T. Buchanan Read's "Sheridan's Ride" and George Boker's "Cavalry Sheridan." Smith, the main performer, had recited another poem by abolitionist Boker, "The Black Regiment," at the December organizational meeting of the Pennsylvania State Equal Rights League. Often put to music, "The Black Regiment" was first published by the Supervisory Committee for Recruiting Colored Regiments and recognized the bravery of black soldiers at the siege of Port Hudson, Louisiana, in the summer of 1863. The last verses of the poem, which, according to the *Christian Recorder,* young Smith recited in "an able and masterly style," make a plea for fair treatment:

> O, to the living few,
> Soldiers, be just and true!
> Hail them as comrades tried;
> Fight with them side by side;
> Never, in field or tent,
> Scorn the black regiment![51]

Through this event, the battlefield accomplishments of black soldiers were acted out in the elocutionary performances of the next generation.

Political Literacies

After the war, one site of rhetorical education developed in the practices of the Union or Loyal League Movement sponsored by the Republican Party. During the Radical Reconstruction period, African Americans acquired new access to political power, access that not surprisingly sparked a great deal of resistance. The Union League, organized in Philadelphia in 1862, established a Republican Party presence in the South as an extension of its organized support of the party and of President Lincoln. The league used its existing structure to promote membership among newly enfranchised black men. Less experienced in political strategizing, these men were attracted to the league and the opportunities it offered for their direct involvement, although many of these leagues were segregated and others were led primarily by white members.[52] This movement was particularly active in the South between 1867 and 1868, following the passage of legislation establishing the Freedmen's Bureau, the Civil Rights Act of 1866, and several Reconstruction acts, which, among other moves, gave former enslaved males the right to vote and hold public office. Thus, black men denied any voice in their own civil condition since birth now found themselves in a position to use that voice to assert and maintain their civil rights.

Leagues frequently met a night and formed a system of night schools. At these meetings, the leagues served a variety of educational functions, and information was disseminated through long speeches, lectures, and discussions on current topics.[53] The participants were catechized in the ways of political participation and in the benefits of supporting the Republican Party. A good deal of time was spent reading newspapers and pamphlets aloud to members, who would listen at length, an activity particularly beneficial to members just learning to read. Many often committed the material to memory, in a process similar to the one followed by the slave mission preachers discussed above.[54] Of course, as historian John Hope Franklin notes, the leagues, surrounded in secrecy, ritual, and a rhetoric of freedom and equal rights, attracted large numbers of African Americans, many of whom looked to league leaders for voting advice, but long after league popularity declined, leaguers who had been indoctrinated into politics through it carried their acquired skills into other political and economic arenas.[55] As with other scenes of rhetorical education, blacks took advantage of literacy opportunities and shaped them to their own purposes.

Postbellum Workplace Literacies

As a coda to this chapter, I consider one end-of-the-century workplace site where rhetorical education thrived—cigar factories in Florida. In many of these factories, both black and white Cuban émigrés worked while lectors read novels, newspapers, and other material chosen by the workers. The issues these materials raised frequently generated heated discussions and thus opportunities to hone argumentative skills. The conversations that took place during the breaks and before and after these reading sessions, along with the sessions themselves, qualify as the kind of literacy event referred to by Moss and Heath, where printed texts are produced or interpreted, mentioned in the opening of this chapter.

In the late 1850s, cigar makers in Havana instituted the custom of *la lectura* in support of literacy and political awareness and in pursuit of common goals.

Cuban cigar workers became educated, in large part, as a result of this tradition of lectors or readers, one of the most prestigious professions of the cigar industry. Readers were paid by contributions from the cigar workers themselves. The more popular they were, the higher the salary they could demand. Lectors' seats were usually elevated above the cigar roller tables in a factory so their voices could be easily heard throughout the room. They usually began the workday by reading excerpts from the local newspaper, or a Spanish newspaper, followed by readings from a novel or the works of a political philosopher while workers sorted tobacco leaves and rolled cigars. The cigar workers voted on the book selection or reading topic. As a result of this practice, many workers who may not have been able to read or write could easily quote Shakespeare, Voltaire, Émile Zola, Leo Tolstoy, and Alexandre Dumas. The lectors also made the workers aware of politics and world events, acquainting them with the political issues and questioning the political authority of Spain. Passionately interested in self-education, they discussed what they had learned during rest periods. As the Cuban cigar industry prospered, the Spanish authorities viewed lectors with increased suspicion.

This tradition of *la lectura* was a predominant feature of the occupational culture of cigar factories not only in Cuba but in Puerto Rico and in immigrant enclaves in such U.S. cities as Key West, Tampa, and eventually Ybor City and New York City. In the 1860s, many manufacturers left Cuba to avoid U.S. import taxes as well as the tension of the war with Spain. The shop floor, therefore, served as an important site of rhetorical education and political mobilization among members of the workforce and, by extension, the larger class, ethnicity, race, and geography groups that they drew from. While many of the cigar workers did not read, their factual and analytical knowledge of the politics that concerned their communities, at home and abroad, was vast. The workers, brought up in a tradition of talking politics, were passionately interested in self-education.

This practice of *el lector* became a symbolic source of conflict between the workers and management throughout Ybor City's cigar industry history. Highly skilled readers, they were selected for their ability to engage an audience and commanded good salaries. Workers paid fifteen to twenty-five cents per week each to support the reader. Since the workers selected the reading material, it reflected their interests.[56] In some factories, the lector, a professional speaker, would sit in front of a microphone, which was also available to the rollers. Benjamin Menendez, former Cuban cigar maker, reminisced that during the golden days of cigar production, "if someone was unhappy, they could use the microphone. Anybody could get up and give a speech."[57]

It should be noted that Afro-Cubans very likely occupied the lower-level jobs within these racially integrated but hierarchically structured factories.[58]

Although one artist's description of an image of a Tampa cigar factory notes that "women, men, whites and blacks mixed without regard to existing segregation laws," historians of the period describe less egalitarian arrangements in most instances.[59] To claim it as a prominent site of rhetorical education for nineteenth-century African Americans, more evidence of an African American presence in these cigar factories with lectors would need to be provided, but it seems reasonable to assume that blacks were present, even if in small numbers, just as there were probably small numbers of blacks associated with the battlefield literary associations.

Both James Weldon Johnson's novel *The Autobiography of an Ex-Coloured Man* and his own autobiography, *Along This Way,* suggest that an African American presence in such factories with readers would not have been impossible or unimaginable.[60] The protagonist in *Autobiography* ends up working as a tobacco stripper in a Jacksonville, Florida, tobacco factory, having abandoned the pursuit of a college education at Atlanta University. He eventually learns to read Spanish so well that he is selected as reader. Unlike many descriptions of the lector, he is given an active role in the discussions and in the selection of materials by the narrator: "He often selects an exciting novel and reads it in daily instalments. He must, of course, have a good voice, but he must also have a reputation among the men for intelligence, for being well posted and having in his head a stock of varied information. He is generally the final authority on all arguments which arise, and in a cigar factory these arguments are many and frequent, ranging from the respective and relative merits of rival baseball clubs to the duration of the sun's light and energy—cigar-making is a trade in which talk does not interfere with work."[61]

In *Along This Way,* Johnson writes about the experiences of his best friend D—, who, while described as "colored," later in life chose to pass for white.[62] D—, the prototype for Johnson's ex-colored man, worked in a cigar factory owned by his father and another black man, stripping stems from leaves and sorting them; Johnson's brother Rosamond and other young men also learned the trade.[63]

If African Americans, even a small number, owned cigar factories during this period, it seems unlikely that they employed readers for the original purpose of keeping workers abreast of developing political events in Cuba and other Spanish-speaking countries. Patricia A. Cooper points out that very few blacks belonged to the Cigar Makers' International Union and that while most black members worked in New Orleans, black cigar makers established CMIU's first black local in 1884 in Charleston, South Carolina. She adds, "The custom of employing a reader—which became commonly associated with the cigar makers in the public mind—originated in Cuba and never became widespread in the

United States outside the Clear Havana [cigars made with all Cuban tobacco] shops employing Spanish-speaking workers." Cooper also points out that most of those Afro-Cubans, Italians, women, and African Americans who worked in the factories held subordinate positions. They generally handled the jobs that did not directly relate to the manufacturing of cigars, including building maintenance, transportation, and shipping.[64] Thus, while it is clear that there were black workers in cigar factories across the country, whether large numbers participated in the tradition of *la lectura* is a question for further study. In addition, consideration of this turn-of-the-century workplace site prompts us to imagine other ways in which rhetorical education occurred while people earned a living. Further, these sites of free-floating literacy remind scholars to look in nontraditional spaces to understand fully how people develop rhetorical abilities.

2

Private Learners
Self-Education in Rhetoric

> Having obtained a furlough from my boss I remained home today feeling like a happy fish out of water. I began an essay on the situation and requisites of the colored people everywhere.
> —Mary Virginia Montgomery, 1872

> While Mr. Harris was packing up to-day for his Northern trip, I came upon his journal, one which he kept several years ago, and obtaining his permission, I have read a part of it. In fact nearly all. After reading it, I have concluded to write a journal too.
> —Charles W. Chesnutt, 1874

This chapter considers more closely the private learner, a term used in the nineteenth century to describe the individual who engaged in some form of self-education. Nan Johnson observes that this learner was more visible in the late nineteenth century, when rhetorical ability became as much a personal asset as an essential tool of civic activism. During this period, interest in rhetoric—initially understood as an academic course centered on persuasive oratory for use in the church, the courts, and the legislature—spread to nonacademic community settings at the same time that an increasing number of middle-class students entered college, and rhetoric became more broadly defined as a "general expertise in speaking and writing applicable to a wide range of public and professional uses and settings."[1] Understood to have practical, social advantage, of use in private and public life, rhetorical training became a critical part of general self-improvement. This chapter develops around the lives of five such learners who, while they may also have had various kinds of formal school training, also spent a good deal of time on self-improvement, especially in reading, writing, speaking, and critiquing the rhetorical performances of others, and who all recorded various aspects of their private learning in diaries. The lives of Charlotte Forten Grimké, Frances Anne Rollin Whipper, Ida B. Wells Barnett, Mary Virginia Montgomery, and Charles W. Chesnutt move across and function within several sites of rhetorical education, including private lessons, literary societies, journalistic work, self-education, and formal instruction, participating in but not fully engaging all aspects of these sites. These rhetors relied in large part on self-education, along with various levels of formal training, to improve their rhetorical skills, and their diaries record the histories of their self-education projects and, in turn, often served as a physical space in which to practice them. Thus, there is inevitable overlap of sites; for example, although references to literary societies occur in the diaries, we learn about them from the perspective of the participants. And it turns out that soldiers, like Christian Fleetwood, maintained diaries while fighting with the Union army, a fact I discuss in chapter 1. This same overlap occurs in descriptions of oratorical performances. The diaries frequently include the writers' assessment of a speech at some critical point in their lives when their own critical skills were just beginning to develop, while newspaper accounts of performances, generally more sophisticated, are targeted to readers, for education and often political purposes. These multiple perspectives converge to make our understanding of how nineteenth-century African Americans interpreted their rhetorical environment all the richer.

Self-education, as used here, means regular, voluntary, disciplined approaches to rhetorical education, initiated and carried out for self-improvement. The key term is "voluntary." In *The Pursuit of Knowledge under Difficulties*, Joseph F. Kett points out that formal education of any kind, especially for youth, is generally associated with some form of compulsion. Students are "sent" to school, while adults "join" societies for mutual improvement. Kett adds that "[t]hroughout the nineteenth century, self-education was associated with an often strenuous act of the will: to choose a course of mental improvement was to embark upon an ambitious enterprise that involved self-denial, persistence, and resilience," pointing out that diaries and journals frequently contain rich information about self-education projects, including the day on which they started.[2] The five writers treated here kept such diaries in which they account for their chosen pursuits, often sustained in the absence of financial or moral support and to the neglect of other activities, and record their responses to the oral and written rhetoric they encountered regularly.

Given that these were voluntary rather than assigned educational activities, these five writers had to have been highly motivated; yet their backgrounds and the circumstances under which they wrote differed. Although Wells kept several diaries at various periods of her life, the diary she kept during her early days in Memphis, from 1885 to 1887, while a teacher and journalist reveals most about her own rhetorical practices and her views on effective public speaking. Montgomery maintained a diary in Davis Bend, Mississippi, in 1872, the year before she enrolled at Oberlin, and it conveys the extent of her preparation as well as the pure pleasure she took from reading, speaking, and writing. Entries from Rollin's diary were recorded from January to July 1868, while she was in Boston completing a biography of Martin R. Delany, and include comments on the rhetorical performances of several prominent Bostonians as well as an account of her own reading and writing practices.[3] Grimké's diary, rich with rhetorical activities, covers the longest period, extending, with breaks, from 1854, when she moved to Salem, Massachusetts, to attend school, to 1892, when she was living in Washington, D.C.

Although many women kept diaries in the nineteenth century, few black women's diaries remain.[4] The diaries of Grimké, Wells, and Alice Dunbar-Nelson have now been published. In addition to drawing on the published diaries of Wells and Grimké, I take examples of self-education from the published excerpts of Rollin's and Montgomery's diaries and the unpublished manuscript of Montgomery's diary. I also consider one male diarist, author and lecturer Charles W. Chesnutt. Prior to migrating to Cleveland, Ohio, where he was born in 1858, Chesnutt's parents were among a small number of free blacks living in Fayetteville, North Carolina. The family returned to Fayetteville in 1866. Chesnutt kept a diary intermittently between 1874 and 1883. Although only sixteen years old when he began the diary, Chesnutt was already an assistant teacher at the Peabody School in Charlotte, North Carolina. By the time of his last entry at twenty-five, he was principal of the State Colored Normal School in Fayetteville. Wells, Montgomery, and Rollin were in their early twenties at the time of their entries, while Grimké began her diary at seventeen but continued it over several decades of her life.

Of course, these five diarists are not representative of the majority of nineteenth-century African Americans. Grimké, a member of the Forten-Purvis Philadelphia family, all deeply involved in the abolitionist movement, received grammar and normal school education in Salem. Rollin, whose parents were among a small number of prominent free black families who settled in Charleston in the 1840s, was educated in local private schools and in Philadelphia. Though Wells and Montgomery were born into slavery, their families were able to see that they had access to the available means of education, and, as Richard Brodhead points out in the introduction to his edition of Chesnutt's journals, "Given that the black illiteracy rate still stood at 75 percent in North Carolina in 1880, the very literacy of which the journal is constant evidence differentiates Chesnutt from the great mass of his contemporaries."[5]

It could be reasonably claimed, then, that diary-keeping was a practice most postbellum blacks had neither the time nor the skills to observe and that those who did were advantaged in some respect. But the lives of these five diarists tell another story. They all were hard workers, often barely able to pay their bills. While Grimké may have inherited the Fortens' abolitionist zeal, she inherited little of the often-cited Forten wealth, which by her time had apparently diminished considerably. In her journal, she writes of her father's financial difficulties and his request that she return to Philadelphia from Salem, as he could no longer support her there. By 1856, Grimké, whose mother died when she was three, was alienated from her father and his second wife, who had moved to Canada with her step-siblings. The following year, Grimké's father informed her that he was "utterly unable" to help her.[6] Lisa A. Long observes that "though they often sheltered her and gave her a sense of intellectual community, her relatives did not ultimately support young Forten."[7] Similarly, with her father suffering financial loss at the close of the Civil War and Martin Delany no longer providing promised funds, Rollin was forced to support herself while in Boston by sewing and working as a copyist for the Massachusetts legislature. And during her years in Memphis, Wells seemed always in the midst of one financial crisis or another. Aside from the requisite literacy, these diarists' most prominent features were not privilege but some version of the self-denial, persistence, and resilience Kett identifies as being associated with those who take on self-education projects.[8] Further, these diarists shared a reality with other black rhetors located in this site of rhetorical education: they were emblematic of those in the wider cohort of African Americans who engaged in some form of self-education through their use of this private literacy. It is our good fortune that they were motivated to record their activities in diaries, for they provide additional insight into the complex intellectual lives of blacks in the mid- and late nineteenth century.

On Diary-Keeping

The diary or journal, defined here as a text written in the first person with dated, chronological passages in which the writing subject speaks of and comments on certain events, was at the height of its popularity in the late nineteenth century.[9] One nineteenth-century conduct book advised that the regularity of diary-keeping improves facility with language that otherwise "lies merely in the outer court of the memory, and does not enter and make any permanent impression upon the mind, until it is practiced and made useful in every-day life."[10] The literature on the history of diary-keeping centers on the habits of middle-class white women, many of whom kept diaries as outlets for the articulation of ideas in the only available space. Setting information on self-education and literacy practices aside, the diaries of the four black women considered here were no doubt motivated by these same social pressures and others. Mary Helen Washington, in her foreword to Wells's published diary, analogizes the diary genre to the "clearing in Black religious culture, a place where, physically and psychologically, Black people felt free to speak in a setting outside the boundaries of the official church, a private sanctuary where one's truer self is affirmed and authorized."[11] These diarists recorded their hopes and desires, their joys and disappointments, in a safe space, and while my interest is in the literacy practices their entries bring to light, I try to remember that these practices represent just one aspect of their complex lives.

Although very much concerned about propriety and respectability, Wells, on numerous occasions, articulated her frustrations with the societal constraints of nineteenth-century Memphis, especially those placed upon an unmarried, outspoken woman. But these writers also seemed intent on documenting their responses to a variety of language experiences—that is, the material they read and the political speeches they heard—as a matter of record, even if only for themselves. In a foreword to her journal, Grimké offered among her reasons for maintaining a diary the fact that it would "doubtless enable me to judge correctly of the growth and improvement of my mind from year to year" (58). Montgomery seemed always enthusiastic about all her pursuits. Anticipating having to learn more about gardening, she wrote, "I feel like one just embracing the threshold of a new life."[12] Chesnutt was probably the most isolated of all these diarists, with few friends or intellectual soul mates. He wrote at the beginning of his third journal, "Cast, as my lot has been, among a people, or in a place whose people do not enter into my trains of thought and who indeed cannot understand or sympathize with them, I find it quite a relief to take them to my confidant, my Journal, who listens patiently as long as I care to talk, never contradicts my statements, and keeps my secrets religiously."[13] His journal, possibly the most self-consciously written of the five examined here, must have functioned as an affirming companion.

The diary form also invites discussion of motive as well as action, including the why of various rhetorical pursuits—why this lecture, this book, this letter, or this response rather than another. While a discussion of various approaches to interpreting diaries is beyond the scope of this project, any assessment of the contents must take into account the diarists' assumptions about audience. To what extent did they write, knowing that at some point their entries might be read, and how might that awareness of audiences to come have helped to shape their narratives? Even if they were not consciously imagining external audiences, rhetorical theorists Chaim Perelman and Lucie Olbrechts-Tyteca point out that self-deliberators, as I am claiming these diarists were, serve as their own audiences, arguing for a particular understanding of their experiences in the same way that they might with another person, and that "it is immaterial whether or not the subject [writer] is unaware of the real motives for his conduct."[14] Questions concerning audience awareness and intent notwithstanding, these records of literacy encounters expose a great deal about the writers' habits of mind and level of rhetorical sophistication.

Rather than focus on the educational contributions of diary-keeping and drawing on these diarists' practices for examples, I have chosen to discuss each diarist separately, highlighting their practices one diarist at a time. This choice runs the risk of shifting the gaze away from diary-keeping as a site of rhetorical education and calling more attention to the diarists, but it has the advantage of presenting a more complete accounting of the rhetorical practices of these five diarists and of emphasizing the ways in which these practices are interwoven. To return to my definition of rhetorical education as various combinations of experiences influencing how people understand and practice effective communication, I see diary-keeping as a primary site of rhetorical education in that it provides such combinations of experiences: diarists write out their thoughts on issues and respond in their diaries to what they have read, heard, or experienced, thereby developing their critical skills. Secondarily, diaries also yield information on the kinds of educational activities these diarists engaged in outside of keeping diaries, for example, their participation in literary clubs and elocution classes. In my discussion, I place the contents of diary entries into one or more of these educational categories. As mentioned earlier, there are only a few extant diaries by African Americans. Part of my initial curiosity about how African Americans learned to speak in the nineteenth century can be satisfied on a case-by-case basis only. By looking at these five diarists separately, I attempt to understand better the circumstances leading to their keeping of a diary—how they found the time, what models they used, and what they hoped to accomplish, if anything. It could be misleading to treat them as if they are representative of some larger collection of diaries. At the end of this section, I identify common features that help to account for how diary-keeping serves rhetorical education.

Charlotte Forten Grimké

Across her five extant journals, maintained intermittently between 1854 and 1892, Grimké recorded innumerable historically rich accounts of rhetorical activities. They include her constant reading and writing habits; her participation in a literary society and antislavery sewing circles; and her responses to sermons, elocutionist performances, and abolitionist lectures. The determined tone and attention to a variety of rhetorical activities in her entry of February 8, 1857, are typical:

> Finished "The Autobiography of a Female Slave."[15] To me it is deeply interesting. The writer's style has not, perhaps, that perfect elegance and simplicity which distinguishes the *best* writers, but she evidently *feels* deeply on the subject, and her book is calculated to awaken our deepest sympathies. I thank her for writing it. Hers must be a brave, true soul thus to surmount all obstacles, to soar above all the prejudices, which, from childhood must have been instilled into her mind, and take upon herself the defense of a down-trodden and degraded race! Recommenced Rollin's "Ancient History" which I intend to read regularly, and read several papers of the "Spectator." Committed some poetry to memory. A plan which I shall pursue, as my memory greatly needs strengthening. Mrs. And Mrs. P[utnam] spent the evening. Talked of forming a French class. Probably it will amount to nothing. I shall go on alone with both Latin and French—and *persevere*. (190–91)

The passage outlines a disciplined approach to self-improvement in rhetorical skills. Constantly in pursuit of knowledge, she writes, "I feel grieved and ashamed to think how very little I know of what I should know of what is really good and useful. May this knowledge of my want of knowledge be to me a fresh incentive to more earnest, thoughtful action, more persevering study!" (96).

At age twenty, Grimké had a plan to cultivate her memory, to read regularly, and to learn both Latin and French, all with a determination to prevail. According to a list found with her diary manuscript, Grimké, during the course of one year, read over one hundred books. What motivated her to engage in this determined project of self-education? Ray Allen Billington suggests that race shaped her existence more than anything else, that it was "always uppermost in . . . [her] thoughts," believing that by excelling she would prove herself equal to whites.[16] I agree that she was fully cognizant of her racialized existence and fully invested in abolitionism and race representations. She came from a family steeped in antislavery activism, extending from her grandfather James Forten to her father, Robert Bridges Forten, and her aunts and uncles Sarah Forten, Harriet Forten and Robert Purvis, Margaretta Forten, and James Forten Jr. In Salem, living with Charles L. Remond and his sister Sarah Parker Remond, both antislavery lecturing agents, Grimké had the opportunity to meet many key figures in New England abolitionism. Yet there is something in her passion for learning that seems driven by pure pleasure and self-satisfaction as well. In 1878, twenty-year-old Charles Chesnutt would also write of having "persevered" to accomplish his goal of learning German (93).

On May 31, 1854, just a week after she began her diary, seventeen-year-old Grimké commented on the quality of public speaking at a political rally she attended in Boston with a friend during the time of the trial of fugitive slave Anthony Burns: "We went to the meeting, but the best speakers were absent, engaged in the most arduous and untiring efforts in behalf of the poor fugitive; but though we missed the glowing eloquence of [Wendell] Phillips, [William Lloyd] Garrison, and [Theodore] Parker, still there were excellent speeches made, and our hearts responded to the exalted sentiments of Truth and Liberty which were uttered. The exciting intelligence which occasionally came in relation to the trial, added fresh zeal to the speakers, of whom Stephen Foster and his wife were the principal" (64).

Living during a time of heightened abolitionist activity in a lyceum-driven oratorical culture, Grimké had many opportunities to hear and comment on the rhetorical performances of prominent speakers, like her Salem host Charles Remond, with whom Grimké lived from 1853 to 1857. After listening to his sister Sarah Parker Remond read one of his speeches, Grimké noted that she "like[d] it very much" (77).[17] Two years later, she commented on a talk he gave on the Kansas rebellion, observing that whether every one agreed with him or not, "Still I am glad that *something* has roused the people of the North at last" (166). It is not surprising that Grimké heard in person or read most of the renowned speakers of the late antebellum period, given her location in Salem where the Salem Lyceum Association, established in 1830, sponsored lectures in a hall seating seven hundred, nor is it surprising that she heard at least four of Ralph Waldo Emerson's lectures between 1855 and 1858, since he appeared at the Salem Lyceum more than any other speaker.[18] What is unusual is that in Grimké's journals, we have responses to these speakers from the perspective of a seventeen- to twenty-year-old black woman, committed to a self-education in the rhetorical arts of reading, speaking, and writing, often for pleasure and more increasingly in the service of abolishing slavery and improving living conditions for members of her race.

The speakers mentioned in Grimké's diaries include Henry Ward Beecher ("His manner is not at all polished or elegant, but he says so many excellent things with such forcible earnestness or irresistible humor that we quite forget it" [121–22]), Lucy Stone ("The lecture was earnest and impressive, and some parts of it very beautiful. It was an appeal to the noblest and warmest sympathies of our nature, in behalf of the oppressed" [116–17]), Frederick Douglass ("Uncle W[illiam] read to me some of F[rederick] Douglass' best speeches;—very fine they were. I wish the man had a *heart* worthy of so great, so gifted a mind" [240]),[19] Wendell Phillips ("Mr. Phillips' lecture was worthy of himself. I can bestow no higher praises upon it. Oh! It is a source of some consolation to feel—to know that some of the noblest minds—the greatest intellects of the age are enlisted in our behalf" [143]), essayist and critic Edward P. Whipple ("Whipple's oration is elegant. But I do not like him. He is too conservative" [185]), Theodore Parker ("I have long wished very much to see and hear this remarkable man, and my pleasant anticipation[s] were fully realized" [125]), and, of course, Emerson. She devoted over an entire page of her February 11, 1857, journal entry to comments on his lecture "Works and Days," which includes the following excerpt: "Have just returned from hearing R. W. Emerson.—Subject 'Works and Days' from Hesiod's poem—One of the most beautiful and eloquent lectures I ever heard. . . . Never, never before have I so forcibly felt the *preciousness* of time. And oh, how deeply do the words and presence of such a man as Emerson, make us feel the utter insignificance, the great inferiority of *ourselves*" (192).

Grimké's comments call attention to the critical link between logos and ethos in effective persuasion and acknowledge this connection between rhetorical training and the kind of public performances required of a worker in the antislavery movement. Her reactions to the leading antislavery orators and activists were akin to the responses of present-day teenagers to rock stars. These men and women coming forward in support of "the cause" were her heroes, not only because of the positions they took but also because of the eloquence with which they did so. She takes pride in knowing that "nearly all the finest orators now are anti-slavery" (126). Grimké mentions attending a meeting of an antislavery sewing circle during which members admired an inkstand once owned by Lydia Maria Child. The entry proceeds to praise Child's writing, especially her 1836 romance novel *Philothea*, set in ancient Greece, rather than her antislavery writings, as might be expected: "No one could read *her* writings without the most enthusiastic admiration of the high-souled writer. I am sure that I cannot. . . . I always think of it [*Philothea*] with a feeling of grateful pleasure that it was written" (171). A few entries later, on Christmas Day of 1856, she had the opportunity to meet Child and other "distinguished champions of our cause," noting, "She is not quite so spiritual looking as one would expect to see the author of 'Philothea,' but is a very charming person nevertheless" (175).

Janet Carey Eldred and Peter Mortensen observe that Grimké "comes to expect in antislavery oratory a rhetorical stance undiluted by appeals to a broader range of human rights," pointing, for example, to her general objections to orators who advocate tolerance for slavery-supporting Christians. These authors argue that when Grimké attended an antislavery lecture, she expected "to hear what she would hear in the Remond household or at an antislavery meeting: persuasion aimed at provoking action."[20] At the same time, still quite young and impressionable, Grimké also took much general pleasure in her rhetorical pursuits.

Throughout the journal, Grimké describes being read to or reading aloud to various people, reminding us of the prevalence of this practice at the time. Among those who were not literate, hearing the Bible, newspapers, letters, political tracts, and other forms of literature read aloud provided a valuable means of access to spiritual guidance, pleasure, and information—a function discussed throughout this volume. Jane Donawerth points out that Lydia Sigourney in her conduct book *Letters to Young Ladies* (1833) defended the practice of reading aloud as acceptable for women in promiscuous settings because it provided instruction in morals and could be a service to the family.[21] In her autobiographical textbook, *Reminiscences of School Life, and Hints on Teaching*, written at the beginning of the twentieth century but based on practices she followed during Reconstruction, Fanny Jackson Coppin emphasizes the value of reading to develop both listening and speaking skills in the classroom: "A first-class reader may be called an elocutionist, because he makes the thoughts of the writer live again in the minds of those who hear. . . . But besides training the eye, we should remember that the ear should be trained. Read a short sentence to the class and see who can repeat it correctly; you will be astonished to see how few can reproduce the sentence just as it was given. It is no wonder that our Lord said, 'Take heed how ye hear.'"[22] Coppin, who joined the faculty of the Institute for Colored Youth in 1865, remained there for nearly forty years, bringing about many educational changes.

In one entry, Grimké records that she "read aloud fifty-nine pages of Macaulay, and an interesting sketch of the distinguished philosopher, Sir Humphrey Davy" (116). She apparently read these pages for her own benefit. For Grimké and her acquaintances, reading aloud appeared to be primarily a habit of pleasure rather than necessity, but nonetheless, it served as a source of rhetorical education. Though mainly considered a role for women, while they sewed or socialized, reading aloud as Grimké recounts it in her in the journal was frequently performed by men, and the shared experience of reading served as a starting point for critique or general conversation. Two instances have already been cited of her being read the speeches of Douglass and Remond; she also records being read ghost stories, the poetry of Robert Burns and John Greenleaf Whittier, Charles Dickens, Margaret Oliphant's *Salem Chapel,* sermons, and temperance tracts. Readers included classmates, friends, relatives, and her husband, the Reverend Francis Grimké, whom she married in 1878. She records his reading to her in Jacksonville, Florida, where he served as pastor of the Laura Street Presbyterian Church between 1885 and 1889, before returning to Fifteenth Street Presbyterian in Washington, D.C. She writes on December 16, 1885, that "F[rank] read to me some extracts of speeches by Dr. Hazzard on the Education of the Negro. They are very fine. He seems to be by far the most liberal and the most Christian friend of the colored people" (520).

Grimké's rhetorical education did not lead to her becoming a public activist. Most of her rhetorical work took place in her writing and in her classrooms. During her time in Salem with the Remonds, Grimké attended the Higginson Grammar School, where her comment following the unexpected class visit of a teacher for whom the students were asked to recite suggests an early reluctance to speak publicly: "I do think reading one's composition, before strangers is a trying task. If I were to tell Mrs. R[emond] this, I know she would ask how I could expect to become what I often say I would like to be—an Anti-Slavery Lecturer. But I think I should then trust to the inspiration of the subject" (92). Her reluctance to join "a kind of literary society" stems from a concern that she might be called on "to read or recite" (339). Ultimately, Grimké's race work took place through her writing and in classrooms on the South Carolina Sea Islands, where she taught contraband slaves from 1862 to 1864, rather than from the podium. As a later entry suggests, she apparently was not a spontaneous speaker. Not finding the words to encourage a friend on the Sea Islands, she records, "I longed to say, 'I thank you, for that noble glorious speech.' And yet I *c'ld* not. It is always so. I do not know how to talk. Words always fail me when I want them most. The more I feel the more impossible it is for me to speak" (433).

In addition to the diary itself, evidence of her writing practices are plentiful: letters, essays, poems, and often just writing (though it's not always clear what)—for example, "Have been writing nearly all day" (77) and "Spent nearly all day in writing busily. Determined to finish my story" (271). In May 1858, for her poem "Glimpses of New England," AME bishop Daniel Payne paid her a dollar ("The first money I've ever made by *writing*" [311]).[23] After completing her work at Higginson, Grimké enrolled in the Salem Normal School, the first African American to do so, completing her teacher training and her formal education there in 1856. But Grimké continued to read and write profusely for the rest of her life, detailing both activities in her journals. For Grimké, these activities of literacy do not seem to have been motivated primarily either by duty to the antislavery cause, as central as it was to her consciousness, or by pleasure, as much as she enjoyed reading, writing, speaking, and listening. Rather, the two incentives seemed to have been mutually sustaining.

Frances Anne Rollin

Excerpts from the diary of Frances Anne Rollin reveal this same kind of natural pleasure in an active life of the mind. However, in the case of Rollin, we have only excerpts from entries made over seven months in 1868 while she was in Boston.[24] Rollin received a superior education in antebellum Charleston, South Carolina, as the daughter of Margaretta Rollin and William Rollin, a successful businessman. She was given a Catholic private school education and attended the Quaker Institute for Colored Youth in Philadelphia, where Fanny Jackson

Coppin would later teach. During Rollin's time there in the early 1860s, the institute offered a classical curriculum, with courses covering Caesar, Virgil, Cicero, Horace, and New Testament Greek.[25] She left the institute and returned to Charleston to teach in 1865. Rollin and her sisters, Charlotte, Katherine, Louisa, and Florence, reportedly held influential political meetings at their home in Columbia, South Carolina, where the family moved after the Civil War. Their drawing room was called "Republican Headquarters." Dorothy Sterling points out that such gatherings of the wives and daughters of prominent black men were common in Southern capitals during Reconstruction.[26] These events, shaping the course of Southern politics, also provided numerous opportunities to sharpen argumentative skills. Both Louisa, who addressed the state House of Representatives in 1869, and Charlotte, who spoke at the 1870 convention of the South Carolina Woman's Rights Association in Charleston, were also active in the South Carolina woman's suffrage movement.[27] Thus, Frances Rollin grew up in a family of political activists who understood the critical value of rhetorical abilities.

Rollin was twenty-two years old in 1867[28] when she met Martin Delany, serving as a captain in the Union army and as a Freedmen's Bureau agent, in Charleston. Delany, then fifty-five years old, commissioned her to write his life story. With the promise from Delany of financial support, Rollin moved to Boston in the fall of 1867. Her great-granddaughter Carole Ione writes that Delany had heard that Boston publishers were interested in his biography, and since he knew many there who would support the project, he encouraged Rollin to move to Boston, a city filled with like-minded "aspiring writers."[29] Rollin worked on the biography throughout the winter of 1867–68, completing a draft in March. The book was published in the summer of 1868, by Lee and Shepard, under the title *Life and Public Services of Martin R. Delany*, and Rollin returned to South Carolina to work for the state government. From January 1 to July 28, 1868, while writing the biography, Rollin also kept a diary in which she documented her writing and revising processes, reading practices, and reactions to various public speakers.

Usually working on the biography in the morning, often at the State House library, Rollin speaks of "writing as hard as ever," even though she had no guarantee of publication. She shared drafts with her acquaintance Richard Greener, who was on his way to becoming the first African American Harvard graduate, with abolitionist orator Wendell Phillips, and with William C. Nell. Greener's critique solicited this response: "Mr. Richard Greener has gone over some of it with me, but he is cynical and apt to discourage instead of acting otherwise. He lives in a grand intellectual sphere and is accustomed to only perfection."[30] Rollin never mentioned what Phillips, whom she called "a masterpiece of humanity," thought of it (455).

Rollin read widely during her time in Boston—Thomas Macaulay, Alphonse de Larmartine's *History of the Girondists,* a biography of Josiah Quincy,[31] Whittier's poem "Randolph of Roanoke," and portions of Thomas DeQuincy's letters. She also read the newly published *Behind the Scenes Or, Thirty Years A Slave and Four Years in the White House* by Elizabeth Keckley, noting that it was "well written but not by Mrs. K, that's clear." Later registering further disappointment, she comments on Keckley's reading of excerpts from *Behind the Scenes:* "It was poor to say the least. It is too late in the day for her to attempt it especially without a first class teacher" (460). Rollin probably was wishing that Keckley had had the assistance of a teacher of elocution.[32]

Rollin attended and commented on a variety of speaking events as well. Over a two day period in January, Rollin attended two speech-making occasions—an anti-slavery festival in Boston, staged to support newly emancipated African Americans rather than abandon them in their time of greatest need, and an antislavery meeting. The second sentence of her first diary entry reads, "Speeches tonight at the Tremont Temple, but so terribly rainy that there is no possibility of reaching there."[33] She heard Dickens reading from *David Copperfield;* Emerson, who spoke on the "immortality of the soul"; Phillips, who gave her a copy of his speeches, "as precious to me as the apple of my eye" (458); William Lloyd Garrison; Frances Kemble; and William Wells Brown. While comfortably acquainted with most of Boston's leading statesmen and women, Rollin was also fully aware of her outsider status. She demurred from celebrating George Washington's birthday, observing, "I am no enthusiast over Patriotic Celebrations as I am counted out of the body Politic" (456), although she did write that men like Phillips "reconcile . . . me to Americans" (455).

Rollin had an impressive array of associates reading and critiquing her work, most of them already well-established authors and orators, like Brown and Nell. As mentioned, one of the leading abolitionist orators, Wendell Phillips—whom Grimké praised at least a dozen times in her journal—was Rollin's personal mentor. It is clear from Rollin's diary that he took her under his wing, giving her tickets to various speaking events, offering to listen to her read from drafts of the Delany biography, and providing encouraging feedback. Thus in Rollin's diary entries, we capture a snapshot of rhetorical activities over a brief period but in a setting deeply immersed in postbellum oratorical culture. Rollin interacted with many of the same "Americans" as Grimké, whom she also met with while in Boston. Grimké had been in Boston since 1865, when she moved there to serve as secretary of the Teachers Committee of the New England Branch of the Freedmen's Union Commission. The routines of these two diarists were similar in the blend of the political and the pleasurable. One might say that for Rollin, as for Grimké, the commitment to self-education was closely linked to an abiding concern for bettering conditions for members of her race.

Ida B. Wells

What would the diary of Ida Wells, born into slavery and, upon the death of her parents from yellow fever, the sole breadwinner for her five surviving siblings, reveal about her self-education strategies? In her autobiography, Wells writes that she does not remember when or where she started school but does recall that the children in her family had the "job" of learning all they could there.[34] Until the age of sixteen, she attended Shaw, later renamed Rust College, one of the many schools established by and officially for the formerly enslaved. Rust College in Holly Springs, Mississippi, provided instruction at all levels—elementary, grammar, normal course, college preparatory, and college. An 1896–97 Rust catalog lists spelling, penmanship, advanced grammar, reading, and civil government among the courses offered in the grammar school; medieval history, literature, rhetoric, pedagogy, and ethics in the normal course; and English Bible, Roman history, Greek, Latin, and French in the college preparatory course.[35] In 1896, Wells would have been away from Rust at least fifteen years. Wells writes in her autobiography, however, that she "had no normal training" and worked hard on her own to prepare her daily teaching lessons.[36] Thus, it is difficult to know with certainty what courses Wells took. T. Thomas Fortune, in a biographical sketch, noted that although she did not graduate from Rust, the institution "conferred upon Miss Wells the degree of Master of Arts at the commencement exercises of 1892," an honor possibly bestowed in recognition of her journalistic work.[37]

Wells's role as an activist-orator had roots in the activism of her parents and her community. When the man to whom her father, James Wells, was apprenticed as a builder learned that Wells had voted Republican, he locked him out of his shop. In response, James Wells purchased another set of tools and moved his family to a location nearby.[38] A trustee of Rust, James Wells was probably also a member of the Holly Springs branch of the Loyal League, a Republican-supported political organization established by local Rust College officials and by the Freedmen's Bureau primarily to encourage blacks to vote. The league met at the home of Nelson Gill, local head of the bureau, or at a Baptist church, with "long speakings and demonstrations." During one meeting, Ku Klux Klan members hid themselves under the house in order to shoot Gill, but their plans were foiled.[39] Growing up in this racially charged environment of active participation in community affairs provided an early model for Wells's own subsequent public rhetoric.

Wells kept diaries during three distinct periods of her life. The examples of rhetorical activities that follow come from the diary she kept while living in Memphis between 1885 and 1887. At the age of twenty-four, her reading list included the Bible and works by Dickens, Louisa Alcott, Charlotte Brontë, and

Shakespeare; all influenced Wells's rhetorical training. But she wrote that during her early years, she "never read a Negro book or anything about Negroes."[40] Wells's diary entries suggest a critical interest in oral performance, particularly pulpit oratory. In one passage, Wells criticized a minister's preaching style for lacking the reverence required in "dealing with holy things" and for being too similar in delivery to a lecture he had given earlier.[41] This critique marks Wells's sense of a clear distinction between what Hugh Blair called pulpit oratory and the oratory of the popular assemblies.[42] She wrote: "I went back last night to hear him *preach* in order to come to a decision and came away doubtful as to his holy zeal & fitness for the work. A constant arraignment of the Negro as compared to the whites, a burlesque of Negro worship, a repetition of what he did not believe in, and the telling of jokes together with a reiteration of his text 'ye must be born again' made up his 'sermon.' It was in style so closely allied to his 'talk' of the morning that I detected little difference between the two" (39).

Yet, Wells also wondered why many preachers in their sermons did not give people the kind of practical information needed for everyday living. On the one hand, it appears that Wells wanted sermons to be different in *form* from the discourse people would hear in nonreligious spaces. On the other, she implies that preachers needed to make their sermons more useful by including information congregations could act upon, thus making them similar in *substance* to the oratory of the popular assemblies. In her February 8, 1886, entry, she praises the delivery style of prominent American evangelist Dwight L. Moody: "His style is so simple, plain and natural. He told the old, old story in an easy conversational way that charms the listener ere he is aware and the secret of his success is, I think—that he does not preach a far-away God—a hard to be reconciled Saviour but uses a natural earnest tone and tells in a natural way without any long drawn doctrine or finely spun theology or rhetoric the simple truth that Christ Jesus came on earth to seek & save that which was lost" (41–42).

Years later in her autobiography, Wells takes the time to comment on the speaking ability of another minister she heard in Liverpool, noting, "He was young, eloquent, and inspired, and it is no wonder that he preached to a church full to overflowing." She called his "the most wonderful sermon I had ever heard in my life."[43] Wells's own extant speeches, all direct indictments of the perpetrators of mob violence and all addressed to popular assemblies, certainly met the criterion of relevance. Wells's comments on her own writing process reveal a dissatisfaction with what she considered to be her inability to vary her prose style: "I think sometimes I can write a readable article and then again I wonder how I could have been so mistaken in myself. A glance at all my 'brilliant?' productions pall on my understanding; they all savor of dreary sameness, however varied the subject, and the style is monotonous" (100).

Because oratorical performance was valued highly in the nineteenth century, many ordinary citizens, not preparing to be lawyers, preachers, or public servants, took private elocution lessons to improve themselves. Elocution, "the study of the artful delivery of speech or poetry," including "training the body and voice," would have been particularly useful to teachers, like Wells, whose work required daily public performances before a class.[44] Wells took elocution lessons in Memphis from a Mrs. Fannie J. Thompson, a Memphis public school teacher, at two dollars a session, even when she had little money.[45] Her diary mentioned intermittent lessons dependent upon her finances, but clearly these lessons were important to her, as she noted that lack of funds resulted in her not going out one day, "not even to take a lesson" (44). Additional entries find her critiquing her own literary meeting performances and those of others: "Went to Literary meeting at LeMoyne Friday night to see Macbeth played but they read it thro [*sic*]. It was exceedingly dull & tiresome & some of the pronunciation was execrable in the extreme. Took my 3rd lesson of the season from Mrs. T[hompson] yesterday. The weather was miserably cold as the second 'blizzard' came sometime Friday night after we got home, but I went as I realize I am losing valuable time by not going. Did not know it [her assigned reading] thoroughly but got along very well" (34).

Wells gave dramatic readings, like the soliloquy of Lady Macbeth, at the literary society meetings at LeMoyne Normal Institute and other venues: July 4, "Went to Mrs. H[ooks]'s concert & recited 'The Letter Reading' & Sleep-walking scenes from 'Lady McBeth.' The first was loudly applauded[;] the last, given in my Mother Hubbard was not so effective as I could have wished" (84). The one constant throughout these early entries is reference to taking or having to miss taking lessons with Thompson, for example, "Took no lesson last Saturday as my book had not come" (60).[46] The activity of taking lessons is listed along with what were considered to be other routine events: "Took lessons Tuesday and tried on my dress this evening" (61); "Went to the Literary Friday night. Went to recite Saturday but have made no choice of a piece yet" (66).

Wells's entries here with respect to her performance at lessons and at the literary meetings contrast sharply with those made during this same period by Laura Hamilton Murray, a young Alexandria, Virginia, mother, who kept a diary between February 1885 and February 1886. Murray was much less enthusiastic about attending such meetings and about her performances once there. She probably participated out of a sense of duty, since her husband, Freeman Murray, was president of the "Literary" at the time. She wrote in a July 9, 1885, diary entry: "I finished my lawn dress. Went to Literary at night. It is as bad as usual. I was given an essay for next time. It is very discouraging."[47] Two days before the next meeting, she noted that she copied the essay "Expectations" to read at "Literary."[48] Following the meeting, Murray wrote: "Finished a dress for baby. Went to Literary read essay to a very slim crowd" (476), adding, probably with little regret, that the club would adjourn for ten months (7/23). Still, it is notable that successful performance at these society events did matter to her, perhaps in part because of her husband's position but also because she perceived these performances as a means of self-validation, as a confidence builder. Unlike Wells, Murray was first and foremost a homemaker and mother rather than an activist for race and women's rights.

Murray took occasional trips into the city, referring in her diary to such events as the February 22 dedication of the Washington Monument. On March 4, she attended Grover Cleveland's first inauguration and a week later took the train into Washington to see *Uncle Tom's Cabin* "played." She also mentions "reading a great deal' (2/28) and, on one day in March, writing thirteen letters. Laura Murray's diary serves as a reminder that many of the black women who kept diaries were ordinary women. We have access to her diary only because it is included among the papers of her husband, who went on to become a civil rights activist, author, and publisher who survived her by over fifty years. Her rhetorical education did not lead to the publication of a biography or a newspaper, nor did she become a schoolteacher. The mother of five children, Murray died at thirty-four. She lived a short life as a hardworking homemaker who also kept a diary in which she inscribed her literacy practices.

Mary Virginia Montgomery

Another Mississippian who kept a diary—though some thirteen years before Ida B. Wells began hers—was Mary Virginia Montgomery. In 1891, Wells visited Mound Bayou, Mississippi, an all-black town established by Isaiah Montgomery, Mary Virginia's brother.[49] Wells mentions him in her autobiography as one of those who assisted her during state tours to promote her paper, the *Free Speech,* and they became "the best of friends," even though Wells disagreed with his acquiescence, as the only black member of the 1890 Mississippi Constitutional Convention, to the "Understanding Clause," which provided a way around the Fifteenth Amendment that granted all male citizens the vote.[50] Wells probably met Mary Montgomery during her visit.

Montgomery's early rhetorical education exceeded that of most Southern men or women, black or white, in the years surrounding the Civil War. Born in 1849, Montgomery spent the first sixteen years of her life in slavery on the Hurricane plantation run by Jefferson Davis's brother, Joseph. Hurricane and Brierfield plantations were located on the Davis Bend peninsula near Vicksburg, Mississippi, some 150 miles south of what would later become Mound Bayou. Montgomery's father, Benjamin, was given certain opportunities on the Davis plantation not usually afforded to slaves. He helped to run the plantation and encouraged Mary Virginia and all of his children to pursue their interests. When only five years old, she and Isaiah were tutored by a well-educated white man Benjamin met who had moved to the area to teach local black and white children. However, this rare mixture of black and white, free and enslaved students being schooled together in antebellum Mississippi was soon dissolved.

Her brother wrote of having ready access to the Davis library and to all the reading matter that came into the household as a consequence of his position as "private secretary and office attendant" to Joseph Davis. He noted, "I read a great deal, but it was without method and served only to give a fair knowledge of history and current events, of language and composition by familiarity and use, which has stood me well in hand to this day for I have never studied either."[51] The Davis family came to rely on Isaiah Montgomery for war news he acquired during his trips to town, an interesting reversal of the opening scene in Frances Harper's novel *Iola Leroy,* where the enslaved engaged in subversive eavesdropping as slaveholders discuss the progress of the war. Mary Virginia, no doubt, had similar access.

Since black codes did not allow the sale of property to blacks, Joseph Davis sold in a secret deal the Hurricane and Brierfield plantations to Benjamin Montgomery in November 1866 for $300,000, to be paid over ten years. Davis Bend developed into a thriving black community even during the turbulent years of Reconstruction. After the Montgomerys took ownership of the Davis Bend property, Mary Virginia held a full-time job at the family store, assisting the bookkeeper and the mail clerk.

Frances Harper, an older contemporary, commented on the lifestyle she observed in Davis Bend during an 1871 visit there of several days, just months before Mary Virginia began her diary. Harper was especially impressed with the kinds of work women like Mary Virginia, whom she described as "an intelligent young lady," and her mother performed. At the same time, Harper acknowledged that the Montgomerys were an exceptional case, "one of the most interesting families I have ever seen in the South."[52]

Information as to her self-education activities comes primarily from extant portions of a diary, covering the period from January 17, 1872, to December 28, 1872, which are filled with rich examples. The diary is an uncommon record of the daily activities of a young black woman, living a relatively comfortable but busy life on a postwar former Mississippi slave plantation. It has been described as depicting "a life so fully programmed with improving activities that it resembles the regimen of the great female Transcendentalist, Margaret Fuller."[53] Montgomery observed a rigid schedule driven in part by household responsibilities, her job at the family store, and an ambitious self-education project. She read widely during every spare moment, especially at night before retiring. A good deal but not all of this reading may have been based on her hopeful anticipation of matriculation at Oberlin College, where she and her sister Rebecca matriculated for two years. But it is also clear that she derived a great deal of pleasure from her intellectual pursuits.

She arose early, often reading before breakfast, performed household chores, and on certain days went to work in the family store. What is immediately apparent is her passion for learning. Mary Virginia sewed, played the piano, and worked in her mother's flower garden, but her ultimate pleasure seems to have been reading. She wrote as the first entry, "Beautiful morning. I have so much to do that I hardly know how to begin" (1/17).[54] She calls reading "a great recreation" (4/12), and at the close of one early entry she tells of having to "forgo book pleasure" because of illness (1/26). One summer evening, she gleefully notes that she "had leisure to read a small book," adding "I have so much to read and so little time, that I often wish the days were twice as long" (8/17). As in Grimké's journals, there are frequent references to reading aloud, especially with Montgomery reading aloud to her father and to communal silent reading: "Read Politics [?] to Pa until too late to do anything else" (8/19) and "Tonight we have a supplement to the N.Y. Times so full of political interest. We read until time to retire" (467).

Of all the material she particularly enjoyed reading over this twelve-month period, works on the interrelated topics of phrenology and self-culture attracted her most. Interest in phrenology, the popular nineteenth-century science of determining a person's mental strengths, abilities, and personality traits from the shape of the skull, frequently merged with an interest in self-improvement under the belief that a knowledge of one's mental strengths and weaknesses would aid in developing self-improvement strategies. In line with this thinking, as Janet Sharp Hermann suggests, Montgomery probably felt that if she could gather enough information about her own capacities, she could improve herself more effectively.[55] On March 25, she mentions having had "a splendid opportunity for studying phrenology . . . almost memorized my chart" and that she had examined the heads of a dozen persons, probably for entertainment. In addition to subscribing to Orson Fowler and Samuel Wells's *American Phrenological Journal,* Montgomery mentions reading and having her father read two works titled "Self-Education" and "Self-Culture." No authors are given for either title, and it is not clear that she refers here to two different works or one, since "self-education" and "self-culture" were often used interchangeably to refer to self-improvement of the mind.[56]

Other topics mentioned include the Ten Commandments, mineralogy, the Punic Wars, zoology, chemistry, United States history, and parallel histories of the construction of Babel. She enjoyed reading William Cowper's "The Task" and Plutarch, whom she found "difficult for fast reading" (6/20). She also read Alfred Lord Tennyson, John Dryden's translation of Virgil, Lord Byron, and Charles Darwin's *On the Origin of Species,* noting that "[i]t bids to be interesting and will entertain me many nights " (4/16). Continuously pursuing her "great recreation," she enjoyed the *Times, Harper's Bazaar,* and *Demorest's Illustrated Monthly Magazine.*

Montgomery also wrote her own compositions and critiqued the written and oral productions of others. In the evenings, she practiced and studied composition using Richard Green Parker's *English Composition.*[57] On an unexpected day off, she began an essay on the "situation and requisites of the colored people everywhere" (4/26). In a later entry, she mentions working late on an essay on progress, one with which she was not pleased. After a walk in the garden one morning, she wrote an essay on flowers. One source of ideas and inspiration was Maturin Ballou's compilation *Treasury of Thought,* an encyclopedia of quotations, which she noted would "serve as a reference when engaged in composition" (10/1).

Diary entries also demonstrate attention to public speaking and politics. She read a great deal of history and the *New York Times* during the summer months. She commented on the controversy surrounding the election of local politician George C. McKee.[58] The family attended public meetings. At one, Mary Ann Shadd Cary's brother Isaac D. Shadd spoke. Shadd had earlier given Montgomery a book of Sir Walter Scott's poetry. After hearing one political speech, Montgomery commented regretfully that the speaker was "intellectually unable to do the subject justice" (10/16). On the Fourth of July, all the workers on the large farm were invited to the Montgomery home for dinner, at which time "several made short speeches." It is clear that the family often read and discussed their readings together. Her father also read "Self-Culture" and, according to Montgomery, was "highly pleased with it" (4/3). Once she enrolled at Oberlin, her reading was mainly related to class assignments with other study time devoted to grammar lessons, recitations, and rhetorical exercises.[59]

Montgomery returned to Davis Bend from Oberlin in 1874 and became a teacher. In 1887, after a financial loss and the deaths of her parents, the Jefferson Davis family reclaimed the plantations. When her brother Isaiah subsequently established the all-black town of Mound Bayou, Montgomery joined him and other family members there and served as postmistress until 1902. Throughout the diary, she expresses thanks for the pleasure she derived from reading. The March 6, 1872, entry closes, "Now with sincere gratitude for all blessings lay me down."

Charles W. Chesnutt

It must be acknowledged that Charles Chesnutt offers an unusual case of rhetorical training for his time and location, which he developed as fully as the circumstances allowed. His journals present an early example of rhetorical education in rural North Carolina at the end of Reconstruction. His own self-education project supplied much of his education, but he also had the benefit of sound training at the postbellum Howard School in Fayetteville, established in 1867, where he attended between the ages of nine and sixteen. The school was a product of the general postwar push to educate the newly freed, but it turned out to be an exceptional one. It was well-staffed, free, public, and graded, unlike the white schools in the area. In addition, it was funded by the Freedmen's Bureau, the American Missionary Society, the Peabody Educational Fund, and members of the Fayetteville black community. The Howard School was so successful that North Carolina's segregated white graded schools, established some years later, were modeled in part on it.[60] In 1874, when he began writing in his first journal, he was serving as an assistant teacher at the Peabody School in Charlotte, North Carolina, under the tutelage of Cicero Harris, the brother of Robert Harris. Cicero Harris's journal served as a model for his own.

The Harris brothers, in fact, played a major role in shaping the course of Chesnutt's education. To improve their situation, the Harris family, members of the Fayetteville antebellum community of free blacks, migrated to Ohio in 1850, eventually settling in Cleveland. Cleveland had a reputation as one of the few cities in Ohio particularly welcoming to African Americans. One historian of the period points out that the Cleveland of 1912 was described as "the negro's Paradise," boasting that from its establishment in 1835, Cleveland admitted black children into its schools "on equal terms with whites."[61] Thus, the Harris brothers attended the integrated Central High School, which adhered to the traditional classical curriculum they carried with them when they returned to Fayetteville to establish the Howard School. It was this curriculum that molded Chesnutt and accounts in large part for the kinds of reading materials he refers to in his journal. He began his second journal in 1877 when the state legislature established two normal schools. The one for whites was part of the University of North Carolina at Chapel Hill. The Howard School was chosen as the site for the State Colored Normal School with Robert Harris as the first principal and Chesnutt as the assistant principal.

More than any of the other diarists considered here, Chesnutt understood his diary as an explicit instrument of his self-education project, thereby requiring less of the kind of "sleuthing" generally associated with research on African American literacy practices, wherein one must examine the daily activities of subjects from a variety of perspectives that help to uncover new ways to characterize those activities.[62] His diary, a collection of three journals maintained for varying periods between 1874 and 1883, is not just a record of his rhetorical engagements but is in fact one of his chief rhetorical engagements, and the act of maintaining a diary his chief means of self-education. Thus, Chesnutt the diarist frequently announces the purpose for a certain entry or series of entries: "I shall confine myself to no particular subject or order of writing. If a bit of poetry strikes my fancy, or may perhaps be of use to me, I shall immediately insert it. If a scientific fact is new, or particularly impressive, it shall be deemed worthy of a place in my note-book" (85). When he began the third journal in 1881, he had become a normal school principal, so that much of the reading he records—Latin, French, rhetoric, ancient history—represents his efforts to acquire a great deal of education rapidly. Chesnutt ends this journal in 1883, before he resigns his post and moves away from the South in search of a more fulfilling life. Few who knew him realized that Chesnutt had accomplished a great deal largely through a strenuous self-education regimen, assisted, as were many nineteenth-century African Americans, by access to a local citizen's well-stocked library.

Further, Chesnutt's position as the only male in the group of diarists examined here prompts us to consider the extent to which nineteenth-century gender roles might have influenced his responses to his experiences of rhetoric and his opportunities for rhetorical education. Throughout his journal, he conveys a sense of isolation from those around him. But he was isolated from the kind of antebellum rhetorical activity Grimké and Rollin wrote about. He lacked the LeMoyne Normal Institute affiliations of Ida Wells and the familial financial support of the Mound Bayou Montgomerys. None of these differences, however, were the consequence of his sex or of societal gender roles. They were mostly a consequence of location. He did have the advantage of the strong mentoring of the Harris brothers, who were responsible for his schooling and his teaching appointments. They might not have been as supportive of a female student in whom they recognized the same potential. At the age of twenty, he married Susan Perry, a teacher at the Howard School, and became the father of three children during the period in which he maintained the journal (his fourth child was born after they moved to Cleveland). He speaks fondly of his wife ("I was lucky in my marriage" [168]) and expresses concern about the quality of education his children would receive. The children would have been too young to participate in rhetorical activities with him, and he does not mention his wife in this regard. It would, therefore, be difficult to make a well-supported claim regarding gender differences, although they were likely.

Chesnutt's early writing practices contain the seeds of his later literary productions. In an August 1874 journal entry, Chesnutt, who would later become a fiction writer, an essayist, and a public speaker, includes an essay he composed after studying George P. Quackenbos's *Advanced Course of Composition and Rhetoric*,[63] first published in 1854. He writes, "As I have been reading 'Quackenbos' Composition & Rhetoric,' I shall write some essay[s], anecdotes, &c. in this book. One is here given" (50).[64] What followed was a brief narrative titled "A Storm at Sea." He abandoned his first attempt to start a second journal, recognizing that he could not give it the time and attention required, adding, "If I wish to improve myself in writing and composition, I must write at some other time than ten o'clock at night, for then my body is fatigued, my eyes are tired, my mind is anything but vigorous and clear, and my hand, as this writing indicates, by no means steady. In order to write well a clear head and a steady hand are prerequisites" (86). Believing that experience is equally as important as training, he later notes that his painstakingly acquired knowledge of the classics, modern languages, and literature; his years of teaching; his life as a family man; and his practice of studying character had prepared him for writing, "not so much [for] the elevation of the colored people as the elevation of the whites." His demonstration of ability, he felt, would advance the "moral progress" of whites (139–40).

He devotes several journal pages to a summary of Blair's *Lectures on Rhetoric and Belles Lettres*. The Brodhead edition includes the sections that Chesnutt discusses—"Lecture X: Style—Perspicuity and Precision," "Lecture XI: Structure of Sentences," and "Lecture XIV: Origin and Nature of Figurative Language"—and Chesnutt here appears to observe the principle that a first step in mastering concepts is basic reiteration of those concepts. He stays very close to Blair's text in his review of the key attributes of perspicuity—purity, propriety, and precision—in his definitions of the periodic sentence, the properties of the perfect sentence, and of tropes.

To practice languages, he wrote some of his entries in German and Latin and, as if in preparation for his later job as a court stenographer, some in phonographic shorthand. He hired a Davidson College graduate to tutor him in Greek. In August 1878, he records his reaction to Homer's *Iliad*. One comment on the work illuminates his search for commonalities across difference: "Yesterday while reading the ante-Homeric history of Troy as given in Dwight's Mythology, we were struck by the story of Iphigenia, and its remarkable resemblance to the scriptural account of the offering of Isaac. The resemblance of many of these legends to the stories of Bible History, as that of Deucalion and Pyrrha, Prometheus, Iphigenia, and others that could be pointed out, only serve to show us that all men come from a common stock and that those events which occurred prior to the dispersion of Babel and shortly afterward, were formerly known to them all, and as Indian and Chinese traditions tell us, were corrupted by the lapse of time and the ignorance of writing" (88). But a few months later, a telling entry finds him lamenting the fact that he lacks intellectual companionship as he continues his self-education, studying French, German, rhetoric, and stenography. There may have been common threads, but in postbellum North Carolina, Chesnutt found them difficult to weave into an intellectual community: "As I have been constantly on my own resources in my solitary studies, I have acquired some degree of *self-reliance*. As I have had no learned professor or obliging classmate to construe the hard passages, and work the difficult problems, I have '*persevered*' till I solved them myself. . . . I have studied and practiced till I can understand and appreciate good music, but I never hear what little there is to be heard. I have studied German and have no one to converse with but a few Jewish merchants who can talk nothing but business. As to procuring instruction in Latin, French, German, or Music, that is entirely out of the question. First class teachers would not teach a 'nigger' and I would have no other sort" (93).

On June 28, 1880, near the end of the second journal, Chesnutt records components of his own invention process, emphasizing the function of memory in extemporaneous delivery, as he prepared for a series of addresses to the school's literary society, organized by Robert Harris: "I am trying to think of a subject for an essay,—critical or Biographical, and I also want subjects for a series of lectures which I propose to deliver to the school, or to the literary society next session. I wish to inspire the young men with ambition—honorable ambition, a earnest desire for usefulness and distinction in life. . . . I shall write the lectures or essay and commit them to memory, so that I can deliver them with ease and effect" (143).

Unlike the female diarists, Chesnutt did not include critiques of political speeches he might have heard during the years he kept the journal. He reports without comment on hearing Senators James G. Blaine of Maine and Zebulon Vance of North Carolina. He does devote several journal pages to effective preaching styles, using as his source Elder J. W. Davis, minister of the local AMEZ church. Davis advised him on the importance of audience accommodation, an essential rhetorical strategy, but in this instance, the audience addressed became the audience invoked, in that over a series of sermons, the congregation would be brought to the point where only a polished style of delivery was acceptable. According to Chesnutt, Davis explained further, "You must first stir them up, which can only be done by excitement. Then you can work on them to greater advantage. It's like getting in new ground—you must first grub at the soil, break it up, and then you can cultivate it" (130–31). Chesnutt's later tribute to Joseph C. Price, a nineteenth-century AMEZ minister and educator, also demonstrates his appreciation for skilled oratory. At least sixty-five years old, the fully matured Chesnutt argued for the value of well-honed oratorical skills from the perspective of his own experience rather than from the advice of a rhetoric textbook. Chesnutt developed the essay around vignettes of Price's numerous oratorical performances, including a response to a politician who spoke at Shaw University, a speech delivered at Chesnutt's AMEZ church in Fayetteville, his passionate international appeals for Livingston College, a sermon delivered at the 1880 AMEZ General Conference in Alabama, a speech at the Prohibition State Convention in Raleigh, an oration at Lincoln Hall in Washington, D.C., and an address to students at Wofford College in South Carolina. Chesnutt folds into his tribute considerable praise of oratory generally, observing that during Price's time, oratory had not yet become the lost art it became with the development of "modern methods of propaganda," which removed the spontaneity of direct audience interaction upon which speakers like Price relied heavily to produce effect. He notes that orators "are not born equipped for effective service," usually being motivated by some cause.[65] Such comments indicate the extent to which the mature Chesnutt recognized the value of training in rhetoric—particularly for a disenfranchised people—training that his journals reveal he worked so diligently to acquire.

Self-Education Manuals for African Americans

Two of the diarists, Montgomery and Chesnutt, refer explicitly to self-help manuals as a source of self-education. Conduct books, variously referred to as success, conduct, self-help, home improvement, and advice manuals, made up a popular genre across the nineteenth century among the white middle class. The belief in the people's ability to improve and educate themselves manifested itself during the Jacksonian era in the growth of the lyceum movement as well. Many of these manuals sought to regulate the behavior of women and included tips on etiquette, courtship and marriage, and homemaking.[66] Others offered advice on conversation, elocution, letter-writing, and other communication practices. These self-instruction guides carried such titles as *The Skillful Housewife's Book* (1846), *The Universal Self Instructor: An Epitome of Forms and General Reference Manual* (1882), *The Golden Way to the Highest Attainments: A Complete Encyclopedia of Life* (1889), and *The Imperial Highway: Essays on Business and Home Life with Biographies of Self-Made Men* (1888). In the period following the Civil War, these manuals targeted African American audiences and were often compiled solely by black authors or by black authors in collaboration with white authors, or were compiled by a white author with an authenticating introduction or foreword by a prominent African American.

Claudia Tate convincingly argues that these conduct manuals, published from the post-Reconstruction era to the turn of the century, were manifestations of the optimism associated with the "Negro improvement" agenda. Engaged in a project of recovery from the devastating effects of slavery, African Americans set about trying to change themselves into acceptable members of white society rather than trying to change society under the belief that such personal change would make a difference.[67] Tate refers specifically to a conduct book by white authors Professor and Mrs. J. W. Gibson, *Golden Thoughts on Chastity and Procreation including Heredity, Prenatal Influences, etc., etc.* (1903), with an introduction by H. R. Butler, black physician at Morris Brown College. This book carries no advice on effective communication except the conversation guideline that one of the qualities of the ideal woman is that she alludes to no subject that would cause pain and, in the section on the "growing boy," the writing guideline that words must be carefully selected, offering the example of William Wordsworth, who was said to have taken an entire day searching for the right adjective to describe the cuckoo.[68] Rather, as the title indicates, the manual focuses on matters associated with reproduction, heredity, and sexuality. African American families at the turn of the century owned a variety of success manuals with such titles as *Sparkling Gems of Race Knowledge Worth Reading* (1897), *Afro-American Home Manual and Practical Self-Educator, Showing What to Do and How to Do It; Being a Complete Guide to Success in Life* (1902), *Beacon Lights of the Race* (1911), *Progress and Achievements of the Twentieth-Century Negro* (1913), and *Hall's Moral and Mental Capsule for the Economic and Domestic Life of the Negro,* compiled in 1905 by Josie Briggs Hall, an African American woman from Texas.

I consider here *The College of Life or Practical Self-Educator: A Manual of Self-Improvement for the Colored Race,*[69] originally published in 1895 by Henry Davenport Northrop, a white Presbyterian minister from Pennsylvania; Joseph R. Gay, a white attorney and publisher; and African American journalist and professor I. Garland Penn. Unlike many of these manuals, this one includes a section on rhetorical concepts. *The College of Life* is divided into two sections, "The Practical Self-Educator" and "The Proper Conduct of Life." The first section contains profiles and images of accomplished African Americans, descriptions of various educational institutions and organizations, and essays on such topics as "honesty," "self-respect," "patience," and "perseverance." "The Proper Conduct of Life" covers rules of etiquette, advice on domestic life ("House-Building"), health ("How to Strengthen the Muscles"), and business matters, ranging from a glossary of business terms to instructions on how to conduct public celebrations. Of particular interest as a site of rhetorical education is book 5 of this section, "Manual of Practical Suggestions and Useful Information for Home and School." Here we find discussions of how to express written thoughts in a correct manner, how to spell correctly, rules of punctuation, illustrations of sign language, and general principles of grammar and style, supported with advice from Hugh Blair on the divisions of style and the methods for attaining a good style[70] and from Richard Whately on the value of revision. Also in book 5 are a list of common errors in writing and speaking, a guide to writing poetry, and a discussion of the care and management of birds and other household pets.

Of course, the volume is a collection of material from a variety of sources, much of it not originally targeted for African American readers. One scholar refers to prescriptive books like *The College of Life* as "strange amalgams which fused representations of black progress with writings by white experts," pointing out that *The College of Life* was republished as *The Afro-American Home Manual and Practical Self-Educator* in 1902.[71] For example, the section "Who Should and Should not Marry" includes images of whites and the advice that "red-whiskered men should marry brunettes but not blonds."[72] In most instances, however, images of African Americans have been inserted. The penultimate section, "Masterpieces of Eloquence," includes excerpts of texts by John Quincy Adams, Daniel Webster, Charles Sumner, Lydia Maria Child, Demosthenes, Horace Greeley, Ralph Waldo Emerson, Charles Dickens, and Robespierre, but none from black orators like Frederick Douglass, Frances Harper, or Bishop Payne. These improvement books, advertised in black newspapers, were quite popular, many going into multiple editions. Both Mary Virginia Montgomery and Charles Chesnutt read self-improvement books, Montgomery from *Self-Culture* and Chesnutt from *A Handbook for Home Improvement* (40) and the *Student's Manual* (88). During a 1937 Federal Writers' Project interview, Mrs. Randall Lee, a formerly enslaved woman living in Florida, still proudly guarded her copy of *The College of Life,* along with a book on the history of the race.[73] This manual took its title seriously, attempting to include instructions on all aspects of living under the guidelines of respectability in postbellum America. The self-help manual *A Handbook for Home Improvement,* from which Chesnutt copied in his journal, was probably a compilation of a series of "pocket manuals" the author Samuel R. Wells published in 1857, since, as Brodhead points out, the pages in each section are numbered separately.[74] The quest for respectability included mastering societal rules for speaking and writing that were laid out in many of these manuals.

Race Improvement through Self-Improvement

Given the nature of their advice, these self-improvement manuals, then, present in formal terms a description of the kinds of lives these young diarists document-ed in their journals. The activities they recorded and the desires they expressed signaled their interest in securing positions of respectability and independence through engagements with language. The diarists reveal what seem to be thoroughly integrated and fairly routinized rhetorical activities. The reader acquires a sense of their passion for language and their critiques of what their passion conveyed. They read widely, attended lectures, took classes, joined literary clubs, exercised their memory, and wrote—diary entries, poetry, biographies, essays, and personal letters. Their recorded rhetorical engagements are frequently communal and inflected by a racialized sensibility. The communal nature of their reading, writing, listening, and speaking practices suggests that self-education in rhetoric was not an entirely isolated endeavor. Even though they functioned singly as individuals pursuing various kinds of knowledge, these pursuits inevitably led them to external audiences and collective engagements.[75] For example, Charlotte Grimké's reticence toward participation in a literary society was based on the possibility that she might be required to recite publicly. She seemed to relish frequent conversations and reading with friends and family members. Recognizing the value of such associations, she asked Bishop Payne about establishing a literary society in Jacksonville, Florida, years later while she was living there with her husband. Frances Rollin frequently shared drafts of her biography of Delany with Boston acquaintances. Ida Wells was active in the LeMoyne Literary Society and other kinds of literary gatherings. Mary Virginia Montgomery, although not involved with a literary group, often discussed reading material and shared her writing with family members, and the Sunday gatherings of other residents of Davis Bend presented opportunities for communicative engagement. Charles Chesnutt, more isolated in his pursuit of a rhetorical education, nonetheless helped to established a literary association and spoke on the benefits of such alliances. Although he rarely mentioned conversations with others about what he read or wrote, he did debate with Elder Davis about politics and effective preaching styles. The alienation his diary conveys, discussed above, though undeniable, seems to have been as much the result of the limited opportunities for African Americans in the area to develop higher order rhetorical skills, during a time when most were still struggling to acquire basic literacy, as it was a product of Chesnutt's sense of superiority. He wished for intellectual companionship and recognized its value, as indicated in this entry on the usefulness of literary societies: "Reading stores the mind with knowledge . . . writing classifies and arranges the results of the reading, but only debate, argument, interchange and criticism of opinion can give one that skill and judgment which is necessary to select the valuable and reject the worthless" (138).

While it would be difficult to imagine that any of these diarists, all born before the abolishment of slavery and maturing in its long and pervasive aftermath, would not have developed a keen sensibility to race matters in general, they were also guided by the conviction that their self-education projects in particular would lead not only to self-improvement but to improvement of the race. Grimké and Rollin were both concerned about how performances by African Americans might reflect on the race, and both applied their rhetorical skills to race improvement and to presenting what they considered to be more favorable images of people of color to dominant culture through their writing and teaching. Montgomery chose to spend her day off drafting an essay on the needs of the race. Wells's entire career in journalism was enabled by her pursuit of rhetorical training and was devoted to exposing racial violence. Chesnutt declares increasingly in his journal that he will go north, write, and show the world that members of his race could achieve. They all imagined that their rhetorical training in some way would serve in race improvement.

3

Mental Feasts
Literary and Educational Societies and Lyceums

> Then, members of this society, as ye cultivate the oratorical, do it diligently, and with purpose; remembering that it is by the exercise of this weapon, perhaps more than any other, that America is to be made a free land not in name only but in deed and in truth.
> —William G. Allen, 1852

> Every winter this church gave many entertainments to aid in paying off the mortgage, which at this time amounted to about eight thousand dollars. Mrs. Smith, as the chairman of the board of stewardesses, was inaugurating a fair—one that should eclipse anything of a similar nature ever attempted by the colored people, and numerous sewing-circles were being held among the members all over the city. Parlor entertainments where an admission fee of ten cents was collected from every patron, were also greatly in vogue, and the money thus obtained was put into a fund to defray the expense of purchasing eatables and decorations, and paying for the printing of tickets, circulars, etc., for the fair.
> —Pauline Hopkins, 1900

African Americans created societies for self-improvement, general racial uplift, and mutual aid as early as 1780, when the African Union Society was organized in Newport, Rhode Island.[1] Black educational societies developed subsequently with expanded goals and were variously called literary, educational, reading-room, or debating societies and lyceums.[2] Their development paralleled but rarely intersected with the history of the white American lyceum movement that usually had a community orientation, in that lectures, plays, and debates were held in public spaces. The first white lyceums on record were established in 1826 to provide a practical and inexpensive education for youth, to keep the community informed, and to train artisans in the practical applications of the sciences.[3] In other words, they were always linked to popular education: in the initial stages in order to have informed workers, but eventually to disseminate practical and useful information community-wide. These early lyceums in the United States were called societies for mutual education and concentrated on education in the sciences. Collective endeavors, they were controlled and supported by the people whom they were organized to educate. They tended to leave political arguments for debating societies.

Carl Bode links the rise of the lyceum movement to the Age of Jackson, beginning in 1828 when Andrew Jackson was elected president, and to the rise of democracy, when the white male population was given more control over government. During this period of populism, Jacksonians pushed to extend voting rights beyond landowners to include all white men of legal age. With the removal of the property requirement, more white American men could vote, and interest grew in having them acquire the education that would better equip them for participation in this new democracy. The lyceum, along with the development of public schools, helped them to acquire it. The lyceum also had the advantage of being cheap, costing nothing, of course, to those who did not participate. As the topic of lectures changed from the application of science to such subjects as biographies of famous persons, the audience included more women and others with broader interests. Bode writes that "[i]f there was ever an American dogma during these decades, it was the desirability of personal improvement."[4] Josiah Holbrook, generally credited with sustaining the lyceum movement, listed several benefits directly associated with the acquisition of literacy, including improving the quality of conversations, establishing libraries, training future teachers, providing an alternative to the "promiscuous assemblage of children" in public schools, and maintaining town histories.[5] The lyceum also provided a legitimate form of evening entertainment; thus, while the education function remained, the lyceum developed into a source of amusement as well.

This overview of the lyceum movement in early-nineteenth-century America provides a framework for considering the ways in which African American lyceum-type societies functioned as sites of rhetorical education.[6] While few African Americans participated in or were welcomed to the meetings of the Anglo-American lyceums, it is important to have a sense of the larger lyceum movement within which these associations developed. The desire for self-improvement, first economic, then intellectual, led African Americans to establish associations of their own to offer mutual support in these endeavors. The organizations had many similar and parallel goals. But the early societies were formed by blacks for blacks, not so much in response to rejection by white societies as in recognition of a need to launch major, generalized literacy initiatives. African Americans in the late eighteenth century established a variety of such collective initiatives for self- and societal improvement, including abolitionist societies that, in the course of arguing against slavery, gave them opportunities to debate and publish treatises and, concurrently, to lecture for the antislavery cause and against colonization. What I will refer to in this chapter as literary societies grew out of these earlier groups and developed, in some instances, along with them. I refer to them as literary societies because this is the term used most commonly across the century to describe associations of this type, even when their purposes were much broader than those we associate with such societies today when many understand "literary" as fictional, imaginary texts and literary groups as readers coming together to discuss these texts. It is helpful to emphasize instead the etymological links to literacy, reading, writing, and letters.

Those groups loosely identified as literary societies or, to use Dorothy Porter's label, "societies for educational improvement" had education as their primary focus.[7] Applying a broad definition of these groups enables us to consider such sites as the home of Lucy Terry Prince, mentioned in the introduction as an early example of rhetoric in action. In his article on Prince, David R. Proper refers briefly to the claim that in the late eighteenth century, young people were attracted to Prince's home in Deerfield, Massachusetts, gathering there for "recitations, music and poetry on the order of an adult literary circle."[8] However, most histories of literary clubs begin in Philadelphia, where African Americans organized the Colored Reading Society of Philadelphia for Mental Improvement, which William Whipper addressed in 1828. A political conservative, Whipper edited the *National Reformer,* the organ of the American Moral Reform Society and the first black newspaper in Pennsylvania. Whipper's address to the Colored Reading Society, discussed below, is emblematic of the linked purposes these societies frequently served of providing a platform to discuss the advantages of developing rhetorical skills and to address pressing political matters. Within a speech in which he outlines the benefits of establishing such a society, he embeds a powerful invective on the evils of slavery, as if to remind his audience of this oppressive exigence for developing rhetorical skills.[9]

As Porter observes, "The lack of economic security, the desire for social contact, the necessity for moral and educational improvement, and the need for spiritual expression constituted the primary reasons for the establishment of mutual aid societies—fraternal, educational, temperance, and religious organizations—by the free Negro in the North and South during the latter part of the eighteenth century."[10] These societies provided libraries, audiences for the practice of public speaking and debating, and audiences to critique written work, all manifestations of rhetorical education. Functioning as blended mutual aid associations and literary societies, they supported the education of selected youths, provided mutual aid, and applied existing abilities to civic concerns. Holbrook's concern for providing alternative activities is echoed in Samuel E. Cornish's 1833 solicitation of support for the New York Phoenix Society's Library and Reading Room: "Many young men, yea' and old ones too, spend their evenings in improper places, because they have no public libraries, no reading rooms, nor useful lectures, to attract attention, and occupy their leisure hours."[11] Cornish, a Presbyterian minister and a founder of *Freedom's Journal,* served as the agent of the Phoenix Society, which also supported a high school for youth and an evening school for young adults. African Americans formed associations, not surprisingly, according to what Alexander Crummell would later call the "social principle" that leads individuals to come together to achieve some common goal for mutual benefit. In a sermon in which he calls for blacks to organize for a variety of social and educational purposes, he writes, "What I mean by the social principle, is the disposition which leads men to associate and join together for specific purposes; the principle which makes families and societies, and which binds men in unity and brotherhood, in races and churches and nations."[12]

In writing this chapter, I set out with the question "What was the impact of literary societies on rhetorical education among nineteenth-century African Americans?" To answer it, I first consider the types and purposes of literary societies that existed across the century. The question of access to these associations is addressed next. It is one thing to demonstrate that they existed, but another to determine the extent to which African Americans were influenced by them. I then analyze five addresses to literary societies delivered over an eighty-three-year period, starting with William Hamilton's 1809 address to the New York African Society for Mutual Relief and ending with Frances Harper's 1892 address to the Brooklyn Literary Union. Based on the kinds of advice these speakers offered, their addresses help to explain how they and these societies understood the function of such groups. They also help us gauge perceptions of rhetoric over time. Next I consider the specific impact of literary societies on prominent black activists, including Frederick Douglass, Mary Church Terrell, and Anna Julia Cooper. I point out that literary societies also appear in the black fiction of the period, reflecting the reality it interpreted. I discuss the decline and shifting roles of literary societies in closing.

All-Male Societies

While both men and women participated in antebellum literary societies, most of them did so in separate associations. I have grouped them below according to this distinction, but in many respects their activities were quite similar, although their motivations were often reputedly different. I follow that separation with an overview of some mixed societies and of early literary societies in California and in the Midwest.

The goals expressed in the constitution of the Phoenix Society of New York, established in 1833, are typical of those for most male societies: "To establish circulating libraries formed in each ward for the use of people of colour on very moderate pay,—to establish mental feasts, and also lyceums for speaking and for lectures on the sciences, and to form moral societies,—to seek out young men of talents, and good moral character, that they may be assisted to obtain a liberal education . . ."[13] Of particular interest as a site of rhetorical education is the Demosthenian Institute. Formed in 1838, its purpose appears to have been primarily to prepare young men—most under the age of twenty-three—for public address. The institute provided a place where members could hone their oratorical skills until deemed ready for public performance, sponsoring twenty-one lectures during one season. Unlike most literary societies, the Demosthenian Institute also published a weekly paper, the *Demosthenian Shield,* starting in 1841 with over a thousand subscribers. Here then is an early example of one site of rhetorical education spawning another.[14] The *Colored American* seems to have assumed a parental relationship with the publication, referring to it as "our infantile protégé," gently chastising its fledgling efforts and even its choice of motto, but also extending encouragement ("the editorials are respectable; the selections are amusing and well arranged; the scissors have been used with judgment").[15]

The Philomathean Society of New York was organized in 1830 "by some of our colored young men, for the purpose of their mutual improvement," in the words of the correspondent to the *Liberator,* who signed the article "A Spectator." He comments on the events at the first anniversary meeting of the society. The meeting opened with a "suitable and well written address" by the president, followed by a reading of the society's constitution. A "collar of distinction" was awarded to a member for his prize essay on education. A recitation by another member of John Dryden's "Ode on Alexander's Feast" earned the praise of being "a fine specimen of Elocution." The meeting ended with another address, this one by Mr. J. G. de Grasse, author of the prize essay, which the "Spectator" deemed "well-written" and "pronounced with much eloquence and animation."[16]

It is important to remember that many of these associations were peopled by young men, like those in the Demosthenian Institute mentioned above, speaking or learning to speak publicly for the first time. They usually recited the works of others but occasionally delivered original compositions. Those performances that were prepared without the aid of teachers were "mainly indebted for their improvement to the mutual suggestions and criticism imparted within their own little circle."[17] Members engaged in a form of peer critiquing. One observer of such a demonstration made the following comments: "We had the pleasure ... to attend an exhibition of exercises in Elocution, conducted by an association who enjoyed the aid of no master in the art, but struggled forward only by their own exertions, and gained what skill they have gained, self-taught. ... We have had constant experience from youth, at many schools, of exercises in elocution, and we must say that these youths of twelve and sixteen have equaled any we have ever seen. In full understanding of their pieces, just emphasis, distinct enunciation, correct action, good management of voices, and natural, unaffected manner, they would stand a comparison with any school in the city."[18]

This commentary resonates with the prevailing discourse of racial improvement, arguing that ability to perform these rhetorical maneuvers demonstrated racial equality. These students, the writer observes, "would stand a comparison with [white students in] any school in the city." As I note throughout this chapter, rhetorical ability as a sign of intelligence and, therefore, as deserving of all the rights of citizenship is a recurring theme in nineteenth-century black discourse—in speeches, letters, and articles in the black press.

The persistence and significance of these literary societies in some cities is evident in the 1869 progress report of a black Baltimorean speaking at a meeting called to petition the city government for better schools. He mentions the total assets of black churches, the financial holdings of black residents, and the seventy-nine beneficial associations that attend to the needy, but the first evidence he offers that the petition merits consideration is that "[f]or a number of years, and through the darkest days of slavery, we have kept in operation seven literary and debating societies."[19] Citing the seven continuous literary societies before ticking off monetary accomplishments suggests that the speaker placed a higher value on this accomplishment as a sign of culture. It is a reminder that the discourse of valuation, in which blacks felt compelled to demonstrate their "merit" for basic human needs and desires, was ongoing. These societies not only provided a site in which to develop the rhetorical skills needed to argue for their rights; their very existence helped to make the case.

Based on this attention to elocutionary excellence, we know, then, that these organizations were created to provide a venue for cultivating and enhancing various kinds of rhetorical skills that would be used to argue for important causes. In addition, charging admission to association-sponsored rhetorical "exhibitions" often generated funds to support these initiatives. For example, a notice in the September 14, 1839, *Colored American* announced a joint exhibition of the Philomathean and Phoenixonian Societies for the benefit of "the unfortunate captives of the schooner Armistead [*sic*], now lying in jail at New Haven, awaiting their trial for alleged piracy."[20] For the occasion, they assembled a ten-piece orchestra, which rendered several musical selections grouped around three addresses, and the recitation of John Greenleaf Whittier's poem "Slave Ship." *Frederick Douglass' Paper* for November 3, 1854, carried a notice of a course of literary exhibitions, composed of eleven speeches, at the First Congregational Church, with proceeds benefiting the church and the sponsoring Young Men's Literary Productive Society.[21] The *Provincial Freeman* advertised a "Mental Feast for the Benefit of Miss Amelia Freeman" to help purchase a stove, desks, and other supplies for a schoolhouse, during which the audience would be treated to "brief but pertinent speeches."[22]

These literary associations were not limited to the eastern United States. Records indicate emerging literary societies in Michigan, Ohio, and across the country.[23] In 1853, the San Francisco Athenaeum, the first black literary society in California, was organized by Jacob Frances, Jonas Townsend, and William Newby. It served as a forum for debate on a variety of racial and political issues. During the five years of its existence, the society established a library and reading room and launched the city's first black newspaper, *Mirror of the Times*.[24] In 1855, Newby, who served as San Francisco correspondent to *Frederick Douglass' Paper*, described in one communication the establishment of a "Musical and Literary Society" by the "young men of Sacramento (colored)," as well. In the mid-1850s, blacks in California had ample opportunities to put their rhetorical skills to work in such public venues as the state conventions, inaugurated that same year.[25]

Female Societies

Women's societies tended to be smaller, and many initially convened in the homes of members. The meetings generally opened and closed with prayer and included readings and recitations. Describing the activities of Philadelphia's Female Literary Association (FLA), William Lloyd Garrison writes in the *Liberator*'s "Ladies Department" column of June 30, 1832, "Nearly all of them write almost weekly, original pieces, which are put anonymously in a box, and afterwards criticized by a committee." Garrison took the liberty in his position as editor to publish many of their pieces, especially those surrounding debates on colonization and emigration to Mexico. Thus, more is known about the activities of this black women's literary society than any other.[26]

At some literary society meetings, a young, inexperienced speaker would often be invited to address the group, providing an interested but sympathetic audience before which the beginning rhetor could practice and creating thereby a site of rhetorical education for all involved. At the third anniversary celebration of the FLA, an address was delivered by "a colored youth," who opened with the following ingratiation: "Trusting that you will extend to me your forgiveness for any errors that may be committed by me, this being, as you are all well aware, no doubt, the first time that I have ever embarked in any subject of this nature." The youth, not identified as to sex, goes on to expand upon the accomplishments of writers from antiquity to Phillis Wheatley, encouraging the women to continue their own course of self-improvement.[27]

African American emigrants to Canada took the tradition of literary societies with them. Mary Bibb, after she became the widow of abolitionist fugitive slave Henry Bibb, formed the Windsor Ladies Club, also referred to as the Mutual Improvement Society, in 1854. Apparently, this was the first female literary society in Canada. Heather Murray points out in her work on Canadian literary societies that unlike Anglo-Canadian women, who established literary clubs some twenty-five years later, the first black women migrating to Canada would have known of and may have been members of women's literary societies in the United States.[28] They drew on that tradition as their need for self-improvement and community action increased. These black Ontario societies engaged in both cultural and political work.

One advantage of these separate societies was that the women could build their self-confidence and leadership skills away from the frequently domineering presence of men. Many of the women's societies grew out of the home sewing circles and mutual aid societies, established to provide aid for those in need. Even when the purpose was broader, the rationale was often that developing rhetorical skills would help women have a greater moral influence on their children and husbands. Consider, for example, this passage detailing the particulars of that influence from an address to the FLA, delivered shortly after it had been organized in 1831: "It is nothing better than affectation to deny the influences that females possess; it is their part to train up the young mind, to instill therein principles that may govern in maturer years; principles that influence the actions of the private citizen, the patriot, the philanthropist, lawgivers, yea, presidents and kings."[29] Although these organizations did not reject the traditional roles assigned to women, the organizers did see them as opportunities for increased community activism as well. In her address to the FLA, Sarah Mapps Douglass, one of the chief organizers, requested that the "readings and conversation should be altogether directed to the subject of slavery."[30] The women understood that finely tuned rhetorical skills could serve the abolitionist cause, and many used the societies as training grounds for, if not sites of, antislavery work at the same time. Julie Winch reminds us that it was "hardly coincidental that members of the literary societies also enrolled in the Philadelphia Female Anti-Slavery Society" and points to the dual activities of women like Sarah Douglass, her mother, Grace Bustill Douglass, Sarah Forten, Harriet Forten Purvis, and many others.[31]

Mixed-Gender Societies

Membership in some societies apparently always included men and women. The Gilbert Lyceum, organized in 1841, admitted both men and women, as indicated by a list of those present at the first meeting, which included the names of Sarah Douglass and Harriet Purvis, along with names of prominent Philadelphia men. The April 23, 1858, edition of the *Liberator* announced the organization of the Histrionic Club, with William C. Nell as president. The "literary association" was established "by a few of the most enterprising colored men and women for their own improvement and elevation." At the meetings, they read their own pieces or those from the "best authors." The fact that the association included the participation of both men and women is mentioned three times, suggesting that this promiscuous activity in 1858 was still worth noting.[32] William J. Watkins, outspoken abolitionist and cousin of Frances Harper, reviewed a debate sponsored by the Union Literary Association in 1855. Watkins, who served as associate editor of *Frederick Douglass' Paper,* noted that the association was "composed of young gentlemen and ladies of color." The debate was on the relative merits of George Washington and Christopher Columbus, during which Watkins decided that the disputants "acquitted themselves very creditably."[33] The first mixed-sex literary society in Ontario was the African Canadian Wilberforce Lyceum Educating Society, established in 1850.[34]

An 1852 letter to *Frederick Douglass' Paper* provides one example of black women's participation in an institution-based society and in rhetorical education generally. The communication concerns the hiring and teaching practices at Central College in McGrawville, New York, founded in 1849 by the American Baptist Free Mission Society, as both interracial and coeducational. Three blacks served on the faculty during its twelve years of existence, and one of the senior commencement speakers at the June 1858 ceremony was John B. Reeve, an African American.[35] The writer observes: "The sexes here obtain the same mental discipline. All are required to take the same part in rhetorical exercises. I found the young ladies as much engaged and interested in preparing for their declamations as I have ever known young men to be; and from all accounts given both of their weekly and yearly exercises in this direction, they prove themselves to be as susceptible to improvement, and as capable of attaining to a high degree of perfection."[36] It is likely that some of these "young ladies" were black women, given the school's progressive agenda. An underground "station" was even operated on the college grounds. Grace A. Mapps, a cousin of Sarah Douglass, is credited with being the first black woman to graduate from the McGrawville school in 1852, the same year the letter was sent to *Frederick Douglass' Paper.* The writer adds that a "literary society in connection with the college, in which ladies and gentlemen are received upon terms of equality, has been voluntarily organized by the students." The letter goes on to quote one of the women students: "I am not expecting to be a public speaker; but I should like to be prepared to express myself intelligibly, either before a society of ladies or in a mixed assembly, if I should ever be called to do so unexpectedly."[37] The student carefully constructed her desire for rhetorical training within midcentury societal boundaries for women. The literary society may have received both sexes "upon terms of equality," but all did not necessarily use their developing abilities for the same purposes.

In an issue of the *Colored American,* Samuel Cornish's eulogy for Henrietta D. Ray, first wife of New York abolitionist Charles B. Ray, provides further evidence of society activity among women. He observed that Ray was "first president of a society of young ladies, formed for the purpose of acquiring literary and scientific knowledge, and though not blessed with an extended systematic education, yet she possessed a giant mind for improvement, and persevering industry in making investigations."[38] Cornish here refers to the New York Ladies Literary Society. A subsequent *Colored American* article gives notice of the society's third anniversary celebration and posts the "Order of Exercise," listing the typical sequence of events at these society anniversary celebrations: (1) a reading, (2) the constitution, (3) an opening address, (4) two musical selections, (5) a dialogue, (6) another musical selection, (7) an address on the improvement of the mind, (8) a musical selection, (9) a poem, (10) a musical selection, (11) a dialogue, (12) a musical selection, (13) an epilogue, (14) a musical selection, (15) a closing poetic address, and (16) a musical selection.[39]

These associations were valued for entertainment as well as for educational purposes. A post–Civil War correspondent to the *Christian Recorder* laments the lack of "a literary and debating society" in Chillicothe, Ohio, adding that it is "one thing they need very badly here. . . . For there is no enjoyment whatever for the young in this city. There are some very talented and nice young ladies and gentlemen in this city, that would deem it a great pleasure if there was something of the kind here."[40] It is interesting to note the concern here for providing a source of amusement rather than an opportunity for racial uplift or self-improvement, as in so many of the calls for literary societies.[41]

Many of these associations were formed within black churches, especially in the late nineteenth and early twentieth centuries. They too promoted learning in their efforts to challenge notions of black inferiority. A report on the proceedings of one church-sponsored society in Washington, D.C., highlights the competitive nature of rhetorical performance in these sites. The Washington correspondent to the *Christian Recorder* narrates the events of a meeting of the Israel Lyceum of Israel AME Church, where during a "Grand Literacy Demonstration," Mrs. Lydia Maddon from Baltimore delivered a "presentation address" with "the best of elocution" while bestowing the gift of a Bible. The correspondent goes on to mention a rivalry between the Baltimore and Washington women with respect to oratorical abilities, a rivalry the writer mentions only because "we are not disposed to remain silent when our dignity is unjustly assailed."[42]

The Brooklyn Literary Union of Siloam Presbyterian Church became one of the best known in that city. Organized in 1886, it spawned others, like the Literary Circle of Concord Baptist Church and the St. Augustine Protestant Episcopal's Literary Sinking Fund. They sponsored "debates, lectures, elocution contests, recitations, musical recitals, and discussions of pertinent issues" and followed a prescribed agenda. The agenda for the Brooklyn Literary Union carried specific time limits for each item for debate: no paper should last longer than twenty minutes unless agreed upon; debates should be conducted between four disputants limited to ten minutes each; and papers and debates would be followed by a discussion lasting no longer than forty-five minutes. Frederick Douglass, Frances Harper, T. Thomas Fortune, educator Maritcha Lyons, and physician Susan McKinney were among the prominent persons affiliated with the Brooklyn Literary Union.[43] Fortune's newspaper, the *New York Freeman,* carried regular reports on the activities of this literary society. For example, the June 26, 1886, issue called into question the originality of a paper, apparently taken from an encyclopedia, that had been read to the society by J. A. Arneaux, described in *Men of Mark* as a "Professional Tragedian, 'Black Booth'—Editor—Poet—Graduate of the French Institutions of Learning."[44]

Another column includes a detailed account of a December meeting of the union, providing a clearer sense of what took place at late-nineteenth-century literary club gatherings. The program opened with an essay on "society," followed by a musical selection, leading up to the evening's debate on a question that, with a few minor changes, is still under discussion in the twenty-first century: "Should the Negro be independent in politics?" The first participant spoke in favor of independent voters, "free from political shackles," not tied to any political party. The second speaker responded in the negative, arguing that blacks could not afford to take an independent stand. The third speaker, again taking the affirmative, argued that the "Negro had been used as a political football long enough," and the final speaker took the compromising position that blacks should distribute themselves among the parties at the polls. The literary club voted overwhelmingly against the question. Following the debate, a resolution petitioning Congress to pass the Blair Education Bill passed unanimously.[45] At this same meeting, the union also authorized the board of the Brooklyn

Literary Union to publish Rufus L. Perry's paper on the Cushite[46] and to sponsor a fund-raiser, a Liberian Coffee Party, to pay off the church piano. The meeting closed with the announcement that the titles of the following week's lectures were "Heredity in Character" and "Stanley, the African Explorer."

This meeting contained several instances of rhetorical action and opportunities for rhetorical education: the speeches, debate, resolutions, petitions, and approval of a publication. But they primarily represented discursive engagements with a wide range of substantive matters all related in some way to the future of the race and its African connections. Rhetorical education in this setting occurred secondarily as a by-product of political activism. The decision to publish Perry's paper also reminds us of the direct link between these societies and various publication venues, like Fortune's *New York Freeman,* where he often published papers delivered at the meetings, as did the black antebellum newspaper editors. A paper presented at a literary society meeting might be published in a newspaper or by the society itself or, as in the case of Perry's paper, be developed into a book for even wider distribution.

Postbellum literary societies were active in Southern cities as well. For example, the *New York Freeman* reports on a meeting of the Lyceum at the Congregational Church in Raleigh, North Carolina, where a debate was held on the U.S. Senate's rejection of James C. Matthews as Recorder of Deeds for the District of Columbia, as well as a meeting of the Baltimore Monumental Literary and Scientific Association, where a paper on hygiene was read by R. M. Hall.[47]

Literary Societies and the Question of Access

It is clear in looking back over this brief overview of literary societies as sites of rhetorical education that only a small percentage of nineteenth-century African Americans participated in them. The same names tend to recur (Cornish, Douglass, Mapps, Garnet, Forten, Remond, Watkins, Terrell, Fortune) and the same cities (Philadelphia, Washington, Boston, and New York). Yet these facts do not diminish the contribution of literary societies to black rhetorical education, especially when we consider that much good abolitionist work came out of them. I set out to identify a variety of sites without concern for numbers. All African Americans did not participate in any one site. Still, it is worth considering this question of access (my version of the talented-tenth debate) because the answers reveal important links across class, to the extent that class distinctions existed.

In Cornish's call for support of the Phoenix Society's Library and Reading Room, he also described in the plans of operation the practice of listening and responding to texts being read aloud. Classes of 25 to 30 students were to begin in staggered two-hour intervals—4, 6, and 8 o'clock—three evenings per week, presumably to accommodate varying schedules. So on a given evening, up to 90 persons could conceivably participate, or up to 270 per week. Readers would be appointed to read for an hour, after which the auditors would gather in small groups to discuss what they heard and, significantly, to discuss other "occurrences of the day."[48] This aspect of the plan encouraged civic engagement with the day's occurrences as well as with literary materials. Of this practice, Elizabeth McHenry observes that "in the case of the earliest African American literary societies, the emphasis on the performative aspect of literary learning and on the sharing of texts indicates that membership in a literary society and basic literacy—the ability to read—did not necessarily go together. . . . Reading texts aloud fostered an environment in which a truly democratic 'sharing' of texts could take place, and it ensured that cohesive groups could be formed from individuals with widely divergent literacy skills."[49]

It is clear from Cornish's call for support that the reading room invited the participation of all interested parties. The levels of literacy of those who participated would have varied; thus, as McHenry notes, the practice of reading aloud could have been, in part, a way of sharing texts communally, even among those who could not read. John Brewer, in his book on eighteenth-century English culture, observes that with the rise of print culture, the practice of reading aloud "enabled non-readers to share in the pleasures of the literate."[50] But reading aloud was also was an art in itself, and members of reading groups often took turns reading to one another to stimulate discussion, as in the small groups described above—a blending of oral and written forms of expression. Brewer and others also refer to this practice as "intensive" versus "extensive reading," applicable here in that public and private intensive readings occurred in contexts with scarce reading material such that the same material was read over and over and was highly valued.[51] Extensive reading was more casual, leisurely, and personal, because the books were not scarce. It is quite likely that many who participated in reading rooms would be considered intensive readers, who were not necessarily members of the sponsoring society.

The Philadelphia Library Company of Colored Persons, established in 1833, was apparently quite successful at reaching diverse audiences. In a December 2, 1837, article in the *Colored American,* a visitor to one of its meetings reported that the library contained nearly a thousand volumes, "neatly labeled and arranged" in a spacious room. The members met two or three evenings a week to debate in front of "large and improving audiences of young of both sexes, and by many of the aged and patriotic, without distinction of color."[52] Such descriptions suggest that whether all those who participated in these events officially belonged to the sponsoring society or not, the societies nonetheless functioned as sites of rhetorical education. What is important is the notion of sharing texts among individuals with a range of literacy skills.

The author of an article in the *Colored American,* possibly Cornish, who was editor at the time, seems to have been especially attuned to the need for these organizations to reach a wider public and refers to it frequently. Five years after the earlier solicitation of support for a reading room, a particularly urgent article, pointedly titled "Literary Societies," opens with the claim that they are more important than other kinds of associations because they bring people with the potential to become public speakers together in an environment where they can compare their abilities. But after acknowledging the good work already being done by existing societies, the author adds that "there is, unfortunately, an exclusiveness about those associations which deters the stranger from making efforts to gain admission into them; they are more like literary clubs than the *public* Societies; consequently their numbers must necessarily be few." He continues, "We need a literary institution which will be in all its bearing, essentially *public.*" He then puts forth a plan for a "Union Lyceum, for the purpose of establishing a *public* Reading Room and Library." The plan calls for black and white members, yearly dues of about two dollars, a minimum of twenty-five members to draw up a constitution, and fifty members to begin operations.[53] The article does not discredit the existing societies but calls for a different kind of association to provide various forms of rhetorical education to a broader public, a word repeated several times in the article.

In a rare reference to a specific work read during a reading room session, Amos G. Beman recalls knowledge of a small group assembled "to hear David Walker's 'Appeal to the Free people of Color,' read through." The scene he reconstructs here incorporates some of the key elements of effective rhetorical education—the shared experience of a thought-provoking text followed by discussion. This article, third in a series of occasional pieces Beman submitted to the *Colored American* on the sources of mental improvement, expounds upon the benefits of participating in debating societies and "meeting together for the purpose of the free interchange of thoughts and opinions." Beman emphasizes the importance of engaging in stimulating conversation as a kind of mental exercise, along with the less interactive rhetorical activities of reading, listening to others read, speaking, or debating—a more structured form of exchange.[54]

Literary societies had their purposes; reading rooms and public lyceums others. As mentioned, the distinction between actual dues-paying members of these societies and those they reached through the kinds of activities they sponsored, such as the reading rooms and lecture series, is worth remembering when we consider access. Rhetorical education took place nevertheless.

Addressing Literary Associations

In this section, I consider implied and explicit rhetorical principles in five addresses to literary societies. We can develop a clearer sense of these associations by paying attention to what speakers said in addressing them. William Hamilton delivered the first address considered at an 1809 meeting of the New York African Society for Mutual Relief on the anniversary of its founding. While not strictly a literary society, this kind of group represents the base upon which many of them were founded. William Whipper's 1828 address to the Colored Reading Society of Philadelphia for Mental Improvement is considered next. In it he critiques the florid style of delivery as an essential component of activist rhetoric. William G. Allen, a professor at New York Central College and, according to one anthology, "the earliest known [African American] to have taught rhetoric," delivered a formal lecture on rhetoric and rhetorical practices to the college's Dialexian Society in 1852.[55] In this address, Allen combines a review of basic rhetorical principles with a call to apply them in service to justice and equality. Charles Chesnutt's 1881 postbellum address at a meeting of the Normal Literary Society of Fayetteville, North Carolina, offers evidence of the changing roles of these organizations. Finally, "Enlightened Motherhood," a speech Frances Harper delivered before the Brooklyn Literary Union in 1892, prescribes traditional roles for literary clubwomen in order to rear sons for public life.[56] These addresses span the century and serve as instructive models of the rhetorical practices they promote.

Hamilton's Address to the New York African Society for Mutual Relief

In 1809, William Hamilton spoke on the anniversary of the founding of the New York African Society for Mutual Relief. It was also a celebration of the anniversary of the abolition of the Atlantic slave trade, a piece of legislation that would become the occasion for numerous celebrations and speeches, including several from Hamilton himself. Hamilton, president and cofounder of this mutual aid society, also helped to organize early literary societies in New York, including the Phoenixonian Society and the Philomathean Society.[57] The mutual aid societies often functioned as literary societies as well, with the difference often being only in chief purpose. By acquiring the education that many literary societies provided, members were better positioned to argue for mutual aid. Education supported personal improvement and community development.[58] Hamilton, thirty-six years old at the time of this address, has been described as "the foremost black intellectual of the first quarter of the nineteenth century."[59] He was influential among African American political activists and understood the kinds and modes of arguments that were needed to promote the abolition of slavery and the general progress of the race. It is important to remember

Porter's point that "[t]he lecture platform of these societies was the workshop and the preparatory school for many of the Negro anti-slavery lecturers who later won fame in America and England as public speakers."[60]

In this address, Hamilton gives high praise to a published document he calls "a specimen of African genius." Hamilton's reference to "genius" resonates with the belletristic discourse of the eighteenth and nineteenth centuries, which privileged a kind of native ability over the tactics of imitation or invention drawing on cultural topoi. Hugh Blair, one of the chief proponents of this view, writes, "Genius is a word, which, in common acceptation, extends much farther than to the objects of Taste. It is used to signify that talent or aptitude which we receive from nature, for excelling in any one thing whatever."[61] This possibility of a native "African genius" was still an open question in 1809, and one of Hamilton's motives in delivering this speech was to answer affirmatively, pushing against Blair and others. The publication not named in his speech was *Peter Williams's Oration on the Abolition of the Slave Trade: Delivered in the African Church in the City of New York, January 1, 1808. With an Introductory Essay by Henry Sipkins*. The audience would have nodded knowingly in agreement with this epithet and smiled at the two young rhetors, Williams and Sipkins, both about twenty years old, who were almost certainly in the audience. Some had doubted Williams's ability to produce the oration Hamilton held up, one of the earliest abolitionist speeches to be published.[62] Nineteenth-century black activists knew that oratory was their chief way of communicating with large audiences. By publishing their speeches separately in pamphlet form or in the press or by including them in their autobiographies, they were able to extend the reach of their messages and at the same time provide tangible proof of intellect for the benefit of what John Ernest calls their "always implicit white audience of judgment."[63] Speeches like Hamilton's, several of which were also published as pamphlets, were almost always addressed to these two categories of hearers and readers: the physical audience of literary society members, who would be expecting a certain kind of epideictic rhetoric combined with a push for social action, and skeptical white readers and auditors, who were not fully persuaded of their rhetorical ability.[64] The rhetors and the black members of their primary audiences acquired rhetorical education in the process of delivering, hearing, and reading such speeches on numerous occasions.

Especially in the years immediately following the abolition of the slave trade, black speakers like Hamilton felt compelled to offer "proof" of black intellectual ability, evidence of the race's humanity. After commenting on the significance of the occasion, Hamilton, as if to disprove white theories of black inferiority, held up the publication as an example of the kind of rhetorical work needed to counter such claims. Of the document, he observes the following:

"[T]he address or frontispiece to the work is a flow of tasteful language, that would do credit to the best writers; the oration or primary work is not a run of eccentric vagaries, not now a sudden gust of passionate exclamation, and then as sudden calm and an inertness of expression, but a close adherence to the plane of the subject in hand, a warm and animating description of interesting scenes, together with an easy graceful style."[65] For Hamilton, the strength of Williams's prose is its evenness of style and the avoidance of excesses. It may represent his attempt to privilege a cerebral over a more emotional delivery, generally associated with black worship in some churches. Hamilton concludes this praise of rhetorical invention and style with the hope that such evidence of genius will silence white assertions of "superiority of souls" (37). Some disagreed with the strategy of seeking equality through demonstrations of intelligence, arguing instead that engaging in that contest elided the truth that equality was a natural right. Still, of interest here is Hamilton's singling out of rhetorical abilities as proof of genius, a clear indication that early-nineteenth-century activists held oral and written eloquence in high regard. Hamilton, at thirty-six, was claiming a space in public discourse for his younger black activist colleagues. He recognized fully the importance of an effective black public voice, one that influenced through argument and evidence. His address goes on to exhort the officers and board members of the New York African Society for Mutual Relief to persevere in their good works.

Related to Hamilton's notion of "African genius" are these two excerpts from subsequent speeches. In her 1837 address to the Ladies Literary Society of New York, schoolteacher Elizabeth Jennings, who would later win a lawsuit against New York's Third Avenue Railroad Company, also spoke about the need for women to develop "powers and dispositions of the mind" lest "our enemies will rejoice and say, we do not believe they [people of color] have any minds; if they have, they are unsusceptible of improvement."[66] An excerpt from an 1840 speech by Austin Steward, president of the African American State (New York) Convention, addressed "to the [white] People of the State," provides another near-midcentury example of the push to demonstrate merit and intelligence to whites by pointing to "our people['s]" participation in literary associations: "In all parts of the state, from Montauk to Buffalo, literary and debating societies and clubs exist among our people, in city, town, and village. In some instances, these societies are adorned and made more useful by libraries and reading rooms. Our schools and associations are continually sending forth a host of youth, with strong determination and purpose of subserving the best and highest interests of their proscribed race."[67] Of particular significance here is that this proclamation was addressed to the citizens of the State of New York as part of the general epideictic project that blacks during this period seemed invested in—to provide what many counted as evidence that African people were intelligent and educated, or becoming educated, and consequently formed literary societies.

William Whipper's Address to the Colored Reading Society of Philadelphia for Mental Improvement

Jacqueline Bacon and Glen McClish observe that extant texts from meetings of these societies often reveal a keen awareness of the importance of applying rhetorical principles in the process of acquiring this much-needed education.[68] Among other examples, the authors point to William Whipper's 1828 address to the Colored Reading Society of Philadelphia for Mental Improvement, in which he speaks about the level of rhetorical training that such societies might support: "I am well aware that the age in which we live is fastidious in its taste. It demands eloquence, figure, rhetoric, and pathos; plain, honest, common sense is no longer attracting. No: the orator must display the pomp of words, the magnificence of the tropes and figures, or he will be considered unfit for the duties of his profession" (107). Coming early in the address, the statement can be understood as part of Whipper's engagement in a form of introductory *insinuatio,* wherein through the modesty topos, he enhances his ethical appeal. In the paragraph preceding this quote, Whipper offers an "apology for my inadequacy" and "regret[s] that the task of awakening these reflections in your minds had not devolved on some one more competent to do justice to the important subject" (107). This statement could be understood as supporting a view of rhetoric as window dressing, a "pomp of words," or flowery but necessary emotional language lacking substance. It expresses sentiments that resonate with Hamilton's in his praise of Peter Williams's speech ("not a run of eccentric vagaries, not now a sudden gust of passionate exclamation") cited above. Bacon and McClish, however, offer a reading that does not support what they refer to as an "antirhetorical stance": "At first glance, this pronouncement resembles the late seventeenth-century antirhetorical stance championed by the likes of Bishop Sprat of the Royal Society and John Locke. As Whipper continues, however, it becomes clear that his ostensible attack on rhetoric is more probably a means of simultaneously laying claim to the spirit of the Scots rhetoric of the previous century ('plain, honest, common sense') and of supporting a self-acquired, democratic eloquence particular to radical antebellum discourse. . . . Whipper transforms the belletrists' notion of taste into a democratic principle that empowers previously marginalized African Americans to participate in the civic sphere."[69]

About half of Whipper's speech expands upon the cultural benefits of creating a reading society. He discusses the general advantages of mental improvement and counters the objections of those who say there are better ways to spend their time. He also points to the ways in which such a society contributes to the cultivation of taste. Bacon and McClish have traced the influence of eighteenth-century Scottish rhetorical theory, including faculty psychology, education, and industry in contrast to genius, the cultivation of taste, and the use of a variety of "stylistic pyrotechnics."[70] Whipper concludes this portion of the speech affirming the importance of a rhetorical education:

> It is therefore not without good reason that in a system of education so much attention is required to the study of belles lettres, to criticism, to composition, pronunciation, style, and to everything included in the name of eloquence.
>
> 'Tis vain to reject these things as useless ornaments; taste is the gift of God, and was given to be used. In the present state of society, attention to these things is absolutely necessary to usefulness and respectability. (112–13)

Yet Bacon and McClish caution that his rhetoric should not be understood "as merely imitative of Scots theory or complacent about current inequities in discursive power."[71] I agree. Whipper's speech is indeed as much a political document as an Enlightenment-inflected treatise on the benefits of a sound rhetorical education. The second half of this text can be understood as an enactment of the benefits expounded upon in the first half in that Whipper addresses his early-nineteenth-century audience on a matter of grave concern. In 1828, America was a slaveholding republic with close to one-fifth of the U.S. population enslaved. Halfway into his speech, Whipper launches into a powerful antislavery invective in which he attacks Southern lawmakers and slaveholders in particular. His chief evidence is the contradiction between the freedom many invoke as justification for the revolution that severed the United States' ties to Great Britain and the enslavement of Africans in this same freedom-founded nation. In Jeremiadic fashion, he predicts destruction of the defenders of slavery if they continue along this path in clear violation of "the letter and spirit of the constitution of the United States" (114). He charges the members of this newly formed literary society to increase their ambition as a catalyst for change, ambition "to be possessed by every useful citizen" (118).

Approximately twenty-four years old at the time of this address, Whipper grew up in Columbia, Pennsylvania, in the home of a lumberman for whom his mother worked. He became a well-to-do lumberman himself and a public voice in abolitionist discourse. Little is known of his early education, but as he indicates in his address, he had knowledge of rhetorical practices and principles derived from his reading of "Scotch philosophy" and the "ancient classics" (111) and absorbed from nineteenth-century oratorical culture in general. Letters authored by Whipper also routinely appeared in *Freedom's Journal,* the *Christian Recorder,* the *Colored American,* and *Frederick Douglass' Paper.* These letters, usually contentious, were based on the unpopular position of the American Moral Reform Society that developing the morality of African Americans would gain them acceptance into white institutions.[72]

William G. Allen's Address to the Dialexian Society of New York Central College

A quote from Allen's address to the Dialexian Society—"Then, members of this society, as ye cultivate the oratorical, do it diligently, and with purpose; remembering that it is by the exercise of this weapon, perhaps more than any other, that America is to be made a free land not in name only but in deed and in truth"—articulates his belief in the power of rhetoric to effect change.[73] He calls "the oratorical" a weapon, implying that it can be used for protection against an enemy. Allen, however, had specific kinds of enemies in mind and charged his auditors to study rhetoric "with purpose." He implies that this ability was not to be used wantonly or to do harm. One clear difference between this literary society speech and Hamilton's and Whipper's above is that there is less emphasis on performance for dominant culture, although there is some reference to it in his discussion of black orators. Instead, the emphasis in on a rhetoric of political activism. Allen had grown up in an environment shaped by harmful rhetoric, such as that of U.S. congressman Henry Clay, whom he mentions in his speech.

A sketch of his formative years will help to explain how he came to address the Central College Dialexian Society, having been "called to Professorship of Greek and German languages, and of Rhetoric and Belles-Lettres."[74] Allen, born in the Tidewater area of Virginia, writes in his personal narrative that he was considered a quadroon, being the son of a half-white mother and a white father. Left an orphan at a young age, he was adopted by a couple who provided this future teacher of rhetoric with a solid grade-school education. He describes his teacher as "a preacher of rare eloquence and power."[75] His education ended abruptly on the heels of the slave rebellion of literate Virginia preacher Nat Turner, when all black schools in the state were closed. Allen was forced to engage in a more intentional self-education project by soliciting instruction from several rank-and-file soldiers at Fort Monroe, many of whom turned out to be highly educated foreigners. From them he learned several languages, including German. One slaveholder, also a soldier, gave Allen free access to his library, and another gave him the small library of his dead son.

When Gerrit Smith, a wealthy abolitionist, learned of him through an associate, he invited Allen to move to New York and attend college at his expense, if necessary. Allen described Smith as "a great orator" with "a great heart" (102), a connection he invokes at the end of his speech to the Dialexian Society as well. At eighteen, Allen enrolled in the Oneida Institute of Science and Industry in Whitesboro, New York, where under the leadership of Beriah Green, it developed into a center for abolitionist activism.[76] Allen was graduated from Oneida in 1844 and studied law in Boston with Ellis Gray Loring, one of the founders of the first Boston antislavery society. Allen also worked with Henry Highland Garnet in editing the abolitionist newspaper the *National Watchman*. A frequent correspondent to *Frederick Douglass' Paper* and the *Liberator,* Allen also contributed an essay on Placido to the first volume of Julia Griffiths's edited collection *Autographs for Freedom* (1853). In 1850, he was called to teach at Central College, an institution that had been established as a kind of social experiment in early-nineteenth-century higher education. As A. L. Brown observed in her 1852 communication to *Frederick Douglass' Paper,* it was "an institution which practically recognizes the rights of humanity without distinction of color or sex.... It is well known that one of the professors is a colored man; yet another statement of a fact so cheering will not be a useless repetition, should it serve merely to stir up 'pure minds' in the antislavery world."[77]

Allen, thirty-two years old when he delivered this address on June 22, 1852, began by announcing his subject, "Orators and Oratory," and assigning the thinker and then the orator to the highest ranks of humankind. His yoking of thinker and orator places emphasis on invention over style, content over form. Based on descriptions of the composition of the student body, there were probably men and women in the audience, although his opening salutation—"Gentlemen and Members of the Dialexian"—might suggest otherwise. After a visit to the college, Gerrit Smith observed that "the sexes are educated together": "about two-fifths of the students are females" and "about one-fifth of the students are colored persons."[78] It seems likely that the literary societies would also be mixed. They certainly invited women to address them. For example, *Frederick Douglass' Paper* of June 30, 1854, announced that as part of the college's annual exercises, Antoinette L. Brown would address the Dialexian Society.

These then are some of the elements making up the rhetorical situation for this address. They result in a speech that is a blend of rhetoric designed to teach, to praise, and to promote action. As McClish observes in his analysis of the speech, "Indeed, the basic components of a conventional instructional presentation on the history and future prospect of oratory—such as those delivered by Blair in Edinburgh a century earlier or Channing at Harvard in Allen's era—are present, but in this speaker's hands they function in service of explicit advocacy."[79] The didactic component is primarily perfunctory, more a review of rhetorical principles than a lecture on them. Allen first recalls that oratory develops in response to some exigence and that it develops best in the movement between liberty and the suppression of liberty. He offers the examples of Demosthenes, Cicero, Patrick Henry, Daniel O'Connell, Frederick Douglass, and Louis Kossuth, moving then into a comparison of the first two, with the conclusion that "Cicero *wins*, Demosthenes *compels*" (234). After evaluating the performances of several of his contemporaries, including Daniel Webster and temperance lecturer John B. Gough, he launches into an extensive critique of Kossuth, leader of the Hungarian independence movement, who was touring in the United States at the time. Allen pronounces him "superior to any orator who has ever spoken, whether of ancient or modern date" (238). Although he is generous in praise for his rhetorical abilities, he criticizes Kossuth's failure to speak out against American slavery in any of his speeches—"Not a word in reference to the wrongs of the American slave has he ever dropped in this country" (237). Allen did not expect him to become an abolitionist, but he did believe that Kossuth should have at least made reference to the practice. Having chastised him thus, he proceeds to spend what must have been at least half of an hour highlighting the strengths of his oratory and quoting a lengthy passage from a speech Kossuth had just given in New York City. Allen seems especially impressed with his breadth of knowledge, his pathetic appeal, and his delivery, even commenting on his "dignified and impressive" personal appearance (241). Allen then moves on to pay tribute to the black orators Samuel Ringgold Ward, Henry Highland Garnet, Frederick Douglass, and Charles Lenox Remond. After brief mentions of the white abolitionists William Lloyd Garrison, Gerrit Smith, and Wendell Phillips, he begins to conclude with a discussion of the types of oratory, ranking the rhetoric of the bar as highest in the development of the speaking faculties and pulpit rhetoric superior in developing the "highest powers" of oratory. Legislative eloquence, he concludes, is no more than "dignified and convincing" (245). He ends this section by adding a fourth category, oratory for the public platform, suggesting that he will discuss it at another time, although it is just this category of oratory that he has been featuring in his previous examples and modeling in his own. After a brief foray into the strengths and weaknesses of various languages because he considered it "not inappropriate in a lecture on oratory" (245), he concludes with a challenge to the members of his audience that they "cultivate the oratorical, do it diligently, and with purpose" (246).

Following the dictates of his closing adage that "he that would be a great orator, must have a great heart" (246), Allen provided the Dialexian Society a lesson in rhetoric that came as much from his heart as from his head. He had obviously been thinking a good deal about responsible rhetoric, rhetoric with a purpose. Kossuth had been in the country since December of the previous year and was preparing to leave after over six months of speaking in front of large, enthusiastic crowds. Allen mentioned in his speech that he himself had traveled ninety miles to hear him speak. The January 1, 1852, edition of *Frederick Douglass' Paper* carries a letter from Allen expressing anger about the reaction of the black citizens of New York to Kossuth.[80] He calls their response "a stupendously foolish thing! Not a word of their own wrongs—their sufferings—their enslavement;—no point, no directness, no nothing except the mere rhetoric. Palaver, the whole of it; and to cap the climax of absurdities, the address winds up with the assurance to the Hungarian that on the day of giving, they (the colored people) will be on hand with at least the 'widow's mite,' if no more. Where did mortal man ever read of such folly as this before[?]" The letter continues in this vein for several paragraphs. By the time of his July address to the college literary society, he had channeled his annoyance into a speech on oratory, challenging the members to exercise this "weapon" that would help America become a truly free land.

Charles W. Chesnutt's Address to the Normal Literary Society of Fayetteville

Some thirty years later, another educator, who titles himself somewhat fancifully in a journal entry a "Professor of Reading, Writing, Spelling &c in the State Colored Normal School of N.C.," addressed an institution-based literary society.[81] Unlike Central College, however, this institution was all-black and located in the postbellum South; yet many of the rhetorical principles outlined are predictably quite similar. In 1881, Charles Chesnutt delivered a speech to the Normal Literary Society of Fayetteville, North Carolina, titled "The Advantages of a Well-Conducted Literary Society." Chesnutt, then only twenty-three—roughly the same age as William Whipper when he addressed the Colored Reading Society of Philadelphia—was principal of the State Colored Normal School at Fayetteville.[82] Chesnutt, who had served as "recapitulator" when the literary society was first organized in 1877, would later deliver addresses to other black literary societies, including the well-known Bethel Literary and Historical Association of Washington, D.C., and the Boston Literary and Historical Association, but it is apparent that in this early literary society address, Chesnutt was helping to establish guiding principles for a newly organized group in which he had invested a great deal of intellectual energy. He opens by defining the literary society as a "valuable auxiliary means of education," not established to replace but to supplement formal training, and quotes from the society's constitution that it "was designed 'for mutual improvement in the arts of composition and debate, and in other literary exercises.'"[83] Thus, we have here a very useful distinction between an institutional and a community-based literary society, the former being understood as supplementing the core curriculum, while the latter, especially in the case of the early societies, often served as the chief source of instruction. In preparation for considering the advantages of a "well-conducted debating society" (13), he talks about the link between the desire to organize an association that would give pleasure and the act of the will that led to its creation, in a section that parallels Francis Bacon's characterization of rhetoric as applying "Reason to Imagination for the better moving of the will."[84]

Modeling good principles of arrangement, Chesnutt next outlines the parts of his address, which are composed of the three main advantages of a literary society, listed climactically from least to most valuable. In teacherly fashion, he embeds four additional numbered lists within this main list. He firsts discusses the advantage that a literary society provides recreation, because "a different set of faculties are brought into play" (14), and the advantage that it "gives its members instruction in practical business knowledge" (15), by which he means the ability to participate in public discourse, facilitated by knowledge of parliamentary procedure. The third and chief advantage of a literary society, he observes, is that it nurtures mental discipline by teaching how to handle oneself before an audience, to control the emotions, to respect authority, and, most important, to develop sound arguments (4–17). We can recognize in these advantages the classical persuasive appeals, ethos, pathos, and logos, along with sound principles of delivery. Delivery, in fact, receives a good deal of attention in this speech as Chesnutt invokes the habits of Demosthenes, Daniel Webster, and Henry Clay to make his a fortiori point that even the great orators had to practice, as does Allen in his speech to the Dialexian Society, except that Allen also points out Clay's misuse of rhetoric. Chesnutt recalled a French statesman's remark that on public matters, it was no compliment to be thought to deliver speeches without preparation, quoting him to say, "I hold it criminal in a man to discuss great public measures without careful thought and study" (18). In support of proper preparation, he attributes to Hugh Blair the advice that beginning speakers should "write their first speeches, and commit them to memory" to capture the "life and fire of the extemporaneous language" (18).[85] Chesnutt argues a strong connection between facility with these rhetorical skills and participation in public discourse: "Under our system of government, the democratic form, every intelligent citizen is likely, almost *certain* to be called upon at some time to take part in a public meeting, or to fill some public office" (16), adding that oratory has never been an art practiced primarily for its own sake but is always associated with some cause. It is worth noting that Chesnutt assumes for himself and his auditors the right to participate in mainstream public spheres to "discuss questions of public moment" and implies that there will be opportunities to do so (18). During this post-Reconstruction period of racial paranoia and denial of civil liberties, such opportunities would in fact have been quite limited. Chesnutt understood that being able to imagine themselves in certain roles was an important first step on the road to full civic engagement. Rhetorical training and social action are here inextricably bound.

The incomplete handwritten text of Chesnutt's lecture ends with a passage from Levi Hedge's 1816 *Elements of Logick, or a Summary of the General Principles and Different Modes of Reasoning,* which he took "verbatim from the excellent little work."[86] It is a section in which Hedge lists the value and rules of argument. Of the twelve included in the incomplete text of the speech, of particular interest is the last point, which speaks to the importance of ethical argument in that the "professed" goal of argument is "a truth, and not victory" (23). This "rule" highlights a distinction between Chesnutt's speech and Allen's. As mentioned, Allen had an agenda well beyond providing an overview of rhetorical principles designed to indoctrinate students in the belief that they needed to learn how to speak and write in ways that would, he hoped, help to improve their lives. Allen wanted his audience to apply these principles in the service of abolition. His was not a neutral assessment of rhetorical abilities. Allen really does seem more interested in truth than victory, while Chesnutt speaks about rhetoric in the abstract.

Frances Harper's Address to the Brooklyn Literary Union

In a paper read before the February 16, 1892, meeting of the Brooklyn Literary Union,[87] New York public school teacher Susan Elizabeth Frazier included the announcement that "Mrs. Harper is now engaged in writing a book called 'Iola,' which is a work on the racial question."[88] Nine months later, Harper herself would speak at a meeting of this same group on the subject "Enlightened Motherhood," an address that could easily have been placed into the mouth of one of the participants in the *conversazione* described in "Friends in Council," a chapter from her 1892 novel, *Iola Leroy.* In the chapter, Iola, the title character, is said to have given a paper on the education of mothers. Although the text of the paper is not provided, the discussion it stimulated centered on the role of mothers in ensuring the survival of the race. One member responds, "I agree . . . with the paper. The great need of the race is enlightened mothers."[89] Harper, sixty-seven years old and an honorary member of the Brooklyn Literary Union, gave this address at the end of a distinguished career as an antislavery lecturer, race and woman's rights activist, and poet. Her novel had probably just been published and some in the audience may have read it, given Frazier's earlier announcement. The address, however, makes no mention of the novel; rather, it emphasizes what Harper claims is the vital role that mothers play in molding the character of children descended from a "legally unmarried race" to train them for "useful citizenship on earth and a hope of holy companionship in heaven."[90] This call to duty borrows from the Victorian discourse of an enlightened domesticity and republican motherhood, informed by science and other kinds of knowledge rather than by blind acceptance of male dictates and desires. Linked to this discourse as well were the concepts of social purity and the "laws of heredity and environment" (289), which were influenced by such "social evils" (288) as alcoholism, prostitution, and sexually transmitted diseases. The social purity movement of the late nineteenth century aimed to suppress what was considered to be excesses of the male sexual drive, such as adultery and pornography, in pursuit of a moral regeneration of society. In the speech, Harper sharply criticized the double standard often applied to boys: "Are there not women, respectable women, who feel that it would wring their hearts with untold anguish, and bring their gray hairs in sorrow to the grave, if their daughters should trail the robes of their womanhood in the dust, yet who would say of their sons, if they were trampling their manhood down and fettering their souls with cords of vice, 'O, well, boys will be boys, and young men will sow their wild oats'" (288).

Harper argues that women should educate themselves in the principles of liberty, independence, and democracy in order to prepare future generations for responsible citizenship and nation-building. In its original iteration, this preparation for motherhood, grounded in a belief in natural sexual distinctions, rarely took into account women or blacks as those being prepared. White women were to nurture white male leaders. Harper, however, takes this concept and applies it to the mothers of black children, male and female, who must extend race work into the future. In her article on Harper, Gabrielle P. Foreman makes the point that "African-American women often fit their writing into what to many contemporary readers seems like conventional generic shells. Their valorization of motherhood, their endorsements of marriage and traditional women's concerns like temperance, and their novelistic use of racially indeterminate protagonists, all characterize later nineteenth-century Black women's writing. Their commitment to these concerns was genuine and political."[91] Harper was claiming for these women of the Brooklyn Literary Union a space in this discourse from which they were often left out as a vehicle for continued racial uplift. She challenges them explicitly in this regard: "Would it not be well for us women to introduce into all of our literary circles, for the purpose of gaining knowledge, topics on this subject of heredity and the influence of good and bad conditions upon the home life of the race, and study this subject in the light of science for our own and the benefit of others?" (290).

Unlike the literary society speeches of Hamilton, Whipper, Allen, and Chesnutt, Harper's does not comment on the occasion or the rules of rhetoric that such a group might promote. Rather, its contribution to the rhetorical education of those who heard it inheres in the ways in which it models the grand style of address, with balanced phrases, repetition of words and syntactic patterns, richly figured language, and antithetical pairings, so typical of Harper by then. The Brooklyn Literary Union, mentioned above, had been established in 1886 and seems to have attracted the black elite from around the country to engage in race work. But even twenty-two years later, the sense of urgency expressed in a 1908 *New York Age* article suggests that such organizations were still needed: "Those of the race who have had intellectual and mental training are to be the levers with which the masses are to be lifted. A literary society in Brooklyn organized with a view to the mental uplift of the community is an imperative necessity."[92] Harper's rhetorical situation responds to this need. She speaks of a larger role, outside of performance, that the society needed to assume and that such black societies had for years assumed: the social role of racial uplift, in this instance as manifested through enlightened mothers.

Prominent Speakers and the Community of Literary Societies

In this section, I discuss the communal impact of literary associations on prominent nineteenth-century black activists who talked about their membership as a site of rhetorical education and as a source of inspiration. The benefit they derived from participation seems to have come as much from being in community with others as from perfecting a skill or a particular set of rhetorical principles. (In chapter 2, I attend more closely to sites located in singular, individualized initiatives.)

Frederick Douglass and Communal Involvement

Still another advantage of these literary societies, given that the most effective rhetorical education benefits from an audience, was that they enabled communal involvement. Those who acquired and developed rhetorical skills most successfully were involved in communities; they participated collectively in activities that helped to hone these skills. It was not just that people worked together to create institutions to advance their communicative abilities, it was also that the coming together itself developed those abilities through *mutual* improvement. This communal, collaborative context yielded perhaps the greatest benefit of literary societies.

In 1871, Frances Harper wrote to William Still of the Philadelphia Underground Railroad about engaging in private conversations with poor women in post–Civil War Greenville, Georgia, women who had had limited opportunities for the kinds of deliberative exchanges that took place in the literary clubs or the antebellum North but who were nonetheless responsive and appreciative: "But really my hands are almost constantly full of work; sometimes I speak twice a day. Part of my lectures are given privately to women, and for them I never make any charge, or take up any collection. But this part of the country reminds me of heathen ground, and though my work may not be recognized as part of it used to be in the North, yet never perhaps were my services more needed; and according to their intelligence and means perhaps never better appreciated than here among these lowly people. I am now going to have a private meeting with the women of this place if they will come out."[93] It is exciting to imagine the intensity of these free and private discussions among freedwomen of the South. What questions might they have had for Frances Harper, then a widow, former antislavery lecturer and poet, acquaintance of William Lloyd Garrison and Frederick Douglass? In these private settings, they would have been more at ease in articulating their concerns about a wide range of issues. Rhetorical education here was achieved through practice in what we today would call a "safe space."

These societies, while improving individual rhetorical abilities, ultimately served the entire community. The notion of community is especially salient in Douglass's discussion of his affiliation with the East Baltimore Mental Improvement Society. Contrary to the prevailing view, Douglass's acquisition of literacy did not alienate him from his community. Rather, it provided new ways of understanding and articulating existing communal relationships. In his article on literacy as communal involvement, Daniel J. Royer points out that the "apparent paradox that pits the slave's efforts to achieve freedom and independence against the slave's efforts to cultivate community is also untangled when black acculturation, especially the central issue of black literacy, is characterized not as a change from the old to the new, but as revitalization, reaffirmation, and recreation within the black community."[94] Royer also notes that the traditional notion that one can't go home again, that learning the rhetorical conventions of another linguistic culture, especially of a dominant culture, will place communicative barriers between the learner and her home culture, has also been questioned by literacy specialist Deborah Brandt. Brandt claims that literacy–and by extension other rhetorical skills—is essentially collaborative in that good communicators become more aware of their audiences and thus better able to relate to them. Literacy enhances Douglass's ability to "intervene in his own context."[95] These associations formed by blacks across the nineteenth century had this communal function. They provided audiences, sympathetic yet critical, bound by a common purpose.

Of the nineteenth-century black activists with literary society affiliations, Douglass was among the few who were enslaved at the time of involvement. Douglass recalls that after being returned to Baltimore from the eastern shore, he became acquainted with free literate black caulkers in Baltimore's Fells Point, who helped to advance his own education. In 1837 or 1838—when Douglass would have been approximately twenty—they formed the East Baltimore Mental Improvement Society, similar, no doubt, to societies that were being formed in many Northern cities with a concentration of free blacks. Antebellum blacks in Baltimore organized literary societies, debating societies, and lyceums that engaged in reading and critiquing famous and contemporary writing, declamatory speaking, and prose writing. They also sponsored lectures on current issues and instruction in grammar, rhetoric, logic, and composition. The first was the Young Men's Mental Improvement Society, formed in the early 1830s and possibly the one to which Douglass belonged. William Watkins, Frances Harper's own teacher and her uncle, organized a literary society to promote the practice of formal and informal debate in midcentury Baltimore. One of the members, William Douglass, published *Sermons Preached in the African Protestant Episcopal Church of St. Thomas', Philadelphia* in 1854. "To this society, notwithstanding it was intended that only free persons should attach themselves," Frederick Douglass writes, "I was admitted, and was several times assigned a prominent part in its debates. I owe much to the society of these young men."[96] So we have here in Douglass's own words testimony as to the role the community of this improvement society played in his rhetorical education. Douglass's literacy was communal. His association with these other members advanced his own facility with language.

Mary Church Terrell's Foundational Community

Mary Church Terrell left explicit testimony on the benefit of literary club membership in her autobiography, *A Colored Woman in a White World*. She recalls her experiences as quite possibly the first black member of the Aelioian Literary Society, which "provided women with a forum for debate and oration" and was founded in 1852 as a more progressive branch of Oberlin College's Ladies Literary Society.[97] Terrell joined while a senior in the preparatory department there, probably in the early 1880s, since she was graduated from Oberlin in 1884. She credits the society with exposing her to some of the best speakers in the country and with enabling her to argue extempore, preside over meetings, and hold her own in formal debates.[98] Terrell went on to have a long and accomplished career as head of the National Association of Colored Women and as a professional lecturer who used the platform over a thirty-year period to represent the race in a series of speeches she recounts throughout her narrative. All of her comments acknowledge the power of rhetoric to bring about change in the sad state of African Americans during that post-Reconstruction period in African American history that Rayford Logan dates from 1877 to 1901. She expressed surprise at how little her Northern white audiences knew about the lives of black people—the difficulty of voting, and the Convict Lease System,[99] and their many accomplishments in the face of oppression—a gap in knowledge she never missed addressing in her speaking opportunities.

Drawing on her early training at Oberlin, Terrell generally spoke without a manuscript in front of her, although she always prepared one. She provides this valuable account of her composing and delivery process: "Because I practically never used a manuscript when I delivered an address, many thought I spoke extemporaneously. But this was not the case, and I attempted to disabuse people's minds of this impression. As a rule, I decided not only what arguments I would make and what facts I would present, but I spent considerable time choosing the language in which my thought should be couched. I took myself very seriously indeed as a public speaker."[100] Understanding the value of having an audience's attention, Terrell, like Chesnutt, had no respect for speakers who gave audiences the impression that they had not thought about or prepared a text for the occasion. When she expressed concern to a lecturer associate that she might say nothing of interest to her audiences, he replied, "Oh, never mind about that. . . . Maybe you won't. But people never go to hear what a woman says anyhow. They simply go to see how she looks."[101] Terrell did not include her response to this advice in the text, but given her concern for substance and purpose throughout her career as a public speaker, it is not difficult to construct one.

Anna Julia Cooper's "At Home" Community

At the other end of the social scale, Anna Julia Cooper recalled fondly her early years in Washington, D.C., where she was called to teach in 1887. She described in detail the weekly informal get-togethers or "at homes" hosted on Friday evenings by Charlotte Forten Grimké and Francis Grimké, pastor of Fifteenth Street Presbyterian Church, and on Sundays by Cooper. These gatherings were attended at various times by other prominent black intellectuals who might have been available, including Jennie Simpson Crummell and Alexander Crummell, then rector of St. Luke's Episcopal Church, Edward Blyden, Mrs. Frederick Douglass, and Richard Greener. Cooper attested to their regularity, writing, "I can safely say not a week passed for thirty years or more that did not mark the blending of those two homes [hers and the Grimkés'] in planned, systematic and enlightening but pleasurable and progressive intercourse of a cultural and highly stimulating kind."[102] They discussed art, politics, literature, and religion. On the days when they discussed literature, she recalled that the material was very carefully selected and that each member purchased the selected reading, all of which was read aloud. Someone was assigned to bring in questions to test comprehension, and then the work was discussed for a full hour. For Cooper, these gatherings served as a forum for the "interchange of ideas" and were for her a source of pure delight: "Here was activity, planned and purposeful, strenuous but joyous, not hunger-driven animal action to appease wants, rather spirit-driven by the inner spur and need for life—the more abundant life."[103] We see, then, opportunities for rhetorical education in the form of impromptu discussions among needy postwar black women in the rural South as well as regularly scheduled meetings of members of the Washington, D.C., black elite.

In the last decade of the nineteenth century, Kelly Miller, Alexander Crummell, and W. E. B. Du Bois helped to establish the American Negro Academy to counter the racist discourse in documents like Frederick Hoffman's 1898 *Race Traits and Tendencies of the American Negro,* purporting to demonstrate the genetic inferiority of blacks. The academy provided a site for the production of a range of rhetorical responses to such claims. Members of this society assumed that those invited to join already possessed the requisite rhetorical skills needed to participate. It was an intellectual think tank for black men. Unfortunately, the organizers did not have the foresight to include women, though at least one woman, Anna Cooper, was invited to address them and may even have been invited to join. This group can be thought of as the realization of the goals of the early societies, although the academy's objectives did include continued support of "youths of genius in the attainment of the higher culture, at home and abroad," along with promoting scholarly publications, archiving black history, vindicating the race from claims of inferiority, and issuing an annual volume of works by selected members.[104] The focus here was not so much on training and improvement of members' rhetorical skills as on applying them in service to the race.

Literary Societies and Public Speaking in Nineteenth-Century Black Fiction

In considering references to literary societies in fiction of the period, I hope to present a sketch of the extent to which these associations were absorbed into black culture such that they appear in the imagined worlds of novelists. Frank J. Webb's 1857 novel *The Garies and Their Friends* provides an abundance of information about the lives of Northern blacks in the pre–Civil War period. Set primarily in Philadelphia, where a number of literary societies were founded, the novel recounts their social activities, business ventures, and attempts to improve their status. In the opening section, a Mr. Winston is visiting the Ellis family when his host's daughters announce their intention to attend a lecture at the "library company's room." In response to Winston's assumption that blacks were not admitted to such events, the host explains: "It is quite true . . . at the lectures of the white library societies a coloured person would no more be permitted to enter than a donkey or a rattle-snake. This association they speak of is entirely composed of people of colour. They have a fine library, a debating club, chemical apparatus, collections of minerals, &c. They have been having a course of lectures delivered before them this winter, and tonight is the last of the course."[105] Webb's fictional family could have been participating members of a society like the Philadelphia Library Company of Colored Persons, which met several times a week.

Sites of domestic rhetorical activity were also re-created in black women's fiction. For example, in "The Sewing Circle," a chapter from Pauline Hopkins's novel *Contending Forces,* women gather at the Smiths' boarding house to sew and to debate "events of interest to the Negro race." In Hopkins's account, these "parlor entertainments" were frequently held to raise money for specific events. Once the sewing tasks had been assigned, the business meeting convened with a review of the past week's events and closed with a talk by a prominent senior woman of the community. At one gathering, a Mrs. Willis spoke on "[t]he place which the virtuous woman occupies in upbuilding a race." Only after the close of the business meeting were the men invited to join them for socializing.[106] The topic would seem to assign women a supporting role in racial uplift work, but a role nonetheless. Their separate discussion of this role gave them a chance to speak openly, as in the case of the women's separate literary societies. In the chapter "Friends in Council" from Frances Harper's novel *Iola Leroy,* mentioned above, she refers to the *conversazione,* in this case a gathering of "some of the thinkers and leaders of the race to consult on subjects of vital interest to our welfare."[107] Both men and women assembled to consider such matters as black emigration to Africa, patriotism, the education of mothers, and the moral progress of the race. Each speaker opened with a prepared paper on the topic, followed by extended critical discussions. It is worth noting that the two women present at the meeting in Harper's novel, Iola Leroy and Lucy Delany, participated in these discussions on equal footing with the men.

Rhetorical performances such as these that took place in parlor rooms rather than in more open spaces gave participants the opportunity to hone their rhetorical skills in alternative public spheres.[108] Lauren Berlant points out that by being "performatively democratic," these gatherings helped make counterpublic spheres "more permeable by women and the ethnic and class subjects who had been left out of aristocratic privilege." She adds that they learned "to construct a personal and collective identity through the oral sharing of a diversity of written ideas."[109] Thus, such meetings existed as sites of rhetorical education.

The 1899 novel *Imperium in Imperio* incorporates another account of rhetorical education in action and, drawing on the tradition of the commencement speech, dramatizes the high value placed upon facility with language. In the narrative, author Sutton Griggs describes the lifelong friendship and rivalry of Belton Piedmont, dark-skinned and impoverished, and Bernard Belgrave, fair-skinned and supported with the financial resources of an absentee white father. On two occasions in the novel, their rivalry culminates in rhetorical battles. The first competition is staged at their high school graduation where the "two oratorical gladiators" had both been asked to speak.[110] Belton, with no help from the teacher, addresses his class on the ironically titled subject "The Contribution of the Anglo-Saxon to the Cause of Human Liberty." Bernard, whose light skin earns him favor with the white judges, speaks last, delivering a panegyric to Robert Emmett, Irish orator and nationalist leader. On the second occasion, at the close of the novel, both men unite behind the Imperium, a black nation within a nation somewhere in Texas. Bernard, having been chosen president, delivers an address to the Congress of the Imperium, calling for armed rebellion in response to recent acts of Southern mob violence: "Let us then, at all hazards, strike a blow for freedom" (149). Belton follows with a chapter-length counterargument that the Imperium should reveal itself to white Americans and work with them for peaceful resolutions: "There is a weapon mightier than either of these [the sword and the ballot]. I speak of the pen. If denied the use of the ballot let us devote our attention to that mightier weapon, the pen" (164). Belton's argument carries the day, and the Imperium is dissolved. Following their performances, Bernard congratulates Belton on his delivery: "Belton, that was a masterly speech you made to-day. If orations are measured according to difficulties surmounted and results achieved, yours ought to rank as a masterpiece" (166).

It's a curious novel of rebellion and accommodation, with rhetoric rather than violence being offered as the proper response to racial oppression. But of significance to this discussion is the extent to which most of the plot centers on rhetorical rather than physical action. Griggs gives considerable attention to the rhetorical training both men received in preparation for their first ceremonial speeches, and many of the characters are described in terms of their oratorical ability. When Belton sought outside help in preparing his high school speech, he chose a local congressman and "polished orator" (26) to correct his diction. According to the narrator, the congressman was so impressed with the "depth of thought" (invention), the "logical arrangement," and the "beauty and rhythm of language" (style) that he allowed Belton to use his library and provided him with constructive feedback (26). Griggs, a graduate of Bishop College and Richmond Theological Seminary, was a Baptist preacher who wrote over a dozen books and established his own publishing company. His father, a prominent Texas activist minister as well, founded the first black newspaper in Texas and edited several others. Thus, Griggs understood the power of rhetoric in its oral and written manifestations. Belton's remarks to the Imperium and to readers of the novel could be a reflection of Griggs's own beliefs.

Why the Decline of Literary Societies?

F. P. Powell observed in 1895 that the lyceum had served its purpose but that its decline did not portend a lack of interest in political or social issues; rather, he suggested that much of the instruction received from outside sources was now being carried out in the homes and in universities. He also pointed to the increasing number of women's clubs, whose programs incorporated discussions of art, music, economics, and literature, a development he attributed to the lecture system. He closed his analysis with the powerful assessment that the "lyceum rose to great power, and fell away and practically died, inside a single quarter of a century. But it killed slavery; it broke the power of superstitious theology; it made woman free; it created a universal demand for higher culture."[111] While Powell here was referring to the more formal New England antebellum lyceum structure, with paid invited lecturers, including Susan B. Anthony, Frederick Douglass, Ralph Waldo Emerson, Henry Ward Beecher, Louis Agassiz, Anna Dickinson, Wendell Phillips, John B. Gough, and Sojourner Truth, some of these same effects certainly applied to literary societies, more broadly defined, which often fulfilled the same purposes. Carl Bode, writing in 1956, confirmed and extended Powell's conclusions, attributing the decline of the lyceum to the fact that many of its functions had been redistributed—bureaus managed lectures; adult education had been taken over by extension courses, vocational schools, night schools, and in-service training; public schools had taken over specialized training; public libraries collected books; and mass media had taken over entertainment.[112]

Newly formed postbellum black institutions of higher education provided an additional site for literary societies. In 1894, Fisk University's Union Literary Society reported on the activities of its members in the *Indianapolis Freeman;* the Young Ladies and Gents Occidental Literary Club announced a fund-raising event for the Shorter University at Arkadelphia; and students of Fisk and Roger Williams universities and Central Tennessee College held an "Intellectual Love Feast—A Feast of Reason and Flow of Soul," during which one speaker read a paper on female suffrage that "caused the brethren to say many funny things."[113] Debating clubs and literary societies were, in fact, the earliest extracurricular student groups at black colleges. Fisk's Union Literary Society was established in 1868, and Monroe H. Little has documented that between the early 1880s and the beginning of the twentieth century, no fewer than seven additional societies were founded at Fisk alone, adding that most black schools during this period had at least one literary society.[114] Literary societies established during the antebellum period frequently served as substitutes for more formal school training in rhetorical skills. At the end of the century, these college societies often supplemented such training in that they gave students the opportunity to apply what they were learning in discussions on a variety of topics, including woman's suffrage, mentioned above, although evidently not taken seriously by many on that occasion. Little also lists such topics as temperance, migration to Africa, American involvement in Mexico, Phillis Wheatley, Jim Crow laws, and textbooks for black schools by black authors as some of the those discussed by literary clubs at Fisk and Atlanta universities and at Morehouse College.[115] The agenda at one 1878 meeting of the LeMoyne Normal Institute Literary Society, which Ida B. Wells would later join, included a historical paper on Benjamin Franklin, a "poetical" paper on Henry Wadsworth Longfellow, a scientific paper on cell life, and a debate on the topic "Resolved, that the Crusades were a benefit to the world." The LeMoyne Literary Society also enacted an early example of community outreach in that it extended membership to non-LeMoyne teachers and students and added a Friday meeting with a "more devotional character." Sabbath school superintendents from various denominations rotated leadership of the meetings, which always included discussions of "practical" subjects like "Best Methods of Conducting Infant Classes."[116]

During this period of shifting roles for literary societies, two contrasting experiences with collegiate rhetoric and oratory are noteworthy. James Weldon Johnson wrote of his affiliation with two Atlanta University literary societies during his matriculation there in the late 1890s. He joined the Ware Lyceum, a debating society, while in the preparatory department, recalling that during his first debate he was "almost as terror-stricken as when I attempted my first Sunday school recitation," but he went on to win the first prize of thirty-five dollars in an oratorical contest during his sophomore year, speaking on the subject "The Best Method of Removing the Disabilities of Caste from the Negro."[117] As one of the top graduates in his college class and president of the Phi Kappa college literary society, he gave a commencement address in which he attempted to "break through the narrow and narrowing limitations of 'race,' if only for an hour," by speaking broadly on "The Destiny of the Human Race."[118] Johnson went on to deliver many speeches in various professional roles: school principal, lawyer, diplomat, newspaper columnist, author, and field secretary for the National Association for the Advancement of Colored People. Yet in spite of his apparent success as a speaker, he would write astutely but disparagingly of "rhetorical oratory" in his 1933 autobiography at the age of sixty-three. Given his opinion's relevance to this volume, I quote it in full:

Before I left Atlanta I had learned what every orator must know: that the deep secret of eloquence is rhythm—rhythm, set in motion by the speaker, that sets up a responsive rhythm in his audience. For the purpose of sheer persuasion, it is far more important than logic. There is now doubt as to whether oratory is an art—curiously, it is the only art in which the South as a section has gained and held pre-eminence—if it may still be classed among the arts, it is surely the least of them all. Oratory, it cannot be denied, has its uses; it has been of tremendous use to me. But the older I grow, the more I am inclined to get away from it. For rhetorical oratory I have absolute distrust. My faith in the soundness of judgment in a man addicted to opium could not be less than that in a man addicted to rhetorical oratory. Rhetorical oratory is the foundation upon which all the humbug in our political system rests.[119]

It appears that by "rhetorical oratory," Johnson meant rhetorical excess, although he says nothing further about this subject in his narrative. He no doubt distinguished this kind of rhetoric from the kind that he employed so effectively over the course of his productive life.

Although he does not mention belonging to a literary society, W. E. B. Du Bois, Johnson's contemporary, presents a very different college oratorical experience in many respects. Du Bois began his writing and speaking career at Fisk University, where he edited the *Fisk Herald* and "became an impassioned orator." He went on to Harvard, where he took English from American literature professor Barrett Wendell, writing in one of his compositions, "I believe foolishly perhaps, but sincerely, that I have something to say to the world, and I have taken English 12 in order to say it well." While there he won a second place Boylston prize in oratory, and in 1890, he delivered one of the six commencement speeches, on the subject "Jefferson Davis," receiving a favorable review in the *New Nation*.[120] While he does not claim that these experiences made him determined to become a public speaker, he also does not express the same dislike for oratory that Johnson does in his autobiography.

These collegiate societies also provided students a social outlet and issued publications, as did the antebellum societies. Many of the social and service-oriented functions of these collegiate societies were taken over by Greek-letter fraternities and sororities, established in the early twentieth century.[121]

The Social Principle

Whether in a church, in a hall, in the front room of a house in Greenville, Georgia, on a college campus, or in the parlor of Anna Julia Cooper's LeDroit Park home in Washington, D.C., these mental feasts, each in its own way, enacted the social principle of unity and accord that Alexander Crummell expressed in his 1875 Thanksgiving Day sermon "The Social Principle among a People and Its Bearing on Their Progress and Development." Crummell responded to arguments against race-based associations, against the "dogma ... *that colored men should give up all distinctive effort, as colored men, in schools, churches, associations, and friendly societies.*"[122] Crummell, then rector of Saint Mary's Chapel Protestant Episcopal Church in Washington, urged his black congregation to observe the cooperative principle by persisting in organizing associations for mutual support:

> Everywhere throughout the Union[,] wide and thorough organization of the people should be made, not for idle political logomachy, but for industrial effort, for securing trades for youth, for joint-stock companies, for manufacturing, for the production of the great staples of the land, and likewise for the higher purposes of life, i.e., for mental and moral improvement, and raising the plane of social and domestic life among us.
>
> In every possible way these needs and duties should be pressed upon their attention, by sermons, by lectures, by organized societies, by state and national conventions; the *latter not* for political objects, but for social, industrial ends and attainments.[123]

In many respects, the goals ("securing trades for youth," "mental and moral improvement") and the means of reaching people (sermons, lectures, societies) parallel those advanced in early-nineteenth-century African American discourse. The difference here, of course, is that this message could now be addressed to postbellum blacks North and South.

It seems then that literary societies, as I define them here, played an important role in developing the rhetorical abilities of nineteenth-century African Americans. These associations brought people together to pool their resources, first for assistance with basic needs and then for mental and moral improvement. They performed and judged their own works and the works of others in order to perfect their skills and build their confidence. They believed the rhetorical ability these societies helped to develop was one sign of their equality, their "African genius," and that it gave them a powerful way to reach wider audiences, including the majority of African Americans who did not belong to such associations, particularly through society-sponsored reading groups, circulating libraries, and often the publishing of newspapers. Society events frequently generated revenue to support the building of schools and other educational initiatives. The separate societies enabled women to develop their rhetorical abilities among one another, often in the service of traditional roles for women, but also they took the skills developed in literary societies with them when they joined activist groups like the female antislavery societies. They would use rhetoric the way William Allen characterized it, as a "weapon." The postbellum societies, many of them church-based, concentrated more on an activist agenda as access to basic skills grew, and they could devote more of the agenda to substantive discussions, such as the progress of a congressional bill or the state of Liberian politics. Rhetorical education became a significant by-product of this activism as participants developed their skills as they addressed these matters. Later in the century, Charles Chesnutt in his first literary society address would make a distinction between institutional and community-based literary societies as newly founded black colleges formed their own associations with the purpose of supplementing class work. The literary societies declined as other social groups replaced them in colleges and as community groups grew more and more exclusively political. The literary society performed a variety of roles across the century; chief among them was as a site of rhetorical education.

4

Organs of Propaganda
Rhetorical Education and the Black Press

> Until this past year I was one among those who believed the condition of
> the masses gave large excuse for the humiliations and proscriptions under
> which we labored; that when wealth, education and character became
> more general among us, the cause being removed the effect would cease,
> and justice be accorded to all alike. I shared the general belief that good
> newspapers entering regularly the homes of our people in every state could
> do more to bring about this result than any agency. Preaching the doctrine
> of self-help, thrift and economy every week, they would be the teachers to
> those who had been deprived of school advantages, yet were making his-
> tory every day—and train to think for themselves our mental children of a
> larger growth.
>
> —Ida B. Wells, 1893

The first half of the nineteenth century in America has been characterized
as "oratorical," in that the ideals of responsible citizenship were conveyed
largely through the public speaker. The medium of print was employed in part
to reproduce and comment on the oral performance. Gregory Clark and S.
Michael Halloran observe that "the orator had a central cultural role: to articulate a public moral consensus and bring it to bear on particular issues through
forms of discourse—spoken or written—that were more or less classical." They
were classical in that they were based on the assumption that this discourse
established a public, consensual moral authority. The authors explain that over
the course of the century, this kind of oratorical culture was transformed into
one based on the authority of the individual and then on the authority of the
expert; they argue that oratory moved away from a deliberative to an epideictic

or entertainment purpose. Clark and Halloran recognize, nonetheless, that this early-century participatory democracy was limited primarily to white males. As I reiterate throughout this volume, African American rhetoric owes much—but not all—of its development to this exclusion, since as Clark and Halloran also point out, "rhetorics are always a response to 'cultural forces.'"[1] The challenges African Americans faced sustained deliberative rhetoric for much of the century, although we have in the pages of the black press references to performative rhetoric in the activities of the early literary societies, for example, the elocutionary recitations. But even these performances were often understood to serve a deliberative purpose, as, for example, in the case of Mary Webb's performance of *The Christian Slave*—Harriet Beecher Stowe's dramatization of *Uncle Tom's Cabin*—discussed later in this chapter. An advertisement for New York Central College placed special emphasis on the fact that in that "day of Public Speaking," the curriculum included a "rhetorical class with daily exercises in Extemporaneous Speaking."[2] People were accustomed to hearing lengthy speeches in religious, deliberative, and judicial spaces; they had, as a result, developed a critical ear for rhetoric that was effective and for rhetoric that failed. It is not surprising, then, that the pages of black periodicals are filled with references to lectures, rhetorical exercises, speeches, and eloquence in general.

The black press offered multiple opportunities for rhetorical education. For the editorial staff, agents, and correspondents, it provided on-the-job training in rhetoric, but the press also directly and indirectly educated readers in sound rhetorical principles. I use the term "black press" in this chapter to refer to periodical literature edited or published by African Americans, although the readership, backing, and distribution mechanisms varied. As journalist Ida B. Wells observed, along with disseminating information, journalists believed their role was to instruct readers and hearers in how to receive, interpret, and respond to that information.[3] Further, these periodicals carried much more than current events; they carried self-improvement advice and critiques of various kinds of rhetorical performances.

After considering some views on the function of newspapers from the perspectives of journalists Frederick Douglass and Wells, who represent over sixty years of newspaper work, I explore the extent to which the black press functioned as a site of rhetorical education. Principles from rhetorical theorist Hugh Blair's Lecture 34, "Means of Improving in Eloquence," provide a frame for identifying sites. As the five means, he lists (1) development of character or moral improvement; (2) accumulation of a storehouse of knowledge ("a Liberal education"); (3) continuous, habitual, diligent effort; (4) emulation of good models, not for "Slavish Imitation" but for enlightenment; and (5) consistent practice in appropriate writing and speaking, regardless of the occasion. Elaborating upon this last item, Blair observes that literary or debating societies create ideal sites for such practice, if members select substantive topics and avoid ostentation. Blair's final advice is that the best rhetorical theorists to study are the ancients: Aristotle, Cicero, and Quintilian.[4] Guided by these five means, I first consider examples of rhetorical education as disseminated through direct instruction in or promotion of the principles of rhetoric, such as in essays on elocution or eloquence. These examples support Blair's advice to acquire specific rhetorical knowledge and broad general knowledge. In many articles, the information provided qualifies as invocation rather than instruction; the authors understood their role as advocates for rather than teachers of rhetorical skills. Thus, I classify these as instances of rhetorical education in that they promote it, even if they do not provide it. I then look at examples of rhetorical education indirectly enacted through sermons; abolitionist and proslavery advocates; lecturers at events sponsored by literary societies; and the critique of speakers as diverse as Louis Kossuth, William J. Watkins, William Lloyd Garrison, and Frances Harper. This category coincides with Blair's means of studying and emulating good models. Numerous articles encourage activities for moral and mental improvement, in keeping with Blair's first means, but this ubiquitous advice is woven into all other kinds of advice and is not addressed separately.

I have relied chiefly on biographies and autobiographies of newspaper editors, histories of the black press, and, of course, the publications themselves. Copies of many of the publications of the black press across the nineteenth century are no longer extant, as in the case of Wells's *Memphis Free Speech.* For others there are partial sets, especially of the antebellum papers, many of which are now more easily searched electronically, although doing so does not give one a sense of the whole of any one issue. I sampled articles in antebellum and postbellum papers; in papers edited by women and by men; in papers in the eastern cities and in those in other parts of the country; and in nondenominational papers and church-sponsored papers, although this may not be a useful distinction, since the latter generally carried a broad range of articles on morality, literature, and politics as well as on theology and religion. Being primarily interested in African Americans functioning as agents as well as recipients of rhetorical education, I chose to consider publications under their editorial control; thus, William Lloyd Garrison's *Liberator,* for example, while having in 1834 more black subscribers than white, was sampled in most instances only to get a sense of what emphasis the abolitionist white press placed on an issue or on a rhetorical performance.[5] Gamaliel Bailey's abolitionist paper, the *National Era,* published from 1847 to 1860, served the same purpose. Comparable to dipping a thimble into the ocean, this "sampling" makes no claim to representativeness. I am less interested in the quantity of samples than in their authenticity as sites of rhetorical education. Where articles appear as reprints from other papers, I consider that the editors made the choice to include them and thus functioned as agents of any rhetorical education that such articles contained.

It is no accident that many prominent nineteenth-century race leaders and speakers were affiliated in some way with newspaper editing. Along with journalists like Douglass, Samuel E. Cornish, Henry Highland Garnet, and, later in the century, T. Thomas Fortune, we also must consider Mary Ann Shadd Cary and Mary Bibb, African American women who emigrated to Canada, and Ida Wells. The black press was active across the century and especially during the antebellum period. Also often overlooked is that a surprising number of antebellum journalists were formerly enslaved. These were individuals motivated by a desire to reach a wider audience than they had been able to before. After reciting a sizable list of black newspapers and newspaper editors, the author of an 1853 article in *Frederick Douglass' Paper* points to this statistic with some satisfaction: "It is not a little remarkable, that [of] the editors above named, not less than one third were fugitives from the 'house of bondage'; showing that the *vis* which bore them out of slavery carried them into the chair editorial: and it is a curious inference from the above names, that, taking into the account, the proportion of *fugitives* to the *free colored* in the free States, slavery has produced the greater number and the most talented among our editors. Had all this and kindred talent been penned up in the slave States, would not another kind of *mark* have been made in our history?"[6] Rhetorical education then occurred as a by-product of the social activism recorded in the pages of the nineteenth-century black press. Contributors, correspondents, and editors developed their own expertise in rhetoric for action; they encouraged subscribers to become critical readers of political discourse, and they called attention directly to nineteenth-century examples of engaging rhetoric.

The sites discussed here may be classified as primary sites and as secondary sites. I consider newspapers to be primary sites when they publish articles containing direct instruction in the art of rhetoric, the history of rhetoric, or critiques of speeches. They function as secondary sites when they publish the speeches themselves or when they report on rhetorical activities. Most of the information on the activities of literary societies comes from newspaper articles, since most societies left no recorded histories. To avoid unnecessary overlap, I do not consider their activities again here. In addition, the section below on pulpit eloquence as a holy skill will bring to mind the section on pulpit literacies of chapter 1. However, here I discuss the topic only as it is treated in the press. Still, it would be impossible and, in fact, undesirable to avoid all overlap. Overlap serves to reinforce these as credible sites. Many of the same people who read papers also worshiped in churches, attended lectures, participated in literary clubs, and often wrote about their experiences in diaries. This last chapter attempts to capture other kinds of educational rhetorical activities found in the pages of those papers.

Producing a Paper as Rhetorical Education

In this section, examining firsthand accounts of journalistic rhetorical education, I focus on the careers of Frederick Douglass and Ida B. Wells. Douglass's life and his work as a black newspaper editor of four newspapers are emblematic of the ways in which the press can serve rhetorical education. The choice of Douglass is complicated by the fact that Douglass, whom Frances Foster acknowledges is "the most famous African-American journalist of all time"—even as she calls for more attention to others not as well known—was assisted in his initial publishing endeavor by a goodly number of white fund-raisers, printers, financial backers, and subscribers. Martin Delany was co-editor of his first newspaper, the *North Star,* for a brief period but spent most of his time traveling in Ohio, Kentucky, and Pennsylvania advertising and selling subscriptions to the paper.[7] Yet white backers notwithstanding, Douglass conceived the *North Star* as a black newspaper and understood its function as such. This point of view is articulated clearly in a January 7, 1848, article titled "Colored Newspapers," in which he alludes to William Whipper and the American Moral Reform Society's opposition to any form of racial identification—that is, "colored," "people of color," or "African"—in the names of organizations. Douglass writes: "We confess to no such feelings; we are in no wise sensitive on this point. Facts are facts; white is not black, and black is not white. There is neither good sense, nor common honesty, in trying to forget this distinction. So far from the truth is the notion that colored newspapers are serving to keep up that cruel distinction [racial discrimination], the want of them is the main cause of its continuance." Fortunately, some volumes of all of his papers are available electronically or on microfilm, and he wrote about his editorial experiences in his books *My Bondage and My Freedom* and *Life and Times of Frederick Douglass*. Although publication of his final newspaper venture, the *New National Era*, ended in 1874, Douglass continued to contribute items to other newspapers until his death in 1895. By that time he had met Wells and they had collaborated in the 1893 publication of *The Reason Why the Colored American is Not in the World's Columbian Exposition*.

Wells is also an exceptional embodiment of the ways in which a rhetorical education can be acquired and put to good use in newspaper work. She edited her own paper for three years and went on to have her pieces published in a variety of periodicals, including the *New York Age,* the *Detroit Plaindealer,* the

AME Church Review, the *American Baptist,* the *Chicago Defender,* the *Cleveland Gazette, Our Day,* and the *Chicago Inter-Ocean.* Wells reported findings of her journalistic investigations in pamphlets with detailed titles like *Lynch Law in Georgia, with the report of Louis P. Le Vin, The Chicago Detective Sent to Investigate the Burning of Samuel Hose, The Torture and Hanging of Elijah Strickland, The Colored Preacher,* and *The Lynching of Nine Men for Alleged Arson.* Wells also wrote of her journalistic ambitions in her diaries and, like Douglass, in her autobiography, *Crusade for Justice.* In this section, I consider some of the ways in which these two journalists understood their editorial roles as an engagement with rhetorical education. The firsthand accounts of the circumstances that motivated and constrained Douglass and Wells as they entered into journalism demonstrate that their desire to reach a wide reading and listening public with urgent arguments against slavery and mob violence created an exigence that accelerated their own preparation for journalism.

The following passage from *Life and Times of Frederick Douglass* describes the reaction of many New England abolitionists, including Garrison, to Douglass's decision to publish the *North Star* and registers his own initial self-doubt, if we read past his irony:

> I can easily pardon those who saw in my persistence an unwarrantable ambition and presumption. I was but nine years from slavery. In many phases of mental experience I was but nine years old. That one under such circumstances should aspire to establish a printing press, surrounded by an educated people, might well be considered unpractical if not ambitious. My American friends looked at me with astonishment. "A wood-sawyer" offering himself to the public as an editor! A slave, brought up in the depths of ignorance, assuming to instruct the highly civilized people of the north in the principles of liberty, justice, and humanity! The thing looked absurd. Nevertheless I persevered. I felt that the want of education, great as it was, could be overcome by study, and that wisdom would come by experience; and further (which was perhaps the most controlling consideration) I thought that an intelligent public, knowing my early history, would easily pardon the many deficiencies which I well knew that my paper must exhibit.[8]

Douglass recalls the skepticism he faced about his qualifications to edit a paper in the artful manner with which he handles understatement. The reactions he received were among the many expressions of doubt in the intellectual ability of blacks, expressions that black writers and speakers spent an enormous amount of time and energy countering. Douglass understood the task before him—what he needed to learn about journalistic writing. But engaging the modesty topos, he has understated his credentials. Twenty-nine years old in 1847 when undertaking this new enterprise, he already had available to him a considerable storehouse of previous rhetorical activities on which to draw. In 1839, his remarks denouncing colonization were published in the *Liberator;* in 1841, he became a lecturer for the Massachusetts Anti-Slavery Society and secured subscriptions to the *Liberator* and the *National Anti-Slavery Standard;* in 1845, Douglass published his *Narrative of the Life of Frederick Douglass, an American Slave Written By Himself;* and by 1847, he had lectured in Scotland, England, Wales, and Ireland. Still, narrating his journalistic decision some ten years later, when he first wrote about it in *My Bondage and My Freedom* (1855), he would recall some doubts about the venture. Douglass edited four papers over the next twenty-seven years: *North Star* (1847–51), *Frederick Douglass' Paper* (1851–60), *Douglass' Monthly* (1859–63), and the *New National Era* (1870–74).

Here in another passage from *Life and Times,* Douglass recalls some specific aspects of his writing process and sense of audience:

> There were times when I almost thought my Boston friends were right in dissuading me from my newspaper project. But looking back to those nights and days of toil and though, compelled often to do work for which I had no educational preparation, I have come to think that, under the circumstances, it was the best school possible for me. It obliged me to think and read, it taught me to express my thoughts clearly, and was perhaps better than any other course I could have adopted. Besides, it made it necessary for me to lean upon myself, and not upon the heads of our antislavery church—to be a principal, and not an agent. I had an audience to speak to every week, and must say something worth their hearing or cease to speak altogether. There is nothing like the lash and sting of necessity to make a man work, and my paper furnished this motive power.[9]

Douglass confirms the strong influence of audience and timing, his "lash and sting of necessity," on the composing process.

Wells began her career in journalism near the end of the century and on the other side of slavery. She never liked teaching and was anxious to find another vehicle for expression of her race concerns. The following passage from her autobiography describes her entry into newspaper work:

> The editor, who had held a position in the city of Washington for a number of years, was a brilliant man. In the course of time, he got his job back and returned to Washington, leaving the *Evening Star* without an editor. To my great surprise, I was elected to fill the vacancy. I tried to make my offering as acceptable as his had been, and before long I found that I liked the work. The lyceum attendance was increased by people who said they

came to hear the *Evening Star* read. Among them one Friday evening was Rev. R. N. Countee, pastor of one of the leading Baptist churches, who also published a weekly called the *Living Way*. He gave us a very nice notice in his paper the next week, copying some of my matter, and invited me to do some writing for his paper.

All of this, although gratifying, surprised me very much, for I had had no training except what the work on the *Evening Star* had given me, and no literary gifts and graces. But I had observed and thought much about conditions as I had seen them in the country schools and churches. I had an instinctive feeling that the people who had little or no school training should have something coming into their homes weekly which dealt with their problems in a simple, helpful way. So in weekly letters to the *Living Way*, I wrote in a plain, common-sense way on the things which concerned our people. Knowing that their education was limited, I never used a word of two syllables where one would serve the purpose. I signed these articles "Iola."[10]

Wells's statement that she had "no training" except that acquired as editor of the *Evening Star* but that she did have a cause and people she wanted to reach speaks to the motivational force of audience, exigence, and purpose. Wells, focused on the message, reveals here especial concern for reaching readers at all levels of proficiency by writing in a "plain, common-sense way."

Wells's best known journalistic piece is, of course, the May 1892 editorial published in the *Free Speech*, a response to the violent racial climate depicted with such venom in the white Memphis press. It was primarily this direct statement of affairs that led to the destruction of the *Free Speech* office and to her permanent relocation.[11] The significance of this series of events often causes us to overlook her earlier formative journalistic work. Her first articles, based on accounts of her lawsuit against the Chesapeake & Ohio & Southwestern Railroad Company, were the 1884 "weekly letters to the *Living Way*," mentioned above. By 1885, T. Thomas Fortune began to reprint her *Living Way* articles in his paper, the *New York Freeman* (later the *New York Age*), and other national black papers followed. As has been pointed out, the years between 1884 and 1887 were "crucial to her formation as a journalist," a period during which she edited the Memphis literary society's *Evening Star*, read widely, kept a notebook of ideas, wrote to the local and national press, participated in organizations of journalists, and worked as a correspondent.[12] The rhetorical education acquired through such activities laid the foundation for the journalistic activism that would follow. This training in newspaper work was fueled by Wells's own determination to express her opinions on any matter deemed worthy of verbal response. As one of only a few black women in journalism during this period,

Wells did not escape the limiting gender labels and insinuations associated with women in spaces men were reluctant to share. She was labeled "princess of the press," described to be as good a writer as any man, was often told that her forthrightness would prevent her from ever getting a husband, and was accused of questionable liaisons with men. What Wells probably began to understand very early in her journalistic career was that if she was going to fight racism and sexual discrimination effectively with words, she would need to acquire the best possible rhetorical skills to wage an effective battle.

I chose Wells and Douglass as male and female examples of journalists during the first half and near the end of the nineteenth century who, with little formal training in writing, developed journalistic skills in the process of producing their papers and articles. They were motivated by the pressing race and gender issues all African Americans faced in the nineteenth century. But they were obviously also different kinds of rhetors. In a frequently quoted exchange between the two, Wells draws a useful distinction. While they were waiting for a meeting to begin, Douglass asked her whether she was ever as nervous as he before a public appearance. She replied no, explaining, "That is because you are an orator, Mr. Douglass, and naturally you are concerned as to the presentation of your address. With me it is different. I am only a mouthpiece through which to tell the story of lynching and I have told it so often that I know it by heart. I do not have to embellish; it makes its own way."[13]

Reporting on Public Meetings as Sites of Rhetorical Exchanges

In *Democratic Eloquence*, Kenneth Cmiel describes a period following the invention of the printing press when increases in literacy rates among the white upper classes enabled an independent "public" and promoted a variety of publications, coffeehouses, salons, and other spaces where ideas were exchanged in a "'free zone' where opinion could be formed independent of the state."[14] Where might such "free zones" have existed for African Americans in the first half of the nineteenth century, places where they exchanged ideas and expressed opinions independent of dominant culture? It would be misleading to suggest that the conditions Cmiel describes were those of most African Americans during this period. One setting where citizens gathered to discuss matters in a space separate from official governmental sites was the literal space of the public meeting. Mary P. Ryan observes that the public meeting was the "sacred civic act" of antebellum democracy, that by 1835 the city pages of New York papers were filled with calls to meetings, and that the participants in these meetings were all white and male.[15] But African Americans developed argumentative skills as they discussed race issues in other black-controlled public meetings. Articles from the *Colored American* (New York City), the *Provincial Freeman*

(Canada West), *Frederick Douglass' Paper* (Rochester), and the *Palladium of Liberty* (Columbus, Ohio) report on public meetings held between 1840 and 1855. I discuss this site of rhetorical education under the broader heading of the black press not simply because reports on these meetings appeared in black newspapers but because the newspapers actually facilitated the proceedings in several ways. Announcements of these meetings were placed in the papers. Minutes and follow-up activities were published in subsequent issues as a way of involving those who did not attend. Further, as in the examples described below, the press frequently was questioned for its role in reproducing the proceedings of a meeting or served as the medium for communicating with the opponents who could not be reached through other means. Thus, it could be argued that the press itself was a crucial participant in these public gatherings.

These meetings, also referred to as public discussions, mass meetings, and, less frequently, "grand demonstrations," were most often held in churches and were called to consider specific topics. At a Brooklyn mass meeting, a petition to repeal a state law requiring blacks to own a certain amount of property in order to vote was discussed. The issue had been addressed the previous month at a "Great Mass Meeting" at a Baptist church on Anthony Street, with speeches and resolutions presented by a cast of prominent black men.[16] An article titled "Mass Meeting at Chatham" reported that the "colored citizens" of Canada West held a meeting to show support for England in the struggle against Russia and included a resolution of thanks to the "Editress of the *Provincial Freeman*" for her political work.[17] *Frederick Douglass' Paper* (hereafter *FDP*) described a public meeting of "colored people" in a New York church where James McCune Smith raised $100 to purchase a new suit of type for the paper.[18] A public meeting of condolence, chaired by Martin Delany, was held in Pittsburgh's Wylie Street Church to organize the community's response to the 1854 death of John B. Vashon, a prominent abolitionist and leader of Pittsburgh's black community.[19] The editor of the *Palladium of Liberty* responded to complaints that he improperly published the proceedings of a public meeting held in Hamilton, Ohio, asking, "Whoever heard of such nonsense as this—no right to publish the proceedings of a public meeting, when at the same time we do not claim that the citizens did pass any thing at the meeting?"[20]

This next example is emblematic of the ways in which these public meetings facilitated timely response to and engagement with mainstream discourse and served as a venue to disseminate information to various publics. In this instance, *FDP* reprinted an article from the *New Bedford Standard* titled "Meeting of Colored Citizens." The October 11, 1852, meeting was convened to hear the report of a committee charged with composing a reply to a letter that Massachusetts congressman Horace Mann had sent to African Americans attending a Cincinnati convention. The letter stated that since "Africans" were inferior in intellect and that "the Caucasian race" was inferior in "sentiment and affection," their coexistence could be mutually beneficial. When asked in a follow-up letter whether his views had subsequently changed, Mann answered that they had not and went on to elaborate the view that each race had distinct characteristics and were ideally suited to live in distinct geographic regions, which some interpreted as an endorsement of colonization. After hearing Mann's second letter, participants in the public meeting had an "animated discussion"; speeches were given, and objections were put forward. The outcome was a resolution, unanimously adopted, which expressed "deep regret that Hon. Horace Mann ha[d] expressed sentiments inimical to our much oppressed and down trodden race."[21] A report of this meeting also appeared in the *Liberator* on the same date as the reprint in *FDP*. Subsequently, others who did not attend the public meeting weighed in on the matter, including Professor William Allen of Central College and Theodore Parker, clerical activist from Massachusetts, who both felt that the New Bedford citizens had overreacted to Mann's remarks, and Daniel Ricketson, a New Bedford native and Quaker intellectual, who felt that the black community was justified in its reaction.[22] The point here is not that antebellum African Americans held public meetings, common events during this era; rather, the relevance to rhetorical education is that these meetings took place in separate spaces, occupied primarily by African Americans, where they could use their rhetorical skills to develop strategies for change and to counter what they understood to be racist discourse. These meeting spaces were their discursive "free zones," one manifestation of what Michael C. Dawson and others have called a black counterpublic.[23] They also understood the function of the press in enabling cross-cultural conversations. The resolution that came out of that October 11 meeting concluded with the provision that the proceedings be published in the local papers as well as in the *Liberator* and *FDP*.

Praising Rhetoric and Direct Instruction in Rhetoric

In this section, I analyze articles from black newspapers across the century that offer direct rhetorical instruction, usually detached from any particular rhetorical performance. In these articles, the writer speaks directly to the reader about ways to improve abilities in public speaking, preaching, writing, or critical reading. Essays on eloquence, elocution, the merits of female orators, and how to read certain documents critically fall into this category as well.

In evaluating the educational intent of such pieces, sociologist Timothy Shortell's work on antebellum newspapers is useful. He conducted a content analysis of five black newspapers published between 1827 and 1860 in antebellum New York.[24] According to the coding system employed, the themes of "brotherhood," "liberty," "America," "colored," and "slavery" occurred most frequently across all papers, with "brotherhood" emerging as a theme in more paragraphs than any other term.[25] The prominence of this theme suggests a heightened consciousness of the need to construct rhetorically an imagined community of politically astute readers.[26] While the editors were conscious of a wider audience, they were clearly focused on reaching black readers, challenging them to critical engagement with the civic discourse of the time. Shortell also coded selected paragraphs for three rhetorical dimensions—tone, or the use of emotion; basis, or the use of comparison; and mode. The dimension "mode" bears special relevance to journalism as a site of rhetorical education. Shortell's modes, based in part on Geoffrey Leech's theory of pragmatics, are the illocutions or performative utterances of asserting, explaining, and evaluating.[27] These modes are similar to the stases, often employed as a way of sorting arguments. Asserting operates in the stasis of fact; the intent is to establish some understanding about the topic under discussion. Explaining is closely aligned with the stasis of cause or definition; and judging or evaluating, the stasis of quality.[28] Shortell's results, based on four of the five papers in his study, showed a high percentage of the paragraphs (40 percent) to be in the explanatory mode, the illocution most often employed when the purpose is to educate, in that the "arguments make connections that reflect a didactic point of view."[29] At the risk of overgeneralizing from a study of five antebellum papers in one state, the finding that across these papers, the most prevalent theme is brotherhood and the most common illocution is explaining or arguing does provide tentative support for the claim that these editors were especially concerned, from a rhetorical perspective, about creating a community through language and about helping African Americans scattered across the Northern states begin to understand themselves as members of a discourse community, educating themselves for full participation in citizenship.

A critical question associated with fitness for participation in public rhetoric was whether one needed certain rhetorical credentials to speak. There was, on the one hand, the conviction that those who represented African Americans in public discourse needed to be fully articulate and able to defend their positions cogently; on the other hand, there was a sense that anyone who felt wronged had a right to address those wrongs using whatever linguistic abilities were available to her or him. In an article contentiously titled "Why Do Ignorant Colored Men So Often Speak in Public?," correspondent to the *Colored American* E. P. R. (Elymas Payson Rogers) opposes attempts to "speak in public on the part of those who are not duly qualified" in the belief that they do their cause more harm than good.[30] But Rogers understood the circumstances that compelled and entitled oppressed people to voice their opinions and paraphrased a portion of Daniel Webster's 1826 speech on the occasion of the deaths of John Adams and Thomas Jefferson in support of this view: "When great interests are at stake, rhetoric is vain."[31] Rogers's point and Webster's passage highlight a discursive dilemma unresolved to this day; it resonates in Gayatri Spivak's celebrated question "Can the subaltern speak?," inquiring into the advantages and disadvantages of discursive representations of marginalized groups.[32] The editor of the *Colored American* appended the response that he was sympathetic to the need to speak but counsels, "Nothing is more detrimental to us than bringing ignorant, illiterate colored men into comparison with educated, talented white men. Such a course is food to our enemies and bane to our cause. Therefore, while we agree with our correspondent that colored men have the right, and should both speak and act, yet we hold that they should know when and where to speak, and how and where to act."[33] We have, then, a newspaper editor and a religious leader discussing the need for rhetorically skilled speakers to represent the concerns of an oppressed race to "educated, talented white men." Partially in the service of the presumption that those who represented the race in public discourse should be properly trained, articles in the black press included advice on public speaking, elocution, oratory, preaching, and other rhetorical skills. But such articles also reflect a general interest in rhetoric and expressive self-improvement, mentioned previously, which were evident in the private learner, discussed in chapter 2.

The demand for rhetoric manuals, accommodated to popular training in composition, oratory, reading, and elocution, increased from midcentury to the 1920s. Many of the popular rhetoric texts during this period contained varying amounts of theory followed by selected works for practice. For example, Caleb Bingham's *Columbian Orator* opens with a thirty-page introduction titled "General Directions for Speaking," with advice on pronunciation and gesture, followed by 270 pages of speeches, poems, dialogues, and other selections for study and practice.[34] Of these rhetorical skills, elocution attracted the greatest interest. Nan Johnson writes, "Interest in oratory and elocution was especially intense, encouraged by numerous and varied occasions for oratory and elocutionary performances serving a variety of political, cultural, and social functions."[35] Audiences held high standards for speakers, as indicated in the pages of the newspapers, where whole speeches or excerpts were frequently reprinted and were almost always accompanied by critical commentary. A good deal of attention was paid to elocutionary elements of an oration, even when its primary purpose was not performative. In this section, I discuss references in the black press to elocution generally and in the context of specific performances. These performances varied from political speeches on social reform to elocution in the strict sense of a dramatic reading or recitation of the work of others.

The January 23, 1841, *Colored American* announced that a Professor Bronson was in New York to offer a course of lectures on oratory and music.[36] The article calls for the "brethren" to organize a class. Bronson is also listed as one of the speakers in a series of lectures sponsored by the New York Phoenixonian Literary Society on the topic "Oratory—Interspersed with Recitations."[37] The *Christian Recorder*, as the official organ of the AME Church, carried numerous essays on elocution and its impact on the art of preaching. The October 27, 1866, "Essay on Elocution" was submitted by frequent *Recorder* correspondent the Reverend Thomas Strother of Terre Haute, Indiana. The essay contains detailed information on the manner of speaking and the rules governing elocution, which Strother defines as "the uttering of words in such a manner, in reading and speaking as most fully expresses the meaning of them; and to do this successfully, requires a knowledge, first of the organs, and then of the muscles which act upon them." The essay proceeds to provide in brief form just this knowledge, beginning with the proper body positions, the complement of vocal organs, and advice on breathing.[38] An earlier article is more general in its advocacy for elocution, admonishing that its study is essential for those who would be public speakers, especially ministers. The article, a reprint from the *Christian Instructor,* a weekly religious paper published in Philadelphia, laments the fact that so many good sermons go unheeded due to poor delivery and closes with lines on the power of eloquence from English poet Samuel Daniel.[39] "Practical Elocution" is the title of an article in the *North Star* in which W. C. N. (William C. Nell) reports on a performance by D. V. Gates of "recitations and imitations of distinguished orators and delineations of tragic and comic characters." Nell asked that the speaker be encouraged in "his self-taught exertions" and closed with an excerpt from William Ellery Channing's 1837 "Address on Temperance," in which he highlights the value of elocutionary recitation: "Were this art cultivated and encouraged, great numbers, now insensible to the most beautiful compositions, might be waked up to their excellence and power."[40]

An extended essay on rhetoric titled "American Eloquence" appeared in an 1852 issue of *FDP.* The piece was written by Wilbur M. Hayward, occasional contributor to the paper and the Rochester book agent who published a collection of Daniel Webster's speeches in 1853. John Ernest observes that the piece bears several resemblances to William Allen's "Orators and Oratory," published in *FDP* over a month later, in terms of the historical trajectory of the examples, the topics associated with the rise of eloquence, and the names of accomplished orators.[41] Such similarities suggest the existence of a genre associated with praise of various abstract concepts. For example, in the case of eloquence, almost any mention of its merits will include reference to Demosthenes, as in the case of an 1851 article in *FDP,* a reprint from *Bentley's Miscellany,* titled simply "Demosthenes." The article reminds readers that although Demosthenes is best known for his oratorical abilities, he cultivated eloquence only to improve his political influence. He was not a "mere rhetorician" but a man of action.[42] While both Hayward's and Allen's texts serve a didactic purpose, Hayward's is more clearly focused on praise of eloquence in general. He had no other agenda. Allen, in the tradition of Demosthenes, conveyed a specific concern as to whether one used eloquence for good or for harm.

Benjamin Tucker Tanner's essays in the *Christian Recorder* present an interesting variation on the essay of direct instruction in rhetoric. Tanner discusses Cyprian, a native of Carthage, who, like Augustine, spent his early life teaching and practicing rhetoric prior to his conversion to Christianity, then applied rhetorical principles to the service of spreading Christianity.[43] Over a period of at least nine months, from January to September 1863, Tanner, then twenty-eight years old, published a series of articles on Cyprian. Tanner, an AME minister, was pastor of the Georgetown, D.C., church at the time and in 1878 began a sixteen-year tenure as editor of the *Christian Recorder*. As part of ongoing arguments to support black intellectual and moral equality, and in some cases superiority, Tanner may have chosen Cyprian because he was known as the first African bishop, who organized the Catholic Church in Africa.[44] Certainly many of the black churches and lodges in the nineteenth century carried his name, identifying with his continent of origin.

Prior to his conversion to Christianity, St. Cyprian was an orator and teacher of rhetoric influenced by the classical culture that would have given him a solid grounding in rhetoric. Spread out over eighteen articles, the six chapters of Tanner's essay that I have been able to retrieve include a history of Cyprian's early life in Carthage, with a description of Carthaginian pagan society and of Cyprian's early instruction according to the principles advocated by Quintilian, "cradled in Paganism, [and] educated in all that pertained to ancient scholasticism."[45] Tanner's third chapter, "Cyprian the Rhetorician," shows how rhetoric shaped his young adulthood as a teacher and pleader and influenced his life as a church official. The remaining three chapters cover his postconversion life as a bishop and martyr. Having reviewed Cyprian's early education, Tanner, in chapter 2, begins a brief history of rhetoric with Cyprian the teacher of rhetoric in the background. He advances the conventional claim that rhetoric originates in the heart rather than in the head and engages the figure *erotema* to invoke the oratory of Frederick Douglass: "Is not the genius of oppression a master rhetorician?" and "Who so eloquent upon the rights of man, as the black sage of Rochester?"[46] It is the only reference in the series of lectures to one of Tanner's peers, an uncontestable reference all readers of the *Christian Recorder* would affirm. All other persons referenced are figures from classical and medieval periods, including Demosthenes and Tertullian. The history that he traces had been well rehearsed by 1883, but what makes it interesting is its placement here in the *Christian Recorder*. Tanner could very well have decided to submit the information in the context of a defense of Cyprian, African bishop. Primarily written in the mode Shortell refers to as explaining, rather than asserting or evaluating, the essays are informational, not directive. The description of Cyprian's conversion from "pagan rhetorician" to Christian documents the spread of the religion during the first forty years of the third century. Tanner does not quote from or refer to specific texts by Cyprian but holds him up as a rhetoric teacher who converted to Christianity and lived a life "with signal honor to himself, benefit to the church, and glory to God."[47]

On the benefits of reading widely, a *Colored American* article claims that it develops character and independence of thought and enables one to become "conversant with the world, and prepared to lend an influence."[48] Two years later, the same paper carried an article arguing against a "fatal error in the literary studies and pursuits of the female," referring to the "passionate and excessive devotion to fictitious writing, which is the reigning idolatry of the sex." The writer complains that fiction constitutes 75 percent of women's reading, while they ignore biographies of great men, adding further that novel reading does nothing to improve oratorical abilities.[49]

An article in *FDP* titled "The Lecturer" comments on traveling speakers' educational value in the community, due to the "modern invention" of the mass lecture reaching a large number of people efficiently. The article then critiques the rhetorical performances of three persons who had recently lectured in Rochester, pointing out variations in their distinctive styles. Henry Giles, Unitarian minister and Shakespeare scholar, received praise for the "generous humane nature" of his lecture. Wendell Phillips, whom the writer calls "Boston's best rhetorician and finest speaker," presented a lecture described as "happily delivered, admirably arranged and comprehensive, simple, and beautiful." The third lecturer, Theodore Parker, gave a talk on human progress, which the writer believed "was in all the elements of a lecture, vastly superior to many of its predecessors this season." The writer preferred Parker over Phillips for his optimism, observing that Phillips presents a picture of civilization as "rising, falling, advancing, and retreating alternately," while Parker's is an ever-advancing construction of history.[50] Comments on Phillips's rhetorical style also appear the following year in a report on the New England Anti-Slavery Society's convention. *FDP*'s Boston correspondent digresses to discuss the effectiveness of various convention speakers, including Stephen Foster, Charles Sumner, and Phillips. Observing that Foster was an "uncommonly shrewd and able debater," the correspondent contrasts Phillips, the prepared but extemporaneous orator, who speaks with a fire "aimed to destroy an evil," to Sumner, the careful, studied orator, who commits his speeches to memory and delivers them with the force of a "tempest . . . to bear down, over power, and put [the opposing argument] 'on its back.'" One correspondent expressed dismay "more from curiosity than anything else" that Sojourner Truth did not have an opportunity to speak on that same occasion. These interspersed comments on rhetorical performance were quite common, especially during the first half of the nineteenth century when rhetoric was still, as Nan Johnson points out, a public art. Papers frequently carried examples of eloquence accompanied by framing comments. In the *Liberator,* a newspaper subscribed to by many African Americans, one can find articles titled "Eloquence," "Indian Eloquence," "Native Eloquence," "Shameful Eloquence," and "Colored Talent and Eloquence," accompanied by speech excerpts in each instance.[51] Similar articles on eloquence appeared in the black press and helped to shape readers' attitudes towards rhetoric, oratory, and eloquence.

The eloquence of a Fourth of July speech by E. D. Barber is noted in a July 1839 *Colored American* article reprinted from the *Pennsylvania Freeman.* The article, titled "Eloquence," includes introductory remarks and an excerpt from the conclusion of the speech delivered before the Addison County Anti-Slavery Society in 1836. It is not clear whether the framing commentary was written by the editor of the *Colored American* or by the editor or the *Freeman.*[52] Regardless of affiliation, the writer heaps praise upon the excerpt for the ways in which it conveys "moral firmness and inflexible love of liberty," for its "prophetic vision" and for its "rich and beautiful" language, comparing it to Daniel Webster's peroration in his reply to Robert Hayne. Readers of the *Colored American* were being offered a piece of occasional rhetoric from three years earlier for appreciation of its spirit and the power of its language. In the excerpt, Barber, clerk of the Vermont House of Representatives and a popular speaker dedicated to reform, creates a utopic vision of freedom rising, as public opinion against slavery increased, and of a "chorus of millions of voices . . . swelling upon the calm, still air, hymning praises and Thanksgivings."[53]

From the beginning, the editors of these newspapers seemed to have understood their educational function. *Freedom's Journal* in 1827 published a statement on the advantage of newspapers as a teaching resource, including the facts that the cost of books is reduced, students are introduced to new, current material every week, and, at the same time, they learn world history and geography.[54] Two months later, *Freedom's Journal,* through a column by "Mr. Observer," advanced a direct endorsement of rhetorical training in which the writer stresses "the importance of forming a Debating Society, among our brethren of this city [New York]. No one at the present day, will presume to dispute the extensive influence which Eloquence exerts upon mankind." The column holds up St. Paul, Demosthenes, Richard Sheridan, Edmund Burke, and those who argued against the slave trade as exemplars, pointing out that while it is not guaranteed to make all participants Sheridans, a debating club "will enlarge our powers of reasoning by teaching us to express our thoughts as brief as possible, and to the best advantage. It will also enable us to detect at a glance, whatever sophistry is contained in the arguments of an opponent."[55]

FDP presents a history of the first newspaper, expressing surprise that "a means of instruction and amusement so apparent should not have been established until nearly two hundred years after the discovery of printing."[56] The *Provincial Freeman,* in an article titled "Newspapers by Colored People in the United States," laments the fact that although several new papers had come into existence, they were advocating, as did their predecessors, the position that blacks must stay in the United States to "make the white American give to them equal political and social privileges," even though whites themselves immigrated to America to escape European despotism.[57] *FDP* reprinted an article from the *Ogdensburg (N.Y.) Sentinel,* listing the benefits to children of having access to newspapers in the home: they become better readers, spellers, and grammarians; they write better compositions; as they mature, they tend to take the lead in debating societies, with newspapers serving as a source of invention.[58] In a *North Star* article titled "Colored Newspapers," Douglass criticizes a passage from the short-lived paper the *Delevan Union,* published by James Gloucester, for its sloppy editing and the *Northern Star and Freeman's Advocate,* published by Stephen Meyers, for its competitive intent. He calls for more cooperative and carefully produced efforts among black newspaper publishers.[59]

While most of the articles on eloquence, rhetoric, or elocution discuss the merits of a particular rhetorical performance, the value of eloquence, or methods for improving one's speaking ability, portions of some articles call attention to the importance of developing the frequently neglected rhetorical skill of critical reading. One of the best examples of an article with this emphasis was submitted to the *Colored American* by Amos Gerry Beman. Beman, a politically active New Haven Congregational minister and a classmate of Alexander Crummell's at the Oneida Institute, submitted a series of at least seventeen articles on mental and moral improvement of the race to the paper. In one, "Thoughts, No. IX," Beman lays out what he calls those abilities that are "strictly mental" and "do not necessarily influence the heart or moral character of the individual." In this amoral category of study, he includes reading, grammar, and the principles of composition, defining reading not as a basic skill but as "the ability and habit of mind which enables one to read with diligence and attention the best standard authors in the English language, in poetry and prose. To be able to appreciate and measure the depth of an argument, whether advanced from the profound mind of a Webster or arrayed in the sparkling brilliance of a Burke . . . to be able to detect the vein of sophistry and chicanery, though robed in the brightest drapery of genius, or found amid the meretricious flowers of eloquence. . . . We should have such a knowledge of figures as will effectually shield us from the cunning of those base minds which are ever ready to take advantage of the ignorant, who are not qualified to demonstrate with facility any problem that may occur in the business of life."[60] Beman here is calling for, rather than providing, instruction in the kind of close critical reading needed to interpret the discourse that during the 1840s was continuing to oppress African Americans, not only through institutionalized slavery but through isolated acts of discrimination like the one Beman himself experienced in his efforts to receive an education in Connecticut. He calls for the development of critical skills to detect what rhetoric often hides as well as what it reveals. In this same article, Beman states that the rules of grammar and composition are needed most among those who have most to say, adding, "Who ought to thunder in all that is solemn and sublime—all that is powerful in arguments based upon the Rock of Truth—the rights of human nature—in all that is persuasive in eloquence for themselves, and their 'brethren in bonds, as bound with them,' if not colored men?"[61]

After the Civil War, newspaper editors felt a stronger need to educate the larger population of subscribers who now had access to their publications. The first issue of the *New National Era* carries a dialogue between "Objector" and "Progressive" in which the two characters debate the advantages of and objections to black newspapers. "Objector" remarks that "no colored newspaper enterprise has ever yet succeeded," and "Progressive" counters that there are more readers both North and South and a heightened urgency for the kinds of self-improvement that newspapers help to foster.[62] This dialogue anticipates James Weldon Johnson's *New York Age* editorial "Do You Read Negro Papers?" in which he answers the complaint from a potential black subscriber that he "cannot find any news in the Negro newspapers." Johnson observes that it is not the role of the Negro newspaper to disseminate "mere news," adding that "they are race papers. They are organs of propaganda. Their chief business is to stimulate thought among Negroes about the things that vitally concern them."[63] Given these circumstances, one might expect to find more examples of direct instruction in rhetorical education in postbellum papers, except of course that to some extent, oratorical culture itself was changing, and much public rhetoric moved indoors, as Nan Johnson outlined. With emancipation came Reconstruction and more private and government-sponsored educational initiatives that would have incorporated various forms of rhetorical education into the formal curriculum and into the extracurricular. Pages of the *Indianapolis Freeman,* for example, describe the activities of college-based literary associations, many of them meeting in regional as well as campus settings. Reports on their activities would appear more frequently in the black press as the society movement spread to other black campuses.[64]

On Women and Rhetoric in the Black Press

Given the constraints against women speaking publicly in the nineteenth century, eloquence and rhetorical education were generally understood to apply differently to females.[65] Articles from the predominantly male-edited black newspapers reflect this difference. Even the most forward-thinking articles on the subject of women and rhetoric insist upon limited participation in the public sphere lest it "unfit them for the holier duties assigned them in the order of creation," this caution from an 1848 piece in the *North Star* defending abolitionist Abby Kelley's right to lecture. The article, observing that when Kelly spoke in Harrisburg, Pennsylvania, some were more curious about her housekeeping skills than her views on the slavery question, recommends that women should develop the "mental culture" associated with eloquence along with their womanly influence.[66]

The superiority of woman's influence comes through in the "Varieties" section of one of the first issues of *Freedom's Journal* in 1827. Under the heading "Female Temper," women are advised to control their tempers to ensure domestic tranquillity and to dissent without the passion associated with males. It is recommended that women receive a different kind of rhetorical education that will not destroy their natural tenderness.[67] But, as Jacqueline Bacon points out in her study of *Freedom's Journal*, the editors of that newspaper also demonstrated the belief that women should be included in public discussions, especially about their own welfare, in publishing a letter signed by "Matilda," who at least assumed the persona of a woman. In her letter, she first requests that they "allow a female to offer a few remarks upon a subject that [they] must allow to be all-important."[68] This subject is the need for educated women who can not only pass their knowledge on to children but possess it as something not to be taken from them. By submitting her argument for public scrutiny, the writer employed her own rhetorical abilities. In Bacon's words, "She used her literary skills to take male leaders . . . to task in a public forum on an issue that was vital to the community's future."[69]

FDP reprinted Ohio abolitionist Sarah Otis Ernst's letter to the *Christian Press* in which Ernst laments the absence of a "competent female speaker" on the program at the 1853 Cincinnati Anti-Slavery Convention, having observed this deficiency on the antislavery lecture circuit over the previous three years.[70] In a reprint from the *New York Independent*, Harriet Beecher Stowe comments on the stir caused by the sermons and public lectures of Antoinette Brown, who had been "troubling the waters" for many traditionalists but apparently had not performed in an unwomanly manner. Stowe, while supporting Brown's right to speak ("Can one tell us why it should be right and proper for Jenny Lind to sing to two thousand people 'I know that my Redeemer liveth,' and improper for Antoinette Brown to say it?"), concludes that most women will have little interest in public speaking: "It would now appear to be a safe course to allow the experiment which is now being made on the sphere of womanhood, to run itself out to its final results without opposition."[71]

Women, cautioned against direct use of eloquence, were instructed to employ "the soft persuasiveness of [their] embraces, or the more melting eloquence of [their] tears."[72] The *Colored American* noted in its November 17, 1838, issue that much of it was devoted to "remarks on female character, influence, and eloquence" because not enough attention had been paid to the part women played in developing human character and because "colored females, from education, are more especially deficient." The issue includes articles on "Woman's Kindness," "Moral Influence of the Wife on the Husband," and, the one of interest to this discussion, "Woman's Eloquence." This article considers the proper spaces where women should practice "unostentatious" eloquence—in her home and in various interactions with acquaintances through "mere conversation." The writer adds that the cultivation of the powers of conversation could take place through direct "intercourse with polished and intelligent society," formal instruction in conversational etiquette, and practice at home during early childhood. Woman is left with conversation into which she can incorporate entertainment or instruction for the benefit of others.[73] A piece in the *North Star* specifically on conversation advises women, especially as they grow older, to refine their conversational skills through wide reading, for "a large heart, and an eloquent tongue, are among the most precious of human things."[74]

A more general argument for the education of women is advanced in the female-edited *Provincial Freeman* article "Female Education." The argument goes that women first need the advantage of a well-rounded education so that they can become "free, independent, accountable, and intelligent," with the same opportunity for self-development as men. The argument then goes to republican motherhood, the idea that those who have primary responsibility for the rearing of children should be well-informed. The article concludes, "It is not half so important that our legislations be wise as that our mothers be so. . . . Strengthen the woman['s] heart, and you strengthen the world. . . . Cultivate the woman['s] mind if you would cultivate the race."[75]

Pages of the postbellum black press carried more material by and about women that would promote rhetorical education beyond "woman's sphere." The

December 8, 1894, issue of the *Indianapolis Freeman* carried a speech made on the opening night of the Bethel Literary Circle given by Mrs. James T. V. Hill, the wife of the first African American lawyer in Indianapolis.[76] In the article, she constructs an argument based on equity, claiming first that women have no desire to "unsex" themselves; they just want equity in the enjoyment of all the "rights, privileges and immunities accorded unto man."[77] In her column "Our Woman's Department," Gertrude Bustill Mossell modeled the ways in which women could function as advocates for their own participation in public discourse. Mossell, whose writing appeared in the *New York Freeman,* the *Indianapolis Freeman,* the *AME Church Review,* the *Woman's Era,* and many other periodicals, used her column to defend higher education for women, to provide advice on the kinds of rhetorical training needed to survive as a newspaper reporter, and to provide instruction specifically to women interested in journalism. This article, aptly titled "Women as Journalists," even outlines a daily routine based on her own experiences: "Writing of compositions . . . of dialogues, accounts of visits to interesting places, we found of great benefit. Take a picture that impresses you and write out a story from it. If you have talents for versification write in that style, endeavoring to conform to rules, and yet retain some originality. Write a little every day. Read and study the best literature, rejoice in candid criticism, even if given in an unfriendly spirit. . . . Write on what you know something about. Use your own style; imitate no one. 'Despise not the day of small things.' Says one, 'Why do you write only on doings of the colored people or women?' There is no nobler work than to make known the good deeds of our ancestors, and to build up a pure womanhood for the race."[78] The last piece of advice indicates Mossell's sensitivity to her times and the extent to which her advice needed to resonate within the discourse of racial uplift and the gradual emergence of women from the domestic. In keeping with convention, her articles for the "Woman's Department," outspoken assertions of a woman's right to equality, were nonetheless all under the name "Mrs. N[athan] F[rancis] Mossell." Using one's husband's name was, of course, standard practice in the nineteenth century among married women, as in Mrs. James T. V. Hill's argument in support of woman's suffrage. For Mossell, rather than diluting her independence, it helped to avoid the appearance of impropriety and to demonstrate that marital respectability could serve as a source of ethical appeal.

As if in response to Mossell's advice, black women launched their own paper, the *Woman's Era,* in 1894. During the last decade of the century, the *Era* served a vital function in community-building among black clubwomen as the first newspaper published by and for African American women. The Boston publication, started in 1894 under the editorship of Josephine St. Pierre Ruffin, continued for several years as the organ of the Woman's Era Club. Black women's organizations across the country, led by women who believed they could solve the problems of the race through intensive self-help activities, contributed to the *Era*. Along with advertisements for Mossell's book *The Work of the Afro-American Woman* and for the Emerson College of Oratory (now Emerson College) were reports on such activities and commentary on the eloquence of various speakers, submitted from correspondents across the country.[79] They appear in the pages of the *Woman's Era* as evidence of enacted rhetorical education. For example, in the first issue, Medora Gould, the editor of the "Literature" column, encourages women to take advantage of a table reserved in the Magazine Room, Lower Hall of the Boston Public Library, for the use of women.[80] In the May 1895 issue, correspondent Dora J. Cole of Pennsylvania remarks on the eloquence of Fanny Jackson Coppin's memorial tribute to Frederick Douglass. Cole observes that Jackson used the thundering approval of the audience "as a weapon against them and charged all who applauded her sentiments to be responsible for carrying them out," adding that her eloquence provided "a grand object lesson for the detractors of woman's ability."[81] One such detractor, writing some ten years earlier, was the Reverend James H. A. Johnson, former student of William Watkins. In his argument against women preaching, Johnson marshals the standard passages from scripture used to conclude that the "bolstering up of female preachers can but enervate the ministry and damage the church."[82] I now turn to some of the rhetorical advice on preaching put forward in the nineteenth-century black press.

On Pulpit Rhetoric, the Holy Skill

"The Eloquence of the Pulpit," Lecture 29 of Blair's *Lectures on Rhetoric and Belles Lettres,* sketches in broad strokes the principles of effective preaching. Blair observes that pulpit rhetoric has the advantages of its dignity and importance. Preachers speak to large assemblies rather than a few judges and are not interrupted or obliged to reply to extemporaneous responses. They have time to select the subjects of their sermons and prepare for their delivery. The disadvantages are the potential for boredom, since the subjects are not new. Preachers have to make tried and true information appear to have some novelty, primarily through delivery, and deal with abstract concepts that need to be illustrated with concrete applications and examples. In response to those who claim that since the truths of religion stand on their own, preaching should not require rhetorical training, Blair answers that this claim would be valid only if eloquence were an ostentatious and deceitful art calculated solely to please. "True Eloquence," he explains, "is the art of placing truth in the most advantageous light for conviction and persuasion." Blair observes that every sermon has the purpose of persuading others to goodness, but the persuasion should be based on the preacher's and the audience's conviction. Pulpit eloquence must be popular eloquence, accommodated to the people, not over their heads. The effective preacher must be a good person, speaking a personal language of conviction, not a language for display or in imitation of vogue trends in preaching. To avoid digressions, the preacher should employ a combination of notes and memory. In the last section of the lecture, Blair observes that given the many duties of preachers, "there is more reason to wonder that we hear so many instructive, and even eloquent Sermons, than that we hear so few."[83] This is all advice that one might expect preachers out to win souls would naturally consider. Practicing his own advice, Blair has just brought together some of these commonsensical principles in accessible format.[84] The rhetorical wisdom on preaching from the pages of the black press were inspired by these same principles—substantive content developed to persuade people to become good, practical applications and examples, strong conviction, and sincere delivery.

As the organ of the AME Church, the *Christian Recorder* is rich with various kinds of advice on ways to enhance preaching. These articles address the preacher's moral, emotional, and mental state as well as formal rhetorical skills. A good bit of the commentary on preaching is reprinted from other denominational periodicals like the *Watchman of the South*, the *National Baptist*, the *American Presbyterian*, and the *Christian Advocate*; from the writing of religious scholars like professor of systematic theology Enoch Pond, Lutheran pastor W. H. Luckenbach, English divine Frederick W. Robertson, or John Bunyan; and from authoritative theological sources like *Bibliotheca Sacra*. One *Recorder* article goes back two centuries to quote English Puritan preachers William Bates (1625–99) and his contemporary Richard Baxter (1651–91). An article in the December 6, 1862, *Recorder* includes a portion of Baxter's advice to preachers that anticipates much of Blair's: "To preach a sermon, I think, is not the hardest part, and yet what skill is necessary to make the path plain; to convince the hearers; to let irresistible light into their consciences, and keep it there, and drive it home; to screw the truth into their minds, and work Christ into their affections; to meet every objection, and clearly resolve it; to drive sinners to a stand, and make them see that there is no hope, but that they must unavoidably be either converted or condemned; and do all this in respect of language and manner, as becomes our work, and yet as most suitable to the capacities of our hearers. This, and a great deal more that should be done in every sermon, must surely be done with a great deal of holy skill."[85]

The respected preachers Bates and Baxter are frequently invoked as exemplars of pulpit eloquence in the *Colored American, FDP,* and the *North Star,* as well. The *Colored American* carried a reprint from the *Watchman of the South,* a moderate Presbyterian publication originating in Richmond, describing with some amazement the rhetorical abilities of an "African preacher," brought to Virginia as a slave, who learned to read the Bible, had committed extended passages to memory, and had converted many whites in the area. The explanation, in some places, borrows from the "fortunate fall" argument that slavery, for all its disruption, brought the benefits of Christianity and literacy:

> [I]t is important to state that "Uncle Jack," (for so he is universally called,) understands and speaks the English language with much more correctness and purity than any native of Africa I have ever known. His pronunciation is not only distinct and accurate but his style is at once chaste and forcible. And yet he has never been made acquainted with the first principles of Grammar or Rhetoric. I have no doubt his superiority in this respect is to be ascribed to the following causes—First, to his having left his native land at so early an age. Next, to the freedom with which he has been permitted and encouraged to mingle in the best society the country affords. Then to the native vigor of his intellect and above all to this intimate acquaintance with the phraseology of the Bible. The reader will, therefore, be guarded against disappointment at seeing nothing, in what we quote from his own lips of the jargon, so peculiar to the African race. No one ever heard the good old preacher say, *massa* for *master,* or *me* for *I.*[86]

This passage is also interesting for what it reveals about attitudes toward African American dialects of English and the Bible as a source of literacy. The writer wants to ascribe the preacher's rhetorical ability to his exposure to Western culture, "having left his native land at so early an age," and later "encouraged to mingle in the best society." The author of the series of sketches on "Uncle Jack," William Spotswood White, was pastor of a Presbyterian church in Lexington, Virginia, and an apologist for slavery, who would have found this link plausible. Although "Uncle Jack" was enslaved throughout his life, the fact that he apparently was not heard preaching an abolitionist sermon but rather seemed to have offered personal spiritual ministry, isolated from larger social conditions, made him the ideal example of the apparent benefits of slavery. The editor of the *Colored American* includes no framing remarks for any of the three extracts from the *Watchman,* causing one to wonder how the reader might have been expected to read these pieces.

A number of articles express the belief that preachers need to preach a social gospel, especially one calling for the abolition of slavery. The article "What Is the Business of the Church!" addresses Blair's principle of meaningful content in that it challenges preachers to speak out specifically against slavery, such that the current "peace" in the church "will be like the stillness before a terrible earthquake," overturning slavery.[87] Another expresses wonder that some see slavery as a "semi-political question" not suitable for sermons, as if the "purchase and sale of God's image, in the vestments of human flesh, and blood, and bones," was not a moral issue.[88] An article in the October 13, 1855, issue of the *Provincial Freeman* insists that preachers should advocate purging church rolls of "manstealers." In a reprint drawing on the advice of William Bates, another *Colored American* article addresses the principle that the preacher ought to be a good person, cautioning against allowing the flattery of the auditors to cause preachers to "bespangle their discourse with light ornaments, to please the ear," rather than preach in a style designed to "save the soul."[89] The Washington correspondent to the *Colored American* compares the preaching styles of the chaplain to the Senate and the chaplain to the House, with high praise for the eloquence of the former and the wish that all "clergymen would throw all their sermons into the fire, and then go to preaching instead of reading." The correspondent would have the preacher study and compare passages of scripture, seeking the illumination to speak without a prepared text.[90] Late in the century, the *New York Age* carries an article on what the writer considers the "Harm Done by Incompetent Preachers and Teachers." The concern here is with content rather than style or delivery as the author criticizes the sermon of a Charlottesville, Virginia, preacher in which he encourages his parishioners to worry less about voting and acquiring their "social rights" and to concentrate on laboring to supply the needs of the superior white race.[91]

In line with Blair's lecture on pulpit rhetoric, these articles from the black press refer to the importance of effective delivery and the ethos of the speaker and place emphasis on the need to apply the abstractions of religion to important contemporary social issues. I close this section with a discussion of "Deborah and Jael," a sermon by Reverdy C. Ransom, a prominent turn-of-the-nineteenth-century social gospeler, who served as editor of the *AME Church Review* from 1912 to 1924. The sermon was delivered in 1897 at Chicago's Bethel AME Church to members of the Ida B. Wells Woman's Club, along with the regular worshipers. This sermon seemed especially relevant as an example of pulpit eloquence with specific social activist leanings, though this tendency is embodied more fully in the speaker himself than in this sermon. The occasion was perhaps an annual event during which members of service clubs worshiped together at some member's church. The choice of Bethel AME, the church to which Wells belonged, added to the significance of the occasion. Ransom had helped the club establish a neighborhood kindergarten at Bethel and later became involved in settlement house work. Further, the AME pastor and Wells had collaborated on several other projects, including a protest against temperance leader Frances

Willard's remarks on lynching, and together would later lead an investigation into the Sam Hose lynching in Georgia, mentioned above.

Yet the speech itself may disappoint readers hoping for radical departure from prescribed gender roles and Western imperialism. It opens with the biblical stories of Deborah and Jael, two Jewish women who performed courageous acts in defense of the Israelites. These narratives serve as ancient examples of the social gospel Ransom would have the parishioners enact. Next, Ransom claims that Christianity produces a "higher type of man" than Confucianism, Buddhism, or Mohammedism, and that of the Christian nations, America produces "the brainiest man on the face of the earth, and it produces the happiest man on the face of the earth: because the foundation principles of our government rest upon manhood and not upon race, not upon creed, not upon blood: but the manhood of our race has suffered in this land—has been dwarfed in this land." Thus, this superlative ranking has been denied to blacks, and especially to black women. He blames slavery for the suffering of black women and looks forward to the day when the black woman will have only one "lord" and "king," her husband, whom she will then be in a better position to encourage to noble deeds and to provide with needed moral support. But he also recognizes the separate leadership roles of many black women, describing at length the accomplishments of Ida Wells, of course, who was probably there in the audience, and also lifting up the names of other female educators, artists, and performers. He calls on the men to show women traditional respect, protection, and support, reminding them that "our womanhood can never shine in all the beauty and dignity and glory which is in store for it until it has our protection; until our women become our queens at whose feet we lay the richest trophies and highest honors we can win in the field of high endeavor." Ransom was clearly a product of his time, with its discourse of middle-class manliness, but, at the same time, he was one of the leading advocates for the rights of women.

He ends the sermon with an excerpt from a poem by one of his former teachers at Wilberforce and wife of the president during his time there, Mary E. Ashe Lee, whose poems were frequently published in the *Christian Recorder.* The poem, for which Ransom does not provide a title, is "Afmerica." It alludes to a subject few talked about publicly at the turn of the century, amalgamation or race mixing, a process that produced what Paula Bennett refers to as "America's amalgamated national identity."[92] The excerpt Ransom quotes speaks more about the future of this blended woman "of every hue, of every shade," and the way in which she should be honored and protected by "her brothers, husbands, and friends."[93] This example of late-nineteenth-century pulpit rhetoric centers on the accomplishments of black women, who are encouraged to take inspiration from two women of the Bible; the sermon quickly takes off from its biblical underpinnings and becomes a message on the tradition of black women as social activists, a tradition the Ida B. Wells Woman's Club continued.

Instructing through Critical Commentary on Rhetorical Performances
Commentary on Performances of Elocutionists

By the 1840s, black women expanded the professional roles available to them by making a living as elocutionary performers through established institutions, such as lyceums, at no loss of the respectability often jeopardized by women in public spaces. Especially in the Northern states, the lyceum became a popular evening entertainment, and elocution had become the most appealing of the popularized components of rhetoric. This specialization in the study of pronunciation or action included the first large-scale, systematic effort to teach reading aloud. Elocutionists named their study for the third office of rhetoric, *elocutio* or style, partly because elocution, as a distinct performative art, referred to the embellished expression of previously composed material, and both men and women were trained in it. Articles in the pages of nineteenth-century black newspapers were filled with observations on elocutionary performances. For example, in a correspondence from "Hannible" to the *Christian Recorder,* February 10, 1866, the writer comments on the performance of Avery College (Allegheny, Pennsylvania) students: "In elocution, the students evince good taste, but it was the subject matter of the various essays and orations, which attracted my attention." Hannible then goes on to name several women who had performed commendably, focusing on one in particular who "contented herself with portraying a scene of every day life, and so vividly was it presented in all its details, that one felt irresistibly drawn along in opposition with the ideal, picturing to the mind the gorgeous reality, and as the reader concluded, amidst a burst of applause, we involuntarily sighed and wished for more."[94] The emphasis here is on performance and visual presentation by what the *Rhetorica ad Herennium* calls "ocular demonstration," so that what is pictured seems to pass in front of the auditor.[95]

This performance training was fueled in part by the opportunity it offered for performances outside of structured dramatic productions. These events often consisted of lectures and solo readings of literature, and they drew broad popular support, as programs of literary societies also indicate. Dwight Conquergood, in his essay "Rethinking Elocution," provides some useful observations on the impact of elocutionary performances in the nineteenth century. He claims that for those aspiring to the mainstream or for those engaged in linguistic gatekeeping, elocution served as an attempt to discipline speech, "to recuperate the vitality of the spoken word from rural and rough working-class contexts by regulating and refining" it.[96] We generally think of rhetorical education—or any form of education—as a means of leveling the field of available opportunities, especially to African Americans in the nineteenth century. But, considering elocution from the perspective of those "against whom it erected its protocols of taste, civility, and gentility," Conquergood also notes that these oral performances provided access, in some instances, to written texts for those who could not read, using Sojourner Truth's appreciation for Walt Whitman's *Leaves of Grass,* which she had heard read at an elocutionary event, as one frequently cited example. According to the story, after hearing a portion of *Leaves of Grass,* Truth asked who wrote it, interjecting, "Never mind the man's name—it was God who wrote it, he chose the man—to give his message."[97]

The dramatic readings originating within the lyceum setting evolved into separate elocutionary events. Elocutionists migrated from literary societies to establish themselves on the professional stage through performing poetry, short sketches, and dramatic readings for a paying audience. Black women elocutionists, whom I am also calling rhetorical educators, reached black audiences not only through their performances but indirectly through accounts of them in the black and white press.

Two women, Mary Webb and Louise de Mortie, provide important examples of public readers whose elocutionary performances served an educational purpose. Elocutionist Webb was best known for her enactment of scenes from *The Christian Slave,* Harriet Beecher Stowe's dramatized version of *Uncle Tom's Cabin.* These scenes functioned dually as a curious argument against black inferiority and as a recycling of literacy through the oral. Webb was the daughter of an escaped enslaved woman and a wealthy Spaniard, who allegedly had attempted to purchase her mother's freedom. A pioneer among black performers, Webb lived in Philadelphia with her husband, author Frank Webb, when she began her career at the age of twenty-seven. Described as exhibiting a "genius for dramatic reading," Webb's success led her to tour in New England, where she met Stowe, and she subsequently became the solo performer of *The Christian Slave,* expressly written for her. In converting her novel to a dramatic performance, Stowe created speaking parts for more women and black male characters than for white men, and Webb performed all of those parts. Thus, as Susan Clark writes, "the persona of Mary Webb visually and vocally reinforced the gender and/or racial characteristics of 22 of *The Christian Slave's* 27 characters."[98] The inclusion of more female and African American speaking parts no doubt helped to make her performance more credible, better to serve the cause of abolition.

In her 1855 diary, Charlotte Forten Grimké entered this negative review of Webb, after seeing her perform selections from Shakespeare: "I wish coloured persons would not attempt to do anything of the kind unless they can compare favourably with others."[99] Grimké's response, softened in the next sentence with the hope that "if she has talent, it may be cultivated, and that she may succeed in her vocation," reflects the pervasive concern among African Americans, mentioned throughout this text, that only the "best" members of the race become objects of the white gaze. Nonetheless, Webb came to be called the Black Siddons, after the British actress Sarah Siddons. Her readings of *The Christian Slave* carried her to England. The July 29, 1856, edition of the *London Daily News* and the August 2, 1856, edition of the *Illustrated London News* carried the same article on her performances in front of a small but apparently appreciative audience. The writer regretted that most people were out of the city for the summer, adding, "[W]e trust that there will be enough friends of the dark races left in London" to ensure a successful tour.[100]

It is not clear whether Webb's performances of *The Christian Slave* reached a wide audience of African Americans. Charlotte Grimké could not be considered typical of the African Americans who might have acquired any form of rhetorical education from direct experience of her performances. Yet they did read about them in the black press, even though most accounts were reprints from the white press. For example, a telling review of her debut performance as a dramatic reader, reprinted in the *Provincial Freeman*, was published in the *Woman's Advocate*, a Philadelphia-based, all-female-managed newspaper, founded in 1855 by Anna McDowell.[101] The review points out that many in the audience were of the "histrionic profession and some of the best teachers and critics of elocution." It comments on Webb's good fortune to have imperceptible "African" features ("Anglo-Saxon predominates"). Although the review found her delivery of the Gothic poem "The Maniac" by Matthew Gregory Lewis lacking,[102] the performance as a whole was deemed favorable, especially her rendering of "Negro Eccentricities," pieces written in "Negro" dialect. The *Portland Transcript* observed that the "Negro dialect was rendered to the life."[103] *FDP* included reviews reprinted from the *Boston Post*, the *Boston Atlas*, the *Boston Courier*, and the *Evening Telegraph*. An 1855 review in the *Liberator* noted that she had performed to a standing-room-only crowd in Boston's Tremont Temple and to an audience of 1,300 in Worcester.[104] Members of these audiences were primarily whites, many of whom had read Stowe's novel and were curious about how the narrative was represented in *The Christian Slave*.

Rather than serving an educational purpose chiefly among African Americans, it seems more likely that Webb's elocution performed the work of abolition and of "persuading" white audiences in the North and in England of the abilities and humanity of blacks, a project that received much attention during this period of heightened antislavery activism. As Susan Clark notes in reference to *The Christian Slave*, "The combination of powerful literary quality and fervent emotion, voiced by a reader who represented the most oppressed members of the slavery system, became a powerful weapon in the fight to convert public opinion to the anti-slavery cause."[105] Webb and her elocutionary skills might be better known today had her career not been cut short by her death in 1859 at thirty-one.

Louise de Mortie, who also performed readings in Boston, presents another case. Monroe A. Majors in *Noted Negro Women* describes her elocution as "wonderful and puzzling."[106] From the December 27, 1862, edition of the *Christian Recorder* comes this description of de Mortie's performance. Not a reprint, this commentary was addressed to Elisha Weaver, then editor of the *Recorder,* and was apparently originally written for the benefit of its readers:

> New York has been favored with something novel and interesting in the debut of Madam Louise de Mortie of Boston "Reading the classics" to a colored audience. It is truly refreshing to have such occurrences to relieve the mind and drive away the ennui consequent upon a continual round of Concerts, Promenades, Mental Feasts, and Prizes, for "the best-looking colored gentlemen and ladies in the room." To have true genius, learning, study, research, and thought, brought out and encouraged; to listen to true eloquence from the lips of [a] high-toned woman, to have every cord touched with delicate fingers—tuned in symphony with the higher, the immortal life is surely exhilarating. How pleasant to ascend in thought, from the low, the grovelling, the mere animal of life, to revel in a world of ideas. To catch the inspiration of the Poets, and with them, far from the influence of terrestrial things, hie on in pursuit of the good, the gentle, and the lovely. Madam Mortie is a good reader, makes a fine appearance, very commanding in manner, and gave general satisfaction to her audience. She will doubtless be heard from again.[107]

Of particular interest here is the fact that the reading was performed before "a colored audience" and that it represented a change from the usual social amusements, of which the correspondent apparently disapproved.

This reading practice can be understood as another instance of the communal literacy, discussed earlier, allowing for broader participation in the pleasures of the printed text by those who did not read.[108] As a form of what Brewer refers to as "intensive reading," it represents a nineteenth-century African American site of public rhetorical education where orality and literacy merge and where scarce reading materials are made available to those without access or the ability to enjoy them.[109] For example, Ida Wells wrote about her own recognition that this practice enabled her newspaper to reach more people. A correspondent to the *Douglass Monthly*—more than likely Rochester abolitionist Lucy N. Coleman—reports on a dramatic reading de Mortie gave in Boston, in 1862, praising her performance and "cheerfully recommend[ing] her to the patronage of the public."[110] All accounts of Louise de Mortie's activities during her short life of thirty-four years suggest that she was committed to educating members of the black community. The fame of de Mortie—a Virginia native—as a reader reached as far south as Maryland. The *Liberator* reports on her participation in a public meeting of "colored citizens" to celebrate the abolition of slavery in Maryland, held at the city hall in Cambridge where she read two poems on freedom.[111] Jane Donawerth reminds us that elocution "helped give nineteenth-century women a voice" and that, while they were not performing original texts, they selected them and delivered "the words of others" to new audiences in more interactive and instructive ways.[112]

Many of those who were denied literacy acquired access to written material as a result of the practice of reading aloud in domestic spaces as well. Conquergood points out, for example, that Sojourner Truth engaged in "insurgent eaves-dropping" when slaveholders read confidential material aloud around her.[113] A fictional example of this kind of eavesdropping comes from the opening scene of Frances Harper's novel *Iola Leroy,* where those denied literacy overheard the conversations around newspaper reports on the progress of the Civil War and developed a code for sharing the news, embedded in such expressions as "How's butter dis mornin'?" and "Did you see de fish in de market dis mornin'? Oh, but dey war splendid, jis' as fresh, as fresh kin be."[114] Such narratives suggest how marginalized groups subverted the exclusionary purposes of some rhetorical acts, turning them into sites of rhetorical education.

Commentary on Political Speeches

Past political speeches were often held up as models in the pages of the press. For example, the *Provincial Freeman* carried a comparison of the two English statesmen William Pitt and Charles Fox. The piece is an extract from Henry Stanton's 1849 book *Reforms and Reformers of England,* which includes extended passages on the two orators; however, the editor of the *Freeman* chose for her readers one passage that specifically addressed their different rhetorical styles. The section draws a sharp contrast between Pitt's austere, studied manner, with "round, smooth periods," often "pompous and sonorous," and Fox's burly and jovial style, "every word pregnant with meaning." The extract concludes succinctly that Pitt "displayed the most rhetoric" while Fox "displayed the most argument," constructing an interesting distinction here between rhetoric and argument and suggesting that the former is less sincere and more contrived, or as Stanton writes, "Pitt had art; Fox nature."[115] In addition to highlighting excerpts from past oratory, the black press carried comments on and extracts from current speech texts as well, including those of young literary society members, the highly praised Hungarian activist Louis Kossuth, members of the William Watkins family, and Chicagoan Fannie Barrier Williams.

Reporters were generally encouraging in their critiques of the rhetorical activities of young people, many speaking publicly for the first time. The early black press functioned not only as a source of rhetorical education specifically targeting black youth—for example, the *Rights of All* included a literary column for youth—but also as a medium for showcasing their rhetorical performances for the benefit of black and white readers skeptical about their abilities.[116] The two examples that follow both took place in Canada West. Miss L. Gilcrease's speech, printed in the *Provincial Freeman,* predictably articulates the benefits of emigration. The speech puts forth all the standard arguments in support of emigration, comparing the cost of living, recommending occupations to pursue, and comparing the migration of Africans to Canada to the migration of other oppressed peoples around the world. The correspondent benevolently observes that her delivery was "remarkable . . . firm and outspoken never exhibiting the slightest degree of timidity although in the presence of some three hundred hearers."[117] The performance took place at a meeting of the Dumas Literary Association, and the number of attendees is indeed impressive. The Dumas was a mixed-sex group, which the *Freeman* had criticized two weeks earlier as being more social than literary.[118] Perhaps this occasion, drawing three hundred people, offered some of both kinds of activities. The second performance took place at an exhibition in the British Methodist Episcopal Victoria Chapel in the presence of four hundred. There, several musical selections, dramatic pieces, and an address delivered by Miss Mary Ann Sanders, visiting Canada West from Nashville, Tennessee, were given in 1865. Sanders's speech, "Moral Improvement of the Mind of the Young People, and the Spirit of Freedom," opens with ingratiation: "[B]eing a stranger in your midst, and unacquainted with your manners and customs, I feel incapable to address you with your education and elocution." She continues, nonetheless, in grand style, contrasting their existence in a free nation with hers as a former slave and encourages them to take full advantage of their privilege as she intends to do with the end of the Civil War in sight.[119] The *New York Age* much later in the century reports on the performance of another young elocutionist performer, Julia C. Wormley, who, according to the article, was "developing as a public reader." Subsequent references to her popularity confirm the *Age*'s prediction.[120]

Louis Kossuth, leader of the Hungarian independence movement, continued to attract the attention of the American press throughout his 1851–52 visit to the United States, and consistently, it was his oratory that drew the highest commendations. Even William Allen in his speech "Orators and Oratory" praised his eloquence highly, even though he objected to Kossuth's refusal to speak out against American slavery. One typical example of such a critique appears in *FDP*, submitted by "J. T."[121] The article reports on Kossuth's visit to Congress; he apparently tamed both Daniel Webster and Henry Clay with his eloquence, leaving the author to conclude hyperbolically that "within eighteen hundred years no man has so gloriously moved such immense masses of mankind in the right direction."[122]

William J. Watkins served as assistant editor of *FDP* for several years and lectured against slavery throughout his adult life. Watkins grew up under the strict tutelage of his father, the Reverend William Watkins Sr., who headed the Watkins Academy in Baltimore, where Frances Watkins Harper, his niece, also received her early education. A word about this influential educator is in order here. The Reverend William Watkins was a founder of the East Baltimore Mental Improvement Society, also referred to as a "school of oratory, literature and debate," and later became head of the Watkins Academy, where he demonstrated "that rare acquisition, a mastery of the English language."[123] One former student described his pedagogy thus: "As a grammarian according to Kirkham's—the best book ever used—he was so signally precise that every example in etymology, syntax and prosody had to be given as correctly as a sound upon a key-board. In parsing, every rule had to be repeated and accurately applied—every peculiarity of declension, mood and tense readily borne in mind. His pupils were compelled to be correct both in speaking and writing. He was strict from the first letter in the alphabet down to the last paragraph in the highest reader."[124]

Watkins maintained a reputation as a persuasive and eloquent public speaker. He was a frequent contributor to the newspapers, and his speeches were published in a number of abolitionist newspapers, including the *Pine and Palm*, the *Anti-Slavery Advocate*, the *Anti-Slavery Bugle*, the *Philanthropist*, and, of course, *FDP*, which published two of his speeches, delivered at successive August 1 celebrations of the West India Emancipation in 1854 and 1855. They are epideictic speeches accommodated to an audience of African Americans on a day of contemplation and celebration for African Americans, delivered by an African American. They were subsequently published in the black press for wider circulation. The 1854 speech delivered in Columbus, Ohio, includes a passage on the efficacy of oratory as an agent of change. It considers the limits and possibilities of rhetoric, isolated from action, and deserves quoting at length:

> There is no rhetoric in the slave code of this practically atheistic nation. It is a living, breathing, burning reality. When it can restrain the baseness and treachery of the degenerate sons and grand sons of the pilgrims, by a mere flourish of the magic wand of rhetoric; when we can, by a rigid

adherence to the rules of syntax, or of logic, persuade white men into a practical recognition of our manhood, and dissuade colored men from worshipping the foul demon of discord and disunion, who lies but to scatter, tear, and slay, then we shall, probably, endeavor so to model our words and phrases to disarm criticism of its remorseless sting; until we shall be convinced that rounded periods are absolutely necessary as the forerunner of the period when the black wing of slavery shall be broken, and the monster die and be buried, we shall not esteem them quite so highly as the Fourth of July orators of slaveholding America, who take especial pains to blaspheme God by the polished diabolisms of their hypocritical hallelujahs. We as a people, love oratory, but we love Freedom more.[125]

Watkins here is questioning the value of rhetoric in situations where action is called for. He is not disparaging rhetoric but those who understand rhetoric as a style-focused, superficial activity rather than a form of action itself, leading to and spurring on other kinds of action. Watkins himself is modeling the way he would have the audience understand the function of rhetoric. Watkins has the crowd reflect on the limits of oratory and celebration in the ongoing context of slavery. He proposes that the true orators on such an occasion should be the "millions of America's bleeding bondmen," including fugitive slaves Anthony Burns and Stephen Pembroke, whom, using the figure *sermocinatio,* he allows to express their own despair.[126] He discounts the significance of the occasion as an opportunity for oratory in the opening of his 1855 Jefferson County, New York, address, observing, "We trust that no one has mingled in this vast assembly, merely to gratify a vain and morbid curiosity, simply to listen, with a critic's ear, to the words that shall fall from the lips of one half buried in the sepulcher of American Despotism."[127]

In both speeches, Watkins applauds the history of British advancement toward emancipation, asserting the progress that the newly emancipated have made in the British colonies, recalling the hypocrisy of celebrating the Fourth of July, in much the same manner as Douglass in his July 5, 1852, address in Rochester, and calling on African Americans to work tirelessly for abolition in the United States. Watkins's speech provides no direct instruction, nor is it accompanied by critical commentary. The educational value for those who heard the speeches and who read them in *FDP* some weeks later lay in the eloquence they modeled and in the comments on rhetoric they incorporated.

Frances Ellen Watkins Harper was easily the most sought after and critiqued African American woman speaker and writer of the nineteenth century. The spectacle of an articulate black woman in the mid-nineteenth century speaking confidently on a range of controversial topics drew the admiration and curiosity of newspaper correspondents. Pages of the black press are filled with uniform praise for her numerous rhetorical performances, much of it in articles reprinted from white newspapers. Most articles open with general acclaim for her oratory, followed by extracts left to speak for themselves. Sampling these commentaries gives a sense of the extent to which they served a rhetorical purpose. Harper was a poet as well as an orator who often incorporated verses into her speeches; in fact, it is her poetry that first appears in the black press. William Still, Philadelphia leader of the Underground Railroad and a staunch supporter and friend, sent to Mary Ann Shadd Cary two examples of Harper's rhetorical ability for publication in the September 1854 issue of the *Freeman,* assuring her that they both provided evidence of "high intellectual culture, and much merit in the adaptation of her thoughts and faculties to subjects of vital importance." The first piece was "Christianity," an essay in which the subject is personified as a woman to whom all the enlightenment branches of knowledge—philosophy, history, and literature—pay homage and are subordinate. The *Norristown (Penn.) Republican* reporter at first felt that her "style partook too much of the recitative" but came to the conclusion that she "rose to a dignity of style as a public speaker, surpassed by no woman who has been in our midst; it was really beautiful in parts."[128] A report from the Indianapolis correspondent to the *Recorder* includes an extract from a local white paper in which her speech on the war was characterized as "instructive," reflecting "close investigation, extensive reading, and withal a comprehension of liberty and Republicanism remarkable in any woman, no matter what her color."[129] The reviewer's observations begin to move away from focus on her physical presence and toward the logos of her arguments. In the early years of her activism, Harper was frequently referred to as the "Colored Anna Dickinson," but during her later years, her younger contemporaries were being compared to her, as in the case of "Miss F. M. Jackson" (Fanny Miriam Jackson Coppin) after giving a speech at Israel Metropolitan Church in Washington, D.C.[130] In the same issue of the *Recorder,* Harper is compared to Douglass: "We have heard Frederick Douglass, and hesitate not to say that for beauty of expression, richness of illustrations, and, in a word, rhetorical finish, she is his superior."[131]

Reactions to Anna Dickinson were in many respects quite similar, as in this account of a lecture she gave in Fall River, Massachusetts, in 1862: "If to have an audience remain quiet, attentive and sympathizing, during the delivery of a long lecture, is any indication of the ability, tact and success of the speaker, we think it may be claimed for Miss Dickinson, that she is a compeer worthy to be admitted as a particular star in the large and brilliant constellation of genius and talent, now endeavoring to direct the country to the goal of negro emancipation."[132] Harper herself could have been considered another star in that constellation. Further, it does seem that some of the later reviews pay more attention to what she has to say and not to the fact that Harper is saying it. Since many of the early responses printed in the black press were extracts from the white press, one wonders how the editors intended those extracts to be "read."

The critique of a speech by Fannie Barrier Williams in 1894 resonates at a different pitch. The review, reprinted in the *Indianapolis Freeman* from the *Chicago Inter-Ocean,* includes excerpts from the speech interspersed with commentary. Williams delivered the speech at the white Chicago All Souls Church before one of the city's "intellectually recherché gatherings." At the time of this performance, Williams was a well-known race representative and advocate for black women who had given one of the major addresses a year earlier at the 1893 Women's Congress of the World's Columbian Exposition, where Harper had also spoken. This speech reads like a version of that earlier speech and was no doubt part of her repertoire of addresses on the state of black women at the end of the century. She points out that in all instances where they have had opportunity, black women have accomplished at a level equal to white women. What makes this critique interesting are the reviewer's comments about the substance, noting that Williams moderated her use of pathetic appeal and "treated her auditors to a restful departure from the traditional and somewhat ancient methods employed generally by race advocates." The writer is pleased that Williams does not dwell on the specific horrors of slavery and that her references served "not as an irritant, but as a guide and light"; they "interested without offending." Williams's ethical appeal allowed these auditors to experience not pity but "mingled shame and resentment" that they too were connected to those who could be charged with "such shameful truths."[133] Here in the 1890s, the reviewer is paying attention to the propriety of the message for this audience and not to the fact that a black woman was performing a speech, a response quite different from those initial responses to Harper, for example. In this article, the *Freeman* reinforced the importance of accommodating message to audience. Editors and readers of the black press both understood the importance of knowing how to adapt their messages to a variety of audiences and how to read and read through the texts of dominant culture that were shaping their own lives.

Purpose and Pleasure: Some Final Observations

I began this survey of the rhetorical activities that African Americans pursued across the nineteenth century in order to identify their educational aspects, how people learned rhetoric as they lived their lives—worshiped, read newspapers and other types of literature, wrote in diaries, participated in political and social gatherings, fought for their freedom, and earned a living. Whether considering early forms of rhetorical education in slave hush harbor spaces or more structured formalized manifestations in late-century college literary societies, I recognized a common urgency—their need to communicate with one another in a shared language and to respond to society's attempts to deny their humanness. The black Union soldiers, reading, writing, and publishing newspapers as they fought for their right to exist freely, stand out as the most salient example of this urgency in chapter 1. What better image of highly motivated rhetorical education under adverse circumstances can be invoked than that of the black Civil War soldier, not initially allowed to enlist, crawling into a battlefield trench with speller in hand? Further, the encampment of soldiers with varying levels of literacy under these circumstances models communal rhetorical education at its best.

In writing the chapter on self-education, I came to understand that all serious educational pursuits are to some extent self-motivated. This chapter was helpful in understanding individual motivation in the absence of a community of learners, whether that isolation was self-imposed or the consequence of situation. The findings of this chapter, especially in the diaries of Ida B. Wells, Mary Virginia Montgomery, and Charles Chesnutt, suggested that pleasure in the pursuit was a critical characteristic of this site of rhetorical education, regardless of other causal elements. The analysis of literary societies revealed the extent to which these associations were socially and politically as well as educationally advantageous. In the topics of discussion, the locations of meetings, the publications often associated with the societies, the connectional relationships across various groups, and the personal motivations for participating, this site served as a point of convergence for the private learner and the black press. The private learner often sought out the literary society, given that rhetoric generally requires an interlocutor. The press preserved the histories of these societies, carrying in its pages the announcements and minutes of meetings and excerpts from speeches delivered there. The newspaper editors were also involved in the other sites of rhetorical activities. They were deeply invested in the communities about which they wrote, making no claim to distanced objectivity.

Fruitful research into how African Americans developed rhetorical skills in what Anne Gere has called the "extracurriculum of composition" remains in sites not fully explored here.[134] The activities associated with the National Negro Convention movement starting in the 1830s and the women's club movement in the 1890s are two that come to mind. Some of the best-known black speeches, manifestations of rhetorical education, were delivered at meetings associated with these movements. In addition, the sites I do examine here could be explored further. All of the examples of free-floating literacy in chapter 1 represent just the outer layers of the cumulative activities resulting in direct or indirect education in rhetoric. Other nineteenth-century African Americans recorded their language practices in various forms that can tell us more about the private learner. We need to know more about what took place in those meetings of literary societies that specifically promoted language skills, including how recitations were selected and rehearsed. Further, my concentration on antebellum newspapers in the Northern states leaves the rhetorical training enacted in others underexamined.

I do not intend to fast-forward into the twenty-first century in search of claims about the implications this study might have for current teaching practices. The times are quite different. I will, however, return to the question that started me on this project, "Where did they learn to speak so effectively?" I answer with the observation that the most effective rhetorical education seemed to occur in sites when the exigence created a heightened need to communicate, when there was collective effort among a broad range of people, and when there was an element of pleasure or gratification in the process. This observation, it seems to me, is transportable. A 2007 *Washington Post Magazine* article documents an exciting example of liberating language in the twenty-first century. It's a site in which exigence, collective effort, and pleasure converge. The location is the Urban Debate Team in Baltimore, where students gather after school to master formal debate techniques as well as tactics that draw on emotional appeal, frequently mixing in their own unconventional practices. They compete with students from across the country. During one competition, a team member shifted the terms of the debate to a discussion of the incarceration of African American men. Ignacio Evans and Jermol Jupiter, the two debaters featured in the article, both have relatives in jail. Angela Davis, Malcolm X, and Paulo Freire provide support for the assertions of another member. These same two students helped to organize a march on the school board to protest the removal of a popular principal. That they find this rhetorical activity rewarding is evident in one team member's comment about the protest: "Now I can just go out and say, 'This is wrong. What they're doing—or not doing, really—in our schools is wrong' and people listen, because I'm a debater. It's like a qualification, like you're somebody, like you've got ideas and your proof . . . and what you say matters. . . . You can persuade people to fix things."[135]

Notes
Bibliography
Index

Notes

All articles from the *Christian Recorder,* the *Colored American, Frederick Douglass' Paper, Freedom's Journal,* and the *Provincial Freeman* were retrieved from Accessible Archives, Inc., *African-American Newspapers: The 19th Century,* <http://www.accessible.com/default.htm>.

Introduction: "By the Way, Where Did You Learn to Speak?"

1. The signers of this document were some of the "most respectable Characters in Boston," including Thomas Hutchinson, the governor of Massachusetts; seven clergymen; Thomas Hubbard, treasurer of Harvard College; and John Hancock, a signer of the Declaration of Independence. The full text of this frequently quoted letter, "To the Publick," prefacing Wheatley's volume, reads as follows: "We whose names are under-written, do assure the world, that the poems specified in the following page, were (as we verily believe) written by PHILLIS, a young Negro Girl, who was but a few years since, brought an uncultivated barbarian from Africa, and has ever since been, and now is, under the disadvantage of serving as a slave in a family in this town. She has been examined by some of the best judges, and is thought qualified to write them" (Wheatley, From *Poems on Various Subjects,* 216–17).

2. Wheatley, From *Poems on Various Subjects,* 214.

3. Proper, "Lucy Terry Prince," 188. The obituary was originally published in the *Greenfield (Mass.) Franklin Herald* of August 21, 1821.

4. Proper, "Lucy Terry Prince," 200.

5. Ibid., 201; Cushman, "Women Advocates," 69.

6. In his study of the black narrative, *From Behind the Veil,* Robert B. Stepto observes that authenticating documents functioned to guarantee, verify, or legitimate the narrator and that narrator's ability to relate his or her experiences of slavery. Such authentication thus assured the narrative's acceptance as factual evidence.

7. Garrison, "Preface," 6.

8. Ellison, *Invisible Man,* 251. The parallels between Ellison's invisible man and Frederick Douglass are worth noting. The invisible man was employed in the service of the Brotherhood specifically because of his facility with language in much the same way that Douglass was used as an instrument of the antislavery movement, with William Lloyd Garrison as Brother Jack. Further, like Douglass, the invisible man escapes

to the North and "freedom" where the Brotherhood attempts to control what he could say, just as Garrison's attempt to censure Douglass led to Douglass's separation from Garrison's organization.

9. Lynette Clemetson, "The Racial Politics of Speaking Well," *New York Times,* February 4, 2007, sec. 4, 1, 4.

10. See my essay "'When and Where I Enter.'"

11. Burke, *Rhetoric of Motives,* 43.

12. Aristotle, *On Rhetoric,* 1354^a 6–11.

13. Brandt, "Literacy," 392.

14. Nell Painter's article on Truth's sources of knowledge is instructive here. Painter considers the ways in which Truth interacted with and manipulated literate culture in the absence of conventional literacy skills. See chap. 2, n. 8, for further discussion of Painter's article.

15. Royster, *Traces of a Stream,* 45.

16. Royster and Williams, "History in the Spaces Left"; Jarratt, "Race and Space"; Gold, "Nothing Educates Us Like a Shock"; Zaluda, "Lost Voices of the Harlem Renaissance."

17. Glenn, "Rhetorical Education in America," x.

18. Kates, "Literacy"; Schneider, "Freedom Schooling."

19. Ellison quoted in Robert O'Meally, "Slavery's Shadow," 158.

20. Ferreira-Buckley and Halloran, "Editors' Introduction," xxii.

21. Cook, "Remarks," 246.

22. Holmes, "Say What?," 204.

23. Fahnestock and Secor, "Classical Rhetoric," 107.

1. Free-Floating Literacy: Early African American Rhetorical Traditions

1. Piersen, *Black Yankees,* 40.

2. hooks, *Teaching to Transgress,* 170.

3. Allen, *Short Personal Narrative,* 99–100.

4. Ellison quoted in O'Meally, "Slavery's Shadow," 158.

5. Ira Berlin, in *Many Thousands Gone,* reminds us of a distinction from early studies of slavery between societies with slaves and slave societies. In the former, slavery was one of many forms of labor, and slaves were "marginal to the central productive processes." In slave societies, slavery was the chief means of economic production, and consequently slaveholders made up the ruling class (8). The categories I refer to here cut across these distinctions and invoke rhetorical communities among conclaves of the enslaved and between enslaved and free blacks, as, for example, in the case of Frederick Douglass, who, while in bondage, belonged to the East Baltimore Mental Improvement Society.

6. In *Ways with Words,* Heath cites the definition of A. B. Anderson, W. B. Teale, and E. Estrada (386n2). These authors characterize a literacy event as "any action sequence, involving one or more persons, in which the production or comprehension of print plays a role." B. Moss considers the African American sermon the "major literacy event to which most African Americans have been exposed" in her essay on literacy in nonacademic settings like those I discuss in this chapter ("Literacy Event," 137).

7. Harris, "Life Story."

8. Cornelius writes that the name *hush harbor* could have evolved as "an obvious parallel to *brush arbor* or *brush harbor,* names that whites gave to the camp meetings,

revials and places of worship they created in burns or groves on the frontier" (*Slave Missions*, 9).

9. Costen, *African American Christian Worship*, 25, 30–37.

10. Nunley, "From the Harbor to Da Academic Hood," 222–23.

11. Raboteau, *Slave Religion*, 215–18.

12. Joyner, *Down by the Riverside*, 172–73.

13. Costen, *African American Christian Worship*, 21. Costen quotes a declaration crafted by South Carolina missionary Francis Le Jau, which included the clause "[Y]ou do not ask for the holy baptism out of any design to free yourself from the Duty and Obedience that you owe to your Master while you live" (21).

14. Cornelius, *Slave Missions*, 5.

15. Ibid., 5–6.

16. Sidbury, "Reading, Revelation, and Rebellion," 127. See Colossians 3:22, "Servants, obey in all things your masters according to the flesh; not with eyeservice, as menpleasers; but in singleness of heart, fearing God," and 1 Peter 2:18, "Servants, be subject to your masters with all fear; not only to the good and gentle, but also to the froward" (KJV).

17. Sidbury, "Reading, Revelation, and Rebellion," 120.

18. Cornelius, *Slave Missions*, 14.

19. In the fifth century B.C.E. treatise the *Phaedrus*, Plato has the Egyptian god Thamus declare that writing literacy results in loss of the ability to memorize: "For this invention will produce forgetfulness in the minds of those who learn to use it, because they will not practice their memory" (Bizzell and Herzberg, *Rhetorical Tradition*, 165). The example of the preacher supports the reverse claim.

20. Raboteau, *Slave Religion*, 241. Emphasis in the original.

21. Cornelius, *Slave Missions*, 11.

22. Recall, for example, Grace Greenwood's characterization of Frances Harper's style of delivery: "She stands quietly beside her desk, and speaks without notes, with gestures few and fitting" (quoted in Still, *Underground Rail Road*, 779).

23. Lampe, *Frederick Douglass*, 39–40.

24. Andrews, "Frederick Douglass, Preacher," 596.

25. Phillips notes that between 1825 and 1853, Bethel AME enrolled 873 women and 407 men; during that same period, 36 men became class leaders (*Freedom's Port*, 135).

26. A. Smith, *An Autobiography*, 24.

27. Ibid., 29–30. I have not been able to determine what Smith was reading. It could have been something like Parley P. Pratt's "Dialogue between Joseph Smith and the Devil," first published in the January 1, 1844, *New York Herald* and subsequently in other papers and as a pamphlet. See <http://mldb.byu.edu/PPPRATDI.HTM>.

28. Douglass gives much credit to Caleb Bingham's popular nineteenth-century schoolbook *The Columbian Orator containing a Variety of Original and Selected Pieces together with Rules Calculated to Improve Youth and Others in the Ornamental and Useful Art of Eloquence*, first published in 1797, for inspiring him to develop his literacy skills. Bingham took this particular dialogue from John Aiken and Anna Barbauld's 1792 text *Evenings at Home, or The Juvenile Budget Opened*.

29. Douglass, *Narrative*, 35.

30. National Archives, "The Fight for Equal Rights." It should be noted that the Union navy had enlisted black soldiers from the beginning of the war. These included

free blacks and contraband slaves, who generally held menial jobs. But perhaps the best known black navy sailor was Robert Smalls, who, in 1862, surrendered *Planter*, a Confederate ship, to the Union army in the Charleston harbor. See, for example, Aptheker, "Negro in the Union Navy."

31. *Christian Recorder*, January 9, 1864; J. Wilson, *Black Phalanx*, 466–78.

32. Carretta, *Equiano*, 77. Of course, Equiano was still technically enslaved at the time.

33. J. Wilson, *Black Phalanx*, 296.

34. Ibid., 505.

35. *Christian Recorder*, December 17, 1864.

36. Fleetwood, *Diary*, February 4, 1864.

37. K. Wilson, *Campfires of Freedom*, 74.

38. *Christian Recorder*, March 4, 1865.

39. Blackett, *Thomas Morris Chester*, 3–91. One example of the empathy with which Chester wrote concerning newly acquired educational opportunities must suffice. In the following passage, he describes what must have been the state of mind of the children as they anticipated "go[ing] to school publicly and carry[ing] their books openly": "The colored Sunday schools in Richmond were amusing institutions. The children were not allowed any books or to learn their alphabet. They were taught the days of the week, months, and year, and how to count their fingers and toes. When a chapter was read in the Bible, the little ones were required to repeat it after the superintendent. Some of the children can repeat Psalms with great rapidity. There have always been secret schools in this city for the instruction of colored children, but they were conducted with a great deal of privacy. The little boys and girls were obliged to carry their books hid under their clothes, and when school closed they had to pass out singly to keep from attracting attention. The little ones all seem to realize that there is no longer any necessity to learn in secret, and have asked, in many instances, their parents whether they could not go to school publicly and carry their books openly" (Chester quoted in Blackett, from an April 4, 1865, submission to the *Philadelphia Press*, 306–7).

40. Both Robert Hamilton and his brother Thomas Hamilton founded the *Weekly Anglo-African* and the *Anglo-African Magazine*. The magazine, published monthly between January 1859 and March 1860, focused on literature. The weekly became "the foremost black newspaper of the Civil War era." It ceased publication for a brief period in 1861 but was reestablished by Robert under the same name later that same year and continued through December of 1865 (Ripley, *Black Abolitionist Papers*, 5:27–29n4).

41. *Christian Recorder*, December 17, 1864.

42. H. Ford Douglas was a black abolitionist from Illinois who questioned Abraham Lincoln's commitment to black equality and spoke about the subject frequently.

43. K. Wilson, *Campfires of Freedom*, 72.

44. "'Rhode Island' to Robert Hamilton," *Weekly Anglo-African*, January 23, 1864, reprinted in Ripley, *Black Abolitionist Papers*, 5:265–66.

45. In addition to authorizing the deployment of blacks in the Union army, the Militia Act of 1862 also established a salary of seven dollars for all black soldiers regardless of rank. This was roughly half the amount paid to the lowest ranking white soldier. Black soldiers and blacks generally protested, as these letters show. It was not until June 1864 that Congress passed a bill establishing equal pay for all soldiers (Ripley, *Black Abolitionist Papers*, 5:298n1).

46. *Christian Recorder,* June 25, 1864; July 23, 1864; May 20, 1865. I have been able to locate only one subsequent letter to the *Recorder* from Collins, published in the July 8 issue and dated June 20, 1865. In what may have been his final letter to Weaver while on active duty, Collins apologizes for "being silent so long" and describes proudly a review of the Charleston, South Carolina, Home Guard, a local militia, "commanded in full by colored officers." The Fifty-fourth Massachusetts Regiment was mustered out of service in August 1865.

47. K. Wilson, *Campfires of Freedom,* 78.

48. Chenery, *Fourteenth Regiment,* 49, 106.

49. Swisshelm, *Crusader and Feminist,* 241.

50. Perkins, "Quaker Beneficence," 22–25.

51. "Mr. John H. Smith's Reading in Sansom St. Hall," *Christian Recorder,* February 4, 1865; K. Wilson, *Campfires of Freedom,* 220–21.

52. The racial composition of league membership varied according to location. In some Deep South states, the membership was almost entirely black with white Northern leaders. But some of the league organizers were experienced black men from the North, who also followed the Union armies south. Eric Foner observes that "Reconstruction was one of the few times in American history that the South offered black men of talent and ambition not only the prospect of serving the race, but also greater possibilities for personal advancement than existed in the North" (*Short History of Reconstruction,* 126). It seemed to many that every black male voter belonged to a league by the end of 1867.

53. The minutes of the predominantly white Maryville, Tennessee, Union League meetings record discussions of such topics as the impeachment of President Andrew Johnson, whether female education was as important as that of males, and whether East Tennessee should be a separate state (Foner, *Short History of Reconstruction,* 125).

54. Fitzgerald, *Union League Movement,* 61.

55. Franklin, *Reconstruction after the Civil War,* 124–26.

56. Mirabal, "Telling Silences," 52–54.

57. Savona, "Son of Montecristo."

58. Puerto Rican–born Arthur Schomburg, who would later build an impressive collection of material on African American culture, made the following comments about working conditions of blacks in Cuba after a visit there in 1905: "Negroes were welcomed in the time of oppression, in the time of hardship, during the days of revolution, but in the days of peace . . . they are deprived of positions, ostracized and made political outcasts. The Negro has done much for Cuba. Cuba has done nothing for the Negro" (quoted in Perez, *On Becoming Cuban,* 323).

59. Ferdie Pacheco, "The Cigar Factory," Hillsborough County, Florida, Official County Government Online Resource, <http://www.hillsboroughcounty.org/publicart/artlocations/westtampalibrary/cigarfactory.cfm>.

60. For reminding me of Johnson's references to cigar factories, I thank Cherise Pollard at West Chester University.

61. J. Johnson, *Autobiography,* 73–74.

62. In Eugene Levy's biography of Johnson, D— is identified as Judson Douglass Wetmore (*James Weldon Johnson,* 16).

63. J. Johnson, *Along This Way,* 60.

64. Cooper, *Once a Cigar Maker,* 25, 66. Cooper notes that in 1910, less than 1 percent of the women working in the cigar factories were African American.

2. Private Learners: Self-Education in Rhetoric

1. N. Johnson, "Popularization," 140–41.

2. Kett, *Pursuit of Knowledge*, xiii.

3. Dorothy Sterling's invaluable edited collection, *We Are Your Sisters,* includes excerpts from Rollin's Boston diary, held, according to Sterling, by her great-grand-daughter (455), and from Mary Virginia Montgomery's diary, also available in full in the Montgomery Family Papers at the Library of Congress.

4. A list of manuscript holdings on women at the Howard University Moorland-Spingarn Research Center includes diaries by at least five black women: Georgia Goins Fraser, Angelina Weld Grimké, Charlotte Forten Grimké, Laura E. Joiner, and Laura Hamilton Murray (Salzmann, "Guide to Resources on Women").

5. Brodhead, "Introduction," 17.

6. Grimké, *Journals,* 272; hereafter cited in text.

7. Long, "Charlotte Forten's Civil War Journals," 40.

8. The requisite literacy associated with diary-keeping should not cause us to dismiss the self-education projects of those who could not read or write but who developed rhetorical skills nonetheless. For example, Nell Painter suggests that Sojourner Truth, who was illiterate, honed her speaking skills through repeating and memorizing material that had been read to her. She was also attuned to divine inspiration, which many believe a more reliable source of "true" knowledge than that acquired through formal instruction. Truth was often overheard preaching as she carried out her daily chores. She preached at camp meetings around New York City, becoming quite skilled at speaking by the time she affiliated with the abolitionist and women's rights movements (Painter, "Representing Truth").

9. Sjöblad, "From Family Notes to Diary," 517.

10. Arthur, *Advice to Young Ladies,* quoted in McCarthy, "Pocketful of Days," 285.

11. Washington, foreword, x.

12. Montgomery quoted in Sterling, *We Are Your Sisters,* 464; hereafter cited in text.

13. Chesnutt, *Journals,* 157; hereafter cited in text.

14. Perelman and Olbrechts-Tyteca, *New Rhetoric,* 40–42.

15. This pseudo-slave narrative was written by Mattie Griffith, a Kentuckian whose childhood in a slaveholding household provided much of the material for this abolitionist text.

16. Billington, "Introduction," 9, 8.

17. This was possibly the speech Remond delivered on May 30, 1854, a few weeks prior to this entry, at the New England Anti-Slavery Convention (see Nell, *Colored Patriots,* 372–74).

18. *Historical Sketch of the Salem Lyceum,* 23. In their analysis of rhetorical constructions in Grimké's diary, Janet Eldred and Peter Mortensen calculate that she heard and commented on twelve of the nineteen speakers during the twenty-sixth season, 1854–55, alone (*Imagining Rhetoric,* 204).

19. Brenda Stevenson, editor of Grimké's journals, suggests that her criticism was based on Douglass's break with Garrison, whom Grimké greatly admired (Grimké, *Journals,* 578n44).

20. Eldred and Mortensen, *Imagining Rhetoric,* 203, 205. These authors provide an astute, contextually rigorous analysis of Grimké's diary, tracing the rhetorical influences on the developing writer and teacher. They identify a tension in her musings

between rhetoric in the service of civic action and rhetoric, in the belletristic tradition, for pleasure.

21. Donawerth, *Rhetorical Theory by Women,* 142. See the excerpt from *Letters to Young Ladies,* discussing the practice, on page 143 of this anthology.

22. Coppin, *Reminiscences of School Life,* 70–71.

23. Along with the journal, Grimké's other published writings include several poems in antebellum periodicals, an *Atlantic Monthly* article on the South Carolina Sea Islands, and collected works in Anna Julia Cooper's *Life and Writings of the Grimké Family* (1951). She also published a translation of the French novel *Madame Thérèse* (1869). See Peterson's close reading of Grimké's diary, in which she documents her various poetry and short story publication efforts (*"Doers of the Word,"* 176–95).

24. My source is Sterling, *We Are Your Sisters,* 453–61. Rollin's great-granddaughter Carole Ione, owner of the diary, has also woven excerpts from Rollin's diary into a family history, *Pride of Family.*

25. In *Reminiscences on School Life,* Coppin includes an interesting history of the institute during her tenure as teacher and principal from 1865 to 1902. Arriving at the school the year Rollin left, Coppin introduced courses in normal and industrial training, recognizing the need for these more practical forms of education, among other innovations.

26. Sterling, *We Are Your Sisters,* 365.

27. Terborg-Penn notes that Charlotte (Lottie) Rollin's words "became the first from an African American woman, other than Sojourner Truth, to be preserved in writing by the chroniclers of the national woman suffrage movement leaders" (*African American Women in the Struggle for the Vote,* 45).

28. Rollin's birth year varies according to the source. I use 1845, the date listed on the "Family Time Lines" in her great-granddaughter's family memoir (Ione, *Pride of Family,* n.p.).

29. Ione, *Pride of Family,* 107.

30. Rollin, diary manuscripts excerpts, quoted in Sterling, *We Are Your Sisters,* 455; hereafter cited in text.

31. Probably the *Life of Josiah Quincy of Massachusetts,* written by his son Edmund Quincy and published in 1868.

32. In *Behind the Scenes* (1868), Elizabeth Keckley (?–1907) wrote of her relationship with Mary Todd Lincoln, wife of Abraham Lincoln, when she served as her dressmaker, traveling companion, and confidante. Rollin was not alone in believing that Keckley had the assistance of a ghostwriter. Some suspected it was James Redpath, who edited the book and possibly arranged speaking engagements to publicize it. But Keckley is to be admired for her tenacity in the face of slavery and numerous adversities. She acquired literacy, financial independence, and the respect of a president's wife.

33. Ione, *Pride of Family,* 93.

34. Wells, *Crusade,* 9.

35. Edwards, "History of Rust College," 66–68.

36. Wells, *Crusade,* 22.

37. Fortune, "Ida B. Wells, A.M.," 38. Oddly, the 1924 *History of Rust College* does not list her among its outstanding students.

38. Wells, *Crusade,* 8–9.

39. Hamilton, *Holly Springs,* 43.

40. Wells, *Crusade,* 22.

41. Wells, *Memphis Diary,* 39; hereafter cited in text.

42. In *Lectures on Rhetoric and Belles Lettres,* Blair writes: "For every species of public speaking has a manner or character peculiarly suited to it; of which it is highly material to have a just idea, in order to direct the application of general rules. The eloquence of a lawyer is fundamentally different from that of a divine, or a speaker in parliament: and to have a precise and proper idea of the distinguishing character which any kind of public speaking requires, is the foundation of what is called a just taste in that kind of speaking" (288–89).

43. Wells, *Crusade,* 126.

44. Donawerth, *Rhetorical Theory by Women,* xxv.

45. Elocutionists, variously referred to as readers, reciters, characterists, impersonators, monologists, storytellers, and expressionists, were especially popular from the mid-nineteenth century on, opening up performance opportunities outside of structured dramatic productions to larger popular audiences.

46. Wells possibly refers to a "reciter text," like Hallie Quinn Brown's 1880 *Bits and Odds: A Choice Selection of Recitations,* which included general advice on elocution along with recitations from both Anglo- and African American traditions.

47. Quotes from Murray's 1885–86 diary are taken from the original document in the Manuscript Division, Moorland-Spingarn Research Library, and from excerpts in Sterling, *We Are Your Sisters.* Page numbers of quotes from Sterling and date of entry for quotes from the diary will both be cited in text.

48. The name of the author of "Expectations" is illegible.

49. Isaiah Montgomery, who in 1890 became the only black delegate to the Mississippi Constitutional Convention, recalls receiving his first instruction from a former slave of Jefferson Davis's who used a Webster blue back speller. His father taught him writing and gave him lessons each night to be recited the following day.

50. Wells, *Crusade,* 37–39. The legislation required all voters to pass a literacy test, regardless of race or previous condition of servitude. Isaiah Montgomery is said to have supported this action, thinking that it would motivate blacks to educate themselves, a myopic but perhaps more understandable position in the context of his own educational opportunities.

51. I. Montgomery, "Isaiah T. Montgomery Tells His Own Story."

52. Quoted in Still, *Underground Rail Road,* 806.

53. Hermann, *Pursuit of a Dream,* 189. It is well established that Margaret Fuller's father placed her on a strict intellectual regimen that at an early age had her studying late into the night. Montgomery, on the other hand, seems to have been self-motivated, although her father was certainly a supportive inspiration. Hermann's book-length history of Davis Bend, the Montgomery family, and Mound Bayou is a valuable resource for understanding the dynamics of this unique Reconstruction social experiment.

54. Quotes from Montgomery's 1872 diary are taken from the original document in the Montgomery Family Papers in the Library of Congress and from excerpts in Sterling, *We Are Your Sisters.* Page numbers of quotes from Sterling and date of entry for quotes from the Montgomery Papers will both be cited in text.

55. Hermann, *Pursuit of a Dream,* 168–69. For example, Orson Squire Fowler's book *Phrenology and Physiology Explained and Applied to Education and Self-improvement* (1841) dealt with mental discipline, the cultivation of memory, and methods of increasing and decreasing the phrenological organs.

56. "Self-Education" could refer to *Self-Education: or, The Philosophy of Mental Improvement* (1847) by William Hosmer or to William Ellery Channing's 1843 *Self-Culture*, but more than likely to one or more of a variety of books on self-improvement published by some combination of the brothers O. S. and L. N. Fowler and Samuel R. Wells from 1852 until at least 1888.

57. Possibly Richard Green Parker's *Progressive Exercises in English Composition* (1832).

58. George C. McKee was elected as a Republican to represent the Fifth Congressional District and served from 1869 to 1872.

59. On the 1884 Oberlin transcript of Mary Eliza Church (Terrell), a course in "Rhetorical Exercises" is listed in each of the college terms; she matriculated there between 1880 and 1884. I thank Susan Jarratt for sending me Terrell's transcript.

60. See Brodhead, "Introduction," 5–8.

61. Quillin, *Color Line in Ohio*, 154, 33.

62. Elizabeth McHenry observes that sleuthing "insists that the scholar become a detective willing to understand African-American literary history in the 19th century as at best incomplete. This detective must develop an affection for the excitement and frustrations of archival work so as to allow quotidian details of 19th-century life to illuminate the various modes of social action and cultural expression to which African Americans, at various times, for various reasons, have turned. She must be willing to ask tough questions, including questions about the ways we have addressed diversity within the African-American community. Finally, she must be willing to abandon the boundaries that have traditionally divided the disciplines as well as those that have kept scholars from working together." McHenry attributes this coinage of what this kind of research frequently requires to Frances Smith Foster. (See McHenry, "Rereading Literary Legacy," 481.)

63. Rhetoric historian Nan Johnson places Quackenbos's textbook in the tradition established by Hugh Blair of "'second generation' New Rhetorics," giving particular belletristic attention to the role of rhetoric in cultivating taste (*Nineteenth-Century Rhetoric*, 76).

64. The full title of the textbook Chesnutt was reading was George P. Quackenbos, *Advanced Course of Composition and Rhetoric: A Series of Practical Lessons on the Origin, History, and Peculiarities of the English Language, Punctuation, Taste, the Pleasures of the Imagination, Figures, Style and its Essential Properties, Criticism, and the Various Departments of Prose and Poetical Composition; Illustrated with Copious Exercises. Adapted to Self-Instruction, and the Use of Schools and Colleges* (New York and London: D. Appleton and Company, 1859). See page 451.

65. Chesnutt, "Joseph C. Price," 555.

66. See Rose, "Conduct Books for Women," and N. Johnson, *Gender and Rhetorical Space in American Life,* for a discussion of the ways in which conduct literature constructed gender and restrained women during this period. Donawerth, in "Conduct Book Rhetoric," also considers the extent to which these women-authored texts often served as sites of resistance in that they included instruction in conversation and letter-writing and "negotiated the gendered constraints of speech and writing with ingenuity, while not challenging them outright until 1850" (7).

67. Tate, *Domestic Allegories*, 110–12.

68. *Golden Thoughts*, 75, 249. This manual is available and fully searchable on-line at <http://www.openlibrary.org/details/goldenthoughtsonoogibsuoft/> (accessed January 18, 2007).

69. The full title is *The College of Life; Or, Practical Self-Educator, A Manual Of Self-Improvement For The Colored Race, Forming An Educational Emancipator And A Guide To Success, Giving Examples And Achievements Of Successful Men And Women Of The Race As An Incentive And Inspiration To The Rising Generation, Including Afro-American Progress Illustrated, The Whole Embracing, Business, Social, Domestic, Historical, and Religious Education*.

70. See Blair, Lectures 18 and 19, in *Lectures on Rhetoric and Belles Lettres*, 195–218.

71. Mitchell, *Righteous Propagation*, 90.

72. Northrop, Gay, and Penn, *College of Life*, 146.

73. Federal Writers' Project, "Florida Slave Narratives: Lee, Randall."

74. Brodhead, "Introduction," 40n4. For example, WorldCat lists among Wells's publications *How to Behave: A Pocket Manual of Republican Etiquette, and Guide to Correct Personal Habits*, which Chesnutt excerpts; *How to Talk: A pocket manual of Conversation and Debating with Directions for Acquiring a Grammatical, Easy, and Graceful Style*; and *How to Write: A Pocket Manual of Composition and Letter Writing . . . : To which are added forms of letters of introduction, notes, cards, etc., and a Collection of Poetical Quotations*.

75. In chapter 3, I discuss the communal aspect of participation in literary societies and other manifestations of literacy.

3. Mental Feasts: Literary and Educational Societies and Lyceums

1. Porter, *Early Negro Writing*, 5.

2. Throughout this chapter, I generally refer to all such associations as literary societies except where a distinction among the various titles is meaningful.

3. Bode, *American Lyceum*, 11–14.

4. Ibid., 32.

5. Ibid., 24–25. In her work on the nineteenth-century U.S. lyceum movement, Angela G. Ray points out that in the 1860s, the scholar is replaced by the orator as the lyceum became a forum for expressing ideas as much as a site for the dissemination of practical knowledge. The term remained in use even as the focus changed. The shifts reflected different ways of viewing the rhetorical situation. The lyceum-goers, formerly viewed as participants, became the audience for the performers or entertainers, formerly teachers (*Lyceum and Public Culture*, 6).

6. See Porter, "Organized Educational Activities," for a foundational history of black literary societies of the early nineteenth century. McHenry's *Forgotten Readers* continues and extends the historical work begun by Porter, focusing on the activities of selected clubs, the black press, and other organizations.

7. Porter, *Early Negro Writing*, viii.

8. Proper, "Lucy Terry Prince," 197.

9. William Whipper, "Address Delivered before the Colored Reading Society," 113–15; hereafter cited in text.

10. Porter, *Early Negro Writing*, 5.

11. Samuel E. Cornish, "A Library for the People of Color," *Colonizationist and Journal of Freedom*, February 1834, 306.

12. Crummell, "Social Principle," 31.

13. Porter, *Early Negro Writing*, 144.

14. The symbiotic relationship between literary associations and the black press is strong. In this example, members of an association launched a publication, but more frequently calls to organize associations or announcements of association activities appeared in the pages of black publications. Frances Smith Foster calls attention to these links between literary societies and the black press, pointing out that Philip Bell, one of the editors of the *Colored American,* chaired the Philomathean Society's Board; William Whipper, an organizer of the Philadelphia Library Company, also edited the *National Reformer;* and members of the Philadelphia Female Literary Society periodically contributed pieces to Garrison's *Liberator.* These examples of cross-pollination of rhetorical practices certainly help to make my argument that they were mutually beneficial, but it is not surprising that the same names appear in the pages of newspapers, on the membership roles of literary societies and antislavery associations, and among the delegates attending political conventions, given that these affiliations all supported the larger project of self-definition and race advancement. Foster also discusses the indebtedness of both literary societies and antebellum publications to the Afro-Protestant press, a point I return to in chapter 4 (Foster, "African-American Print Culture," 727).

15. Porter, "Organized Educational Activities," 562, and the *Colored American,* April 24, July 24, and July 31, 1841. Du Bois refers to the *Shield* as the first black newspaper in Philadelphia (*Philadelphia Negro,* 45).

16. A Spectator, "Philomathean Society," *Liberator,* December 10, 1831, 197.

17. William C. Nell, "Literary Progress of the Colored Young Men of Boston," *Liberator,* March 27, 1846.

18. "Colored Youth of Boston," *Liberator,* January 7, 1842, 3. The article was signed "W. P.," possibly William Powell, black abolitionist and frequent contributor to the *Liberator.* Powell, active in a number of associations, helped to organize the New Bedford Young Men's Wilberforce Debating Society in 1839 and had received several years of formal education. He would certainly have been in a position to comment on the rhetorical abilities of these young scholars. See Ripley, *Black Abolitionist Papers,* 3:302–3n4.

19. "The Colored Men of Baltimore," *New York Observer and Chronicle,* March 11, 1869, 77.

20. The Phoenix Society and the Phoenixonian Society were different organizations.

21. "Literary Exhibitions in New York City, *Frederick Douglass' Paper* (hereafter *FDP*), November 3, 1854.

22. *Provincial Freeman,* January 3, 1857.

23. See Porter, "Organized Educational Activities," for names of societies in the Midwest before 1846.

24. Ripley, *Black Abolitionist Papers,* 4:238n5.

25. "From our San Francisco Correspondent," *FDP,* May 18, 1855.

26. For detailed discussions of Sarah Douglass and the activities of the Philadelphia Female Literary Association, see Lindhorst, "Politics in a Box"; and McHenry, *Forgotten Readers,* 59–67. Both writers track the debate surrounding a proposal for emigration to Mexico as reproduced in the pages of the *Liberator.*

27. "An Address," *Liberator,* November 29, 1834, 190.

28. Murray, *Come, Bright Improvement!,* 71.

29. "Address to the Female Literary Association of Philadelphia," *Liberator,* June 9, 1832, 91.

30. Sarah Mapps Douglass, "Mental Feasts," *Liberator,* July 21, 1832, 114.

31. Winch, "You Have Talents," 115.

32. "The Histrionic Club," *Liberator,* April 23, 1858, 67.

33. "Union Literary Association," *FDP,* February 2, 1855.

34. Murray, *Come, Bright Improvement!,* 70.

35. The three African American faculty members were Charles Reason, George B. Vashon, and William G. Allen. Frederick Douglass also delivered four lectures there in 1852. See Quarles, *Black Abolitionists,* 114.

36. A. L. Brown, "Central College," *FDP,* November 19, 1852. A. L. Brown was Antoinette Louisa Brown, a woman's rights activist and friend of Douglass's, who the following year would become the first female ordained minister in the United States. She would have had a special interest in the treatment of women at this institution.

37. Ibid.

38. Samuel Cornish, "On the Death of Mrs. Ray," *Colored American,* March 4, 1837. Poet Henrietta Cordelia Ray (1852–1916), daughter of Charles Ray and his second wife, Charlotte, was named after his first wife.

39. "Third Anniversary," *Colored American,* September 23, 1837.

40. "Letter from Chillicothe, Ohio," *Christian Recorder,* December 15, 1866. Chillicothe had been the first and third capital of Ohio and in 1866 had a significant black population.

41. For example, in the same paper a year earlier, a Harrisburg, Pennsylvania, correspondent reported on the founding of the Garnet Equal Rights League, with nearly a hundred members, adding that "*with a view to improvement,* a number of ladies have already prepared essays for several meetings" (emphasis added). The letter also reports plans to establish a reading room where members can spend time "perusing the papers that are edited by colored men" ("Letter from Harrisburg," *Christian Recorder,* October 7, 1865). This is also an example of the reciprocal relationship between these associations and black newspapers. The entertainment function was, no doubt, still very much a factor in their preparations as well.

42. *Christian Recorder,* April 4, 1863. It seems that the Bible was not merely a gesture of friendship. Here are more of the correspondent's comments: "While we do not wish to pass any unfriendly criticisms on the course of procedure of the Lyceum, yet we are not disposed to remain silent when our dignity is unjustly assailed. It is rumored that the reason that the Baltimore ladies made the present to the Lyceum was, because that the Washington ladies did not appreciate literature and the Lyceum sufficiently to present them a memento of their esteem. And the reason that the Baltimore gentlemen did all the speaking was, that they far excelled the Washingtonians in their oratorical powers and literary attainments. If this be true, I say it is humiliating in the extreme. However, I cannot believe it. Hence, I say it is a foul aspersion, for where are those bright and flaming intellects which grace Israel Lyceum? Where is Yunnion, Brown, Costia, Hilleary, and hosts of other Washingtonians, who stand entire in literature; whose strains of burning eloquence gush forth with the ease and facility that the waters glide over the cataract? Why then such nonsensical vilification?"

43. Taylor, *Black Churches of Brooklyn,* 29–30.

44. Simmons, *Men of Mark,* 484; "Guilty of Literary Roguery," *New York Freeman,* June 26, 1886.

45. "Brooklyn Literary Union," *New York Freeman,* December 11, 1886. The Blair Education Bill would have allotted federal funds for schools to states according to

literacy rates, meaning that Southern states would have received more in aid to assist in educating those who had been denied access to literacy during slavery.

46. The union did indeed publish the paper in 1887 under the title *The Cushite: or, The Children of Ham (The Negro Race) as seen by the Ancient Historians and Poets.* In 1893, a longer version was published with an expanded title, *The Cushite, or, The descendants of Ham as found in the sacred Scriptures, and in the Writings of Ancient Historians and Poets from Noah to the Christian Era.* This publication sequence represents just one example of an often overlooked function of many literary clubs, as well as the link between newspapers, literary clubs, and subsequent published works.

47. "A Raleigh Lyceum," *New York Freeman,* March 5, 1877; "Baltimore Letter," ibid., November 13, 1886. See Simmons, *Men of Mark,* 966–77, for a detailed account of the 1886 congressional hearings on Matthews's nomination.

48. Porter, "Organized Educational Activities," 567.

49. McHenry, *Forgotten Readers,* 54. In the section on workplace sites of rhetorical education in chapter 1, I discuss the reading practices of the lector in Tampa cigar factories at the turn of the century, another instance of the democratizing effect of this public sharing of literacy.

50. Brewer, *Pleasures of the Imagination,* 187.

51. Ibid., 169.

52. "Editorial Correspondence," *Colored American,* December 2, 1837.

53. "Literary Societies," *Colored American,* October 5, 1839. Emphasis added.

54. A[mos] G[erry] B[eman], "Thoughts--NO. III," *Colored American,* December 5, 1840. Beman (1812–74), for close to twenty years, served as a Congregational minister in New Haven, Connecticut. Beman's understanding of the function of these rhetorical activities may have been reinforced during his time at Oneida Institute under the tutelage of Beriah Green, as one of the "black Oneidans," a small group of black males who were admitted to school in Whitesboro, New York, between 1834 and 1844. See note 76 below.

55. Foner and Branham, *Lift Every Voice,* 229.

56. The Library of Congress copy of the speech reads "Brooklyn Literary Society."

57. On November 18, 1841, the Phoenixonian Society of New York changed its name to the Hamilton Lyceum in honor of William Hamilton. See *Colored American,* December 4, 1841.

58. The first incorporated black association in New York, the New York African Society for Mutual Relief, was organized on June 6, 1808, as a result of economic unrest in the wake of a U.S. embargo that affected the black seaman laboring class, to support members in need. The organizers included Hamilton, Peter Williams, who later helped to establish a separate black Episcopalian church, and Henry Sipkins. Swan points out that "one of the Mutual Relief Society's unwritten objectives became the establishment of a school offering a quality education" ("John Teasman," 348). Thus we can see here the interconnected influences of labor, education, and, concurrently, religion on the establishment of educational institutions, including literary societies. For further discussion of the evolving black community during this period in New York history, see Swan, "John Teasman."

59. Stuckey, *Slave Culture,* 200–201.

60. Porter, "Organized Educational Activities," 575.

61. Blair, *Lectures on Rhetoric and Belles Lettres,* 23.

62. An article in the February 16, 1855, issue of *FDP* offers a historical account of the event and the surrounding controversy. "The year 1808 was marked by the abolition of

the African slave Trade, which was celebrated throughout the country by the colored people, in meetings, prayers, thanksgivings, and orations, some of which are yet extant in pamphlet form. One of them, delivered by Mr. (afterwards Reverent) Peter Williams, of New York, required the attestation of the bishop of the Diocese, to win credence to the fact that it was composed by a colored man" ("From Our New York Correspondent").

63. Ernest, *Liberation Historiography,* 226.

64. As Foster observes, "African Americans did not create their literature solely in reaction to, or for the enlightenment of, those who were not African American" ("African-American Print Culture," 719). Yet, it should not be difficult to understand why so many of these speeches and other literary club activities seemed to have been focused on demonstrating basic intellectual ability; the skepticism among many white "spectators" was palpable and frequently consequential. Consider, for example, this excerpt from a *Liberator* article, in which an onlooker describes his genuine amazement at the performance of black Philadelphia schoolchildren and offers these words of "praise": "There was to be an examination of the scholars on the different and some of them intricate branches of an English education. I could not repress the curiosity I had to witness such a novel sight as the examination of children of color in Grammar, Geography, History, &c. The idea of a colored child being much more than able to spell through a sentence; as an apology for reading, had scarcely occurred to me as existing at the present day. You may readily imagine my surprise, and I may add unfeigned joy, at finding, under these feelings, 70 neat, clean and intelligent looking children collected together in a fine spacious airy apartment" (A Spectator, "Interesting Exhibition," May 28, 1831, 86).

65. Hamilton, "Address to the New York African Society," 37; hereafter cited in text.

66. Elizabeth Jennings, "On the Improvement of the Mind," quoted in Foner and Branham, *Lift Every Voice,* 168. First published in the *Colored American,* September 23, 1837.

67. Steward, "Address of the New York State Convention of Colored Citizens," 240. Steward (1793–1865) escaped from slavery and eventually settled in Rochester, New York. He became a popular activist speaker, served as an agent for *Freedom's Journal* and the *Rights of All,* and helped to establish the Wilberforce colony in Canada. In 1857 he published his autobiography, *Twenty-Two Years A Slave, and Forty Years a Freeman,* which appears in Ripley, *Black Abolitionist Papers,* 2:53n7.

68. Bacon and McClish, "Reinventing the Master's Tools," 29.

69. Ibid., 28.

70. Ibid., 24–29.

71. Ibid., 26.

72. Samuel Cornish, editor of the *Colored American,* was one of the American Moral Reform Society's chief critics, especially because of its refusal to identify itself by race.

73. Allen, "Orators and Oratory," 246; hereafter cited in text. For ease of access, I have chosen to cite the text as reprinted in Foner and Branham's *Lift Every Voice.* The headnote states that it was taken from the version in the *Liberator,* October 29, 1852, which was itself a reprint from the October 16, 1852, *Pennsylvania Freeman.* The speech was also reprinted in *FDP,* October 22, 1852, and published separately in a pamphlet by the Dialexian Society titled *Addresses Pronounced before the Dialexian Society of New York Central College.* See McClish, "Allen's 'Orators and Oratory,'" 66n4, for a fuller account of its publication history.

74. Allen, *American Prejudice Against Color,* 42. In various references to Allen in the literature, his is titled in a variety of ways. In his own *Short Personal Narrative,* he writes that he "received the appointment of Professor of the Greek Language and Literature" (105), but in the longer version of his life, *The American Prejudice Against Color,* he provides the expanded title I use here.

75. Allen, *Short Personal Narrative,* 99.

76. A number of blacks who attended Oneida would go on to become prominent orators and race leaders, including Henry Highland Garnet, Alexander Crummell, Jermain Loguen, Amos Beman, and William Forten. See Sernett, *Abolition's Axe,* chap. 4.

77. A. L. Brown, "Central College."

78. G. Smith, "Central College of New York," reprinted in Elbert, *American Prejudice,* 15.

79. McClish, "Allen's 'Orators and Oratory,'" 61–62. McClish has written the most comprehensive rhetorical analysis of this speech to date. He traces the possible influences of the eighteenth-century rhetorical theorists Allen no doubt studied at Oneida, including Hugh Blair, George Campbell, and Adam Smith, as well as elements of faculty psychology, pointing out possible subversions along the way. He categorizes the discursive genres shaping the speech as "academic rhetorical pedagogy," "African-American rhetorical forms and experiences, and the social reformist subculture in which he was immersed" (63). I propose a similar division of the types of discourse evident in Allen's address.

80. In the remarks, presented at a reception for Kossuth in New York City, the authors allude to the situation of blacks in America, stating, "In the face of the distinguished example of the Pilgrim fathers, and the many eminent men who have made this their *exile* home, we have steadily maintained this birth-home right during the last third of a century in this our native land, and will continue to maintain it until its ultimate triumph, 'for the first love of man is in his home.'" The signers included James McCune Smith, George T. Downing, and Philip A. Bell ("Reception of Colored Persons," *Liberator,* December 19, 1851, 206).

81. Chesnutt, *Journals,* Summer 1879, 108.

82. The state-supported Colored Normal School of Fayetteville, established in 1877, was the first such school in the country. Although there were more women than men in the first class, Chesnutt refers only to males in this speech, given just four years later.

83. Chesnutt, "The Advantages of a Well-Conducted Literary Society," 13; hereafter cited in text.

84. Quoted in James Zappen, "Bacon, Frances," 62.

85. In Lecture 27 of *Lectures on Rhetoric and Belles Lettres,* Blair discusses the disadvantages, from the standpoint of audiences, of the set speech but does advise careful "premeditation." He adds that "it may be proper for a young Speaker to commit to memory the whole of what he is to say. But, after some performances of this kind have given him boldness, he will find it the better method not to confine himself so strictly; but only to write, beforehand, some Sentences with which he intends to set out, in order to put himself fairly in the train; and, for the rest, to set down short notes of the topics, or principal thoughts upon which he is to insist, in their order, leaving the words to be suggested by the warmth of discourse" (291).

86. Levi Hedge was professor of religion, philosophy, and civil polity at Harvard. The *Elements of Logick* was a popular logic textbook in the early decades of the nineteenth century.

87. The Library of Congress copy reads "Brooklyn Literary Society," but "Brooklyn Literary Union" appears on other contemporaneous sources.

88. Frazier, "Some Afro-American Women of Mark," 381.

89. Harper, *Iola Leroy*, 253.

90. Harper, "Enlightened Motherhood," 285, 286; hereafter cited in text.

91. Foreman, "'Reading Aright,'" 330.

92. *New York Age,* February 27, 1908, quoted in Taylor, *Black Churches of Brooklyn,* 30.

93. Harper quoted in Still, *Underground Rail Road,* 772.

94. Royer, "Process of Literacy," 370.

95. Ibid., 367, 368.

96. Douglass, *Life and Times,* 185–86. William Douglass would later marry Sarah Mapps Douglass.

97. Oberlin College Archives, RG 19/3/4—Ladies Literary Society (Aelioian, L.L.S.), Scope and Content, <http://www.oberlin.edu/archive/holdings/finding/RG19/SG3/S4/SS1/scope.html>.

98. Terrell, *Colored Woman in a White World,* 76–77.

99. Under the Convict Lease System, incarcerated persons of all ages and sexes were leased to plantation owners for profit to the state to perform, in many instances, the same kind of harsh labor as in the days of slavery. Most of these workers were African Americans. The practice continued into the 1930s. See especially Wells, Douglass, Penn, and Barnett, *Reason Why,* 23–28.

100. Terrell, *Colored Woman in a White World,* 225.

101. Ibid., 197.

102. Lemert and Bhan, *Voice of Anna Julia Cooper,* 311.

103. Ibid., 313.

104. A. Moss, *American Negro Academy,* 291.

105. Webb, *The Garies and Their Friends,* 48.

106. Hopkins, *Contending Forces,* 143–48.

107. Harper, *Iola Leroy,* 243.

108. The term "alternative public spheres" resists the notion of one privileged white male–dominated public and recognizes instead the always already existence of many publics. The issues acknowledged as "public" in the nineteenth century were those articulated, recorded, and perpetuated by property-owning, literate white males, who had the ability to endow them with salience. An issue had the potential to become of "public" interest--that is, to be debated openly--when it appeared to affect the lives of those in power. A black counterpublic emerged, in part, in response to exclusion from such public deliberations, but only in part. Sites of black political activism provided not only an alternative space but a much needed separate space in which to deliberate about "race matters" and to develop strategies for entering and thereby disrupting mainstream discourse.

109. Berlant, *Queen of America,* 237.

110. Griggs, *Imperium in Imperio,* 27; hereafter cited in text.

111. Powell, "Rise and Decline," 737.

112. Bode, *American Lyceum,* 250–51.

113. *Indianapolis Freeman,* January 20, January 27, and December 8, 1894. See Simmons, *Men of Mark,* for a detailed account of the1886 congressional proceedings.

114. Little, "Extra-Curricular Activities," 44.

115. Ibid., 44–45.

116. "Le Moyne Normal School," 114.

117. Bacote, "James Weldon Johnson," 338.

118. J. Johnson, *Along This Way*, 121.

119. Ibid., 80.

120. Du Bois, *Dusk of Dawn*, 31, 36–43.

121. See Little's discussion of the changing variety of group formations at black colleges during this period in "Extra-Curricular Activities."

122. Crummell, "Social Principle," 36. Emphasis in the original.

123. Ibid., 41.

4. Organs of Propaganda: Rhetorical Education and the Black Press

1. Clark and Halloran, "Introduction," 25, 4.

2. "New York Central College," *FDP*, March 17, 1854.

3. Wells, "Lynch Law in All Its Phases," 81.

4. Hugh Blair, *Lectures on Rhetoric and Belles Lettres*, 381–89.

5. See Jacobs's discussion of Garrison's estimate that 75 percent of those who subscribed at the end of 1834 were black supporters from Boston, Philadelphia, and New York ("Garrison's *Liberator*," 261n6). On the other hand, Douglass's *North Star* had five times as many white subscribers as black (Ullman, *Martin R. Delany*, 81).

6. "Heads of the Colored People," *FDP*, February 18, 1853. The "editors above named" included William Allen, Amos Beman, Philip A. Bell, Martin R. Delany, Henry Highland Garnet, Samuel R. Ward, Charles B. Ray, Henry Bibb, and Douglass. The article was one in a series submitted to *FDP* under the pseudonym "Communipaw." "Communipaw" was Dr. James McCune Smith, a New York City doctor, pharmacist, and race activist, who often submitted pieces to the paper under this name and who was involved in several editorial ventures himself.

7. Foster, "African-American Print Culture," 732. Foster, developing her argument from the historical perspective that far too many other African American editors and journalists have been overlooked, later adds: "By criteria of being owned, controlled, and edited by an African American, both the *North Star* and *FDP* are part of African-American print culture. But upon closer inspection of primary readership, purpose, employees, consultants, and underwriters, the *North Star*, especially, was a serious abolitionist paper, but, as an African-American newspaper, it is an uneasy fit" (734). See Levine, *Martin Delany*, especially chap. 1, "Western Tour for the *North Star*," 18–57, for a detailed analysis of Delany's contributions to the *North Star*, particularly as demonstrated through his travel letters. Levine, too, argues that more attention to Delany's influence on Douglass and the *Star* is warranted, pointing out that Douglass fails to mention Delany in any of his autobiographies. Douglass does list Delany among the roll call of black editors in the February 18, 1853, *FDP* article but not in connection with the *North Star*.

8. Douglass, *Life and Times*, 259–60.

9. Ibid., 264.

10. Wells, *Crusade*, 23–24.

11. This editorial and the circumstances surrounding its penning have been discussed in numerous publications, including my own anthology, *With Pen and Voice*, 75–79.

12. Wells, *Memphis Diary*, 177.

13. Wells, *Crusade,* 231.

14. Cmiel, *Democratic Eloquence,* 24.

15. Ryan, *Civic Wars,* 96, 119.

16. "Brooklyn Mass Meeting," *Colored American,* January 23, 1841; "Great Mass Meeting," ibid., December 12, 1840.

17. *Provincial Freeman,* June 30, 1855. Mary Ann Shadd (later Cary) was the editor.

18. "A New Typographical Dress for our Paper," *FDP,* March 2, 1855.

19. *FDP,* February 3, 1854.

20. "Editors are Slaves," *Palladium of Liberty,* November 13, 1844.

21. "Meeting of Colored Citizens," *FDP,* October 22, 1852.

22. Allen's response was published in *FDP,* November 5, 1852, and in the *Liberator,* November 26, 1852. Ricketson's comments were published in the *Liberator,* October 29, 1852; Parker's were in the October 22, 1852, issue.

23. See Dawson, "Black Counterpublic?," where he points out that when blacks were formally expelled from mainstream post-Reconstruction public discourse through disenfranchisement, they worked to reinsert themselves into this discourse through political agitation but also shored up and strengthened their own counterpublic. Their post-Reconstruction activities, in my view, represent an extension of a tradition established in these public meetings reported on and advertised in the antebellum black press.

24. The five antebellum New York newspapers were the *Weekly Advocate,* the *Colored American,* the *North Star, FDP,* and the *Weekly Anglo-African Magazine.*

25. Shortell, "Rhetoric of Black Abolitionism," 95, table 2. Shortell's quantitative study employed computerized content analysis and trained coders and various statistical measures to analyze the discursive field in 257 paragraphs from these papers. While other findings were not particularly germane to this search for sites of rhetorical education, they do offer promising leads for those interested in further study of themes in the nineteenth-century black press.

26. Benedict Anderson used this term "imagined community" in his work on nation-building. He writes that "it is imagined because the members of even the smallest nation will never know most of their fellow-members, meet them, or even hear of them, yet in the minds of each lives the image of their communion" (*Imagined Communities,* 6). Surely these early rhetors, separated from one another by space and social condition, needed to imagine a collectivity leading to social change.

27. Shortell, "Rhetoric of Black Abolitionism," 87–88. An illocutionary act is defined according to the work it performs and the way in which it is understood, for example, as an assertion, a demand, or a promise. See also "Speech Acts," 690.

28. See Fahnestock and Secor, "Stases in Scientific and Literary Argument," for a discussion of the ways in which disciplinary discourses are governed by the stases in which they tend to argue. To give special emphasis to arguments about cause, the authors separate them from definitional arguments.

29. Shortell, "Rhetoric of Black Abolitionism," 88 and 101, table 6.

30. *Colored American,* March 16, 1839. The Reverend Elymas Payson Rogers (1815–61) was one of the black Oneidans, along with William Allen, Alexander Crummell, Henry Garnet, and others. Rogers, also a poet and an educator, studied for the ministry at the Institute and went on to pastor churches in New Jersey.

31. Here is the excerpt from Webster's speech: "True eloquence, indeed, does not consist in speech. It cannot be brought from far. Labor and learning may toil for it, but

they will toil in vain. Words and phrases may be marshaled in every way, but they cannot compass it. It must exist in the man, in the subject, and in the occasion. Affected passion, intense expression, the pomp of declamation, all may aspire after it; they cannot reach it. It comes, if it come at all, like the outbreaking of a fountain from the earth, or the bursting forth of volcanic fires, with spontaneous, original, native force. The graces taught in the schools, the costly ornaments and studied contrivances of speech, shock and disgust men, when their own lives, and the fate of their wives, their children, and their country, hang on the decision of the hour. Then words have lost their power, rhetoric is vain, and all elaborate oratory contemptible" (Daniel Webster, "Adams and Jefferson," 109–10). The February 19, 1831, edition of the *Liberator* carried a longer excerpt from this same section of Webster's speech under the simple heading "Eloquence."

32. Spivak, "Can the Subaltern Speak?"

33. "Why Do Ignorant Colored Men So Often Speak in Public?," *Colored American,* March 16, 1839.

34. Caleb Bingham's *Columbian Orator,* first published in 1787, went through numerous editions and is now available online at *19th Century Schoolbooks,* <http://digital.library.pitt.edu/>.

35. N. Johnson, "Popularization," 141.

36. Cotesworth P. Bronson was a well-known teacher of elocution who in 1845 published *Elocution; or Mental and Vocal Philosophy: Involving the Principles of Read and Speaking; and designed for the Development and Cultivation of both Body and Mind, in accordance with the Nature, Uses, and Destiny of Man.* Most reviews of his work as a teacher and voice healer and of his textbook in the white mainstream press are cautiously favorable. See, for example, "Review," *Harbinger, Devoted to Social and Political Progress,* March 14, 1846, 216.

37. *Colored American,* February 6, 1841.

38. The essay ends with the notice that it is to be continued; however, I have been unable to retrieve additional articles that appear to be continuations of this essay.

39. "Elocution," *Christian Recorder,* February 2, 1861. The excerpt is part of Samuel Daniel's poem *Musophilus; containing a general defense of all learning* (1599), which includes the following lines in defense of rhetoric:

> Power above powers! O Heavenly Eloquence !
> That with the strong rein of commanding words
> Dost manage, guide, and master the eminence
> Of men's affections, more than all their swords!
> Shall we not offer to thy excellence,
> The richest treasure that our wit affords?
> Thou that canst do much more with one poor pen,
> Than all the powers of princes can effect;
> And draw, divert, dispose, and fashion men,
> Better than force or rigour can direct! (*Selections,* 148)

40. W[illiam] C. N[ell], "Practical Elocution," *North Star,* May 19, 1848. In the passage Nell quotes, Channing goes on to draw a distinction between recitation and dramatization, preferring recitation because it brings out the author's meaning more effectively.

41. Ernest, *Liberation Historiography,* 379n14.

42. "Demosthenes," *FDP,* December 18, 1851.

43. Augustine, in his defense of Christian rhetoric, includes passages from Cyprian's interpretation of the sacrament of the chalice and his encomium of virginity to demonstrate the moderate style (*On Christian Doctrine,* 475, 476–77).

44. For example, in his 1855 autobiography, Samuel Ringgold Ward includes Cyprian among those who give evidence of early black preeminence: "Nor could I degrade myself by arguing the equality of the Negro with the white; my private opinion is, that to say the Negro is equal morally to the white man, is to say but very little. As to his intellectual equality, Cyprian, Augustine, Tertullian, Euclid, and Terence, would pass for specimens of the ancient Negro, exhibiting intellect beyond the ordinary range of modern literati, before the present Anglo-Saxon race had even an origin" (*Autobiography of a Fugitive Slave,* 87).

45. Tanner's first essay on St. Cyprian appears in the *Christian Recorder,* January 10, 1863. Subsequent essays appear intermittently thereafter, usually at one- or two-week intervals. I retrieved eighteen between that date and September 12, 1863, but some are clearly missing, and there were probably additional ones after the September 12 submission.

46. Tanner, "Life of St. Cyprian, The African Bishop, Martyr and Saint," *Christian Recorder,* March 14, 1863.

47. Ibid., September 12, 1863.

48. "Elevation of Our People," *Colored American,* November 23, 1839.

49. "Novel Reading," *Colored American,* June 5, 1841.

50. "The Lecturer," *FDP,* January 13, 1854.

51. The citations listed respectively are February 19, 1831; May 21, 1841; December 20, 1850; July 18, 1851; and January 29, 1864.

52. This peroration was also printed in the *Liberator* several weeks earlier with a different opening commentary ("Sublime!," *Liberator,* July 5, 1839). Of course, speeches from previous celebrations of events are often retrieved for later display and admiration. Exposure to different readers is the chief advantage of this reprinting of articles, and most readers of the *Colored American* were probably reading the peroration for the first time.

53. "Eloquence," *Colored American,* July 20, 1839.

54. "Newspapers in Schools," *Freedom's Journal,* July 6, 1827.

55. "OBSERVER.—NO. III," *Freedom's Journal,* September 7, 1827.

56. "The First Newspaper," *FDP,* July 31, 1851.

57. "Newspapers by Colored People in the United States," *Provincial Freeman,* June 23, 1855.

58. "Influence of Newspapers," *FDP,* February 2, 1855.

59. "Colored Newspapers," *North Star,* June 29, 1849.

60. Amos G. Beman, "Thoughts, NO. IX," *Colored American,* March 6, 1841.

61. Ibid.

62. The *New Era,* with J. Sella Martin as editor and Douglass as nominal corresponding editor, was launched in January 1870. It became the *New National Era* with the September 8, 1870, issue when Douglass assumed the editorship.

63. James Weldon Johnson, "Do You Read Negro Papers?" (editorial), *New York Age,* October 22, 1914.

64. See, for example, "Union Literary," *Indianapolis Freeman,* January 20, 1894; "Literary Social Club," ibid., January 27, 1894; and "Fifteenth Annual Session," ibid., December 8, 1894. The development of college literary societies is discussed in chapter 3 of this volume; see also Little, "Extra-Curricular Activities."

65. The history of prohibitions against women participating in public discourse has been and is being recovered by feminist historiographers of rhetoric from a variety of perspectives. See, for example, Campbell, *Man Cannot Speak for Her;* Lunsford, *Reclaiming Rhetorica;* Glenn, *Rhetoric Retold;* Logan, *"We Are Coming";* Royster, *Traces of a Stream;* and Donawerth, *Rhetorical Theory by Women before 1900.*

66. "Woman's Sphere," *North Star,* March 17, 1848.

67. "Varieties," *Freedom's Journal,* April 20, 1827.

68. Matilda, "Letter," *Freedom's Journal,* August 10, 1827.

69. Bacon, *"Freedom's Journal,"* 138.

70. "Anti-Slavery Convention," *FDP,* June 3, 1853.

71. "Mrs. Stowe on Female Orators," *FDP,* February 9, 1855. In an earlier account of a speech Brown delivered at a temperance convention, reprinted from the *Randolph Whig,* the reporter assured readers that "she does not wear the bloomer costume, but was arrayed in a dress of plain black silk" ("Miss Antoinette L. Brown," *FDP,* March 4, 1853).

72. "A Word to the Ladies," *Colored American,* March 18, 1837. The quoted text comes from the extract of a speech delivered in Georgia on the Fourth of July.

73. "Woman's Eloquence," *Colored American,* November 17, 1838.

74. *North Star,* September 5, 1850.

75. "Female Education," *Provincial Freeman,* June 7, 1856.

76. I have been unable to determine Mrs. Hill's own name.

77. Mrs. James T. V. Hill, "Shall Women Vote? Yes," *Indianapolis Freeman,* December 8, 1894. In an adjacent column can be found "Woman's Field of Duty," a report on a sermon by a Reverend Chapman, in which he argues that woman's proper sphere is the home, where she has charm and influence, lost when she involves herself in politics. The readers then had the opposing points of view laid out for comparison.

78. Mrs. N. F. Mossell, "Our Woman's Department," *New York Freeman,* June 5, 1886.

79. It is not surprising that the Emerson College of Oratory advertised in the pages of the *Woman's Era.* The school was founded in 1880 by Charles Wesley Emerson, apparently "liberal on race matters." He took Edward Sterling Wright under his wings while he matriculated at the college. In 1913, Wright, an African American, made an Edison cylinder recording of Paul Laurence Dunbar's poetry. Booker T. Washington spoke there in 1900, when other black students were enrolled (Brooks, *Lost Sounds,* 260).

80. Medora Gould, "Literature" column, *Woman's Era,* March 24, 1894, 10.

81. Dora J. Cole, *Woman's Era,* May 1895, 5.

82. J. H. A. Johnson, "Female Preachers," 105.

83. Blair, *Lectures on Rhetoric and Belles Lettres,* 317, 327.

84. See Ferreira-Buckley and Halloran's discussion of the originality of Blair's lectures in their "Editors' Introduction," xxxv.

85. "Richard Baxter," *Christian Recorder,* December 6, 1862.

86. "The African Preacher," *Colored American,* January 19, 1839. White subsequently published these stores about "Uncle Jack" under the title *The African Preacher: An Authentic Narrative* in 1849, by which time the slave preacher, who died in 1843, had become well known in the Amelia County and Richmond areas of Virginia. Unfortunately, all available information about "Uncle Jack" comes, Sojourner Truth–like, through the filter of his white contemporaries.

87. "What is the Business of the Church!," *Colored American,* July 28, 1838. This is reprinted from the *Herald of Freedom,* published by the New Hampshire Anti-Slavery Society.

88. "Methodist Church," *Colored American,* December 16, 1837.

89. "Temptations Peculiar to Ministers," *Colored American,* July 17, 1841.

90. "From our Washington Correspondent," *Colored American,* January 9, 1841.

91. "Barriers to Our Progress: Harm Done by Incompetent Preachers and Teachers," *New York Age,* February 28, 1891, 3.

92. Bennett, *Poets in the Public Sphere,* 67. In a section appropriately titled "The Poetics of Difference," Bennett offers a close analysis of Lee's complete poem, comparing it to other poetry by women on the taboo nineteenth-century subject of amalgamation.

93. Ransom, "Deborah and Jael." The more defiant portions of Mary E. Ashe Lee's poem are found in the complete version, published in the October 1886 *Southern Workman* (Hampton Institute). She comments on the presence of Afmerica, figured as a woman, across America, and her long history of slavery and abuse; her determination to remain in America is a central component of it. The most accessible version is in Bennett, *Nineteenth-Century American Women Poets,* 466–71.

94. The performance was at Avery College, one of the first educational institutions for African Americans, located in what was then Allegheny City, Pennsylvania, annexed by Pittsburgh in 1907.

95. *Rhetorica ad Herennium* quoted in Bizzell and Herzberg, *Rhetorical Tradition,* 281.

96. Conquergood, "Rethinking Elocution," 143.

97. This quotation was taken from a letter written to Whitman by Elisa Seaman Leggett on June 22, 1881, and is quoted in Reynolds, *Walt Whitman's America,* 148.

98. Clark, "Solo Black Performance," 344.

99. Grimké, *Journals,* 144. In a subsequent entry some three years later, Grimké records a more favorable response to Webb's reading of passages from *Uncle Tom's Cabin,* writing, "I thought she read remarkably well" (295), possibly reflecting genuine improvement on the part of Webb and an opinion mellowed as a result of acquaintance on the part of Grimké, whose maternal aunt, Annie Woods Webb, was married to Mary Webb's brother-in-law.

100. "Dramatic Reading by a Coloured Native of Philadelphia," *Illustrated London News,* August 1856, <http://www.iath.virginia.edu/utc/uncletom/xianslav/xsrebo1at. htm>. The August 22, 1856, *Liberator* carried a reprint of this same review under the same title but with the heading "From the *London Daily News,* July 29."

101. *Provincial Freeman,* May 12, 1855.

102. Webb quite possibly used the text as found in an edition of Lucius Osgood's *Reader,* fully titled *Osgood's Progressive Fifth Reader: Embracing A System of Instruction in the Principles of Elocution and Selections for Reading and Speaking from the Best English and American Authors* (1858). See *19th Century Schoolbooks,* <http://digital. library.pitt.edu/>.

103. The *Portland Transcript* article was reprinted in the June 15, 1855, edition of *FDP.*

104. "Mrs. Stowe's Drama," *Liberator,* December 14, 1855.

105. Clark, "Solo Black Performance," 348.

106. Majors, *Noted Negro Women,* 113.

107. *Christian Recorder,* December 27, 1862.

108. Brewer, *Pleasures of the Imagination,* 187.

109. Brewer, *Pleasures of the Imagination,* 169.

110. L[ucy] N. C[oleman], "Dramatic Reading," *Douglass Monthly,* January 1863.

111. "The Abolition of Slavery in Maryland," *Liberator,* December 9, 1864.

112. Donawerth, "Introduction," xxvii.

113. Conquergood, "Rethinking Elocution," 147.

114. Harper, *Iola Leroy,* 7–8.

115. "Fox and Pit[t]," *Provincial Freeman,* September 16, 1854.

116. Hutton, *Early Black Press,* 133. In a chapter titled "Youth: The Ultimate Outsiders," Hutton offers examples of the ways in which the black press provided educational advice to children and their parents, including fables and anecdotes for moral development.

117. "Emigration," *Provincial Freeman,* April 26, 2006.

118. Murray, *Come, Bright Improvement!,* 72; "Dumas Literary Society," *Provincial Freeman,* April 12, 1856.

119. "Letter from Canada West," *Christian Recorder,* January 7, 1865.

120. "Two Washington Artists," *New York Age,* December 7, 1889, 1. See also Abbott and Seroff, *Out of Sight.*

121. For a well-reasoned contemporaneous argument opposing Kossuth's refusal to support the abolitionist cause, see "Kossuth in Faneuil Hall," *FDP,* June 17, 1852, a reprint from the *Nantucket Mirror.* The writer made the point that in speaking out against slavery, Kossuth would have been an even more effective orator; further, it would have cost him nothing, and it could have advanced his own crusade for Hungarian reform.

122. "Kossuth at Washington." *FDP,* January 15, 1852.

123. Morris, "William Watkins," 7.

124. J. H. A. Johnson, "William Watkins," 11–12. The reference here is probably to Samuel Kirkham's *English Grammar in Familiar Lessons,* a popular nineteenth-century textbook.

125. "Speech of Wm. James Watkins," *FDP,* August 18, 1854.

126. Both Burns and Pembroke were fugitive slaves who had escaped to Boston and New York earlier in 1854. Burns's highly publicized Boston trial called needed attention to the consequences of the Fugitive Slave Law. Pembroke, brother of the Reverend James Pennington, was eventually "purchased" and settled in New York. From *Silvae Rhetorica: The Forest of Rhetoric* comes this definition of *sermocinatio:* "Speaking dramatically in the first person for someone else, assigning language that would be appropriate for that person's character (and for one's rhetorical purpose)," <http://humanities.byu.edu/rhetoric/silva.htm>. Frances Watkins Harper, William Watkins's cousin, employed this same figure in an 1858 New York address. In this instance, it is the slave mother who is given voice: "That army [of the enslaved] raise their manacled hands, they lift their imploring eyes, they point to men in this republic, and say, 'You are the cause!' Amid the din of conflicting interests, the cries of 'Lecompton' and 'anti-Lecompton,' I hear the shrieks of the slave-mother, as her child is torn from her bosom and sold to the highest bidder. Amid your declamations about liberty, your Fourth of July speeches, amid the darkness of the Dred Scott decision, I see the mournful light that flashes from the eye of the fugitive as he steps cautiously through your boasted Republic, to gain his personal freedom in a Monarchical land" ("Speech of Miss Frances Ellen Watkins," *National Anti-Slavery Standard,* May 28, 1858).

127. Wm. J. Watkins, "West India Emancipation Address Delivered on the First of August," *FDP*, August 10, 1855.

128. Reprinted in the *Provincial Freeman*, July 11, 1857.

129. "Lecture on the Mission of the War," *Christian Recorder*, May 21, 1864.

130. "Another Mrs. Frances E. W. Harper," *Christian Recorder*, September 15, 1866. Also from Philadelphia, Anna Dickinson was a popular Quaker speaker who at 19 received help from William Lloyd Garrison to launch her career as a woman's rights activist, abolitionist, and political campaigner. One review suggests that the early attraction was, as in Harper's case, "more from the novelty of hearing a woman lecture than from any other reason" ("Lecture of Miss Anna E. Dickinson," *Liberator*, April 18, 1862). She addressed Congress in 1863, but little was heard from her after the war. Frequently, during the nineteenth century, when the practice of comparing a relative newcomer to an established person within a field—a variation on the rhetorical figure *epitheton*—was applied to African Americans, they became the black version of some white performer. Thus elocutionist Mary Webb was called the "Black Siddons"; singer Elizabeth Taylor Greenfield, often compared Jenny Lind, was the "Black Swan"; Sissieretta Jones was called the "Black Patti" and compared to Italian singer Adelina Patti. The practice frequently resulted in a benevolent manifestation of W. E. B. Du Bois's double consciousness of being measured by the "tape" of dominant culture (*Souls of Black Folk*, 45). See also Peterson's reading of the reviews of nineteenth-century black women that reveal a tension between received views of blacks and the contradicting display of ability with which they were presented (*"Doers of the Word,"* 122–23).

131. "Harvest Home at Princeton, NJ," *Christian Recorder*, September 15, 1866.

132. "Lecture of Miss Anna E. Dickinson," *Liberator*, April 18, 1862.

133. "An Eloquent Plea," *Indianapolis Freeman*, August 18, 1894.

134. Gere, "Kitchen Tables and Rented Rooms."

135. Houppert, "Finding Their Voices," 29.

Bibliography

Abbott, Lynn, and Doug Seroff. *Out of Sight: The Rise of African American Popular Music, 1889–1895*. Jackson: University Press of Mississippi, 2003.

Allen, William G. *The American Prejudice Against Color. An Authentic Narrative, Showing How Easily the Nation Got into an Uproar. By William G. Allen, a Refugee from American Despotism, 1853*. Rpt. in Elbert, *American Prejudice against Color*, 35–92.

———. "Orators and Oratory." Rpt. in Foner and Barnham, *Lift Every Voice*, 229–46.

———. *A Short Personal Narrative, by William G. Allen (Colored American)*. Dublin, 1860. Rpt. in Elbert, *American Prejudice against Color*, 93–119.

Anderson, Benedict. *Imagined Communities: Reflections on the Origin and Spread of Nationalism*. London: Verso, 1991.

Anderson, James D. *The Education of Blacks in the South, 1860–1935*. Chapel Hill: University of North Carolina Press, 1988.

Andrews, William L. "Frederick Douglass, Preacher." *American Literature* 54.4 (December 1982): 592–97.

Aptheker, Herbert. "The Negro in the Union Navy." *Journal of Negro History* 32 (April 1947): 169–200.

Aristotle. *The Rhetoric and the Poetics*. New York: Modern Library, 1984.

Augustine. *On Christian Doctrine* (Book IV). In *The Rhetorical Tradition: Readings from Classical Times to the Present*, ed. Patricia Bizzell and Bruce Herzberg. 2nd ed. Boston: Bedford/St. Martin's, 2001. 456–85.

Bacon, Jacqueline. *"Freedom's Journal": The First African-American Newspaper*. Lanham, Md.: Rowman and Littlefield, 2007.

Bacon, Jacqueline, and Glen McClish. "Reinventing the Master's Tools: Nineteenth-Century African-American Literary Societies of Philadelphia and Rhetorical Education." *Rhetoric Society Quarterly* 30 (Fall 2000): 19–47.

Bacote, Clarence A. "James Weldon Johnson and Atlanta University." *Phylon* 32.4 (1971): 333–43.

Baker, Webster B. *History of Rust College*. Greensboro, N.C.: privately printed, 1924.

Bennett, Paula. *Nineteenth-Century American Women Poets: An Anthology*. Boston: Blackwell, 1998.

———. *Poets in the Public Sphere: The Emancipatory Project of American Women's Poetry, 1800–1900.* Princeton: Princeton University Press, 2003.

Berlant, Lauren. *The Queen of America Goes to Washington City.* Durham: Duke University Press, 1997.

Berlin, Ira. *Many Thousands Gone: The First Two Centuries of Slavery in North America.* Cambridge: Belknap Press of Harvard University Press, 1998.

Berlin, Ira, Marc Favreau, and Steven F. Miller. *Remembering Slavery: African Americans Talk about Their Personal Experiences of Slavery and Emancipation.* New York: New Press, 1998.

Billington, Ray Allen, ed. "Introduction." *The Journal of Charlotte L. Forten.* New York: W. W. Norton, 1981. 7–41.

Bizzell, Patricia, and Bruce Herzberg, eds. *The Rhetorical Tradition: Readings from Classical Times to the Present.* 2nd ed. Boston: Bedford/St. Martin's, 2001.

Black, Edwin. "The Aesthetics of Rhetoric, American Style." In *Rhetoric and Political Culture in Nineteenth-Century America,* ed. Thomas W. Benson. East Lansing: Michigan State University Press, 1997. 1–14.

Blackett, R. J. M. *Thomas Morris Chester, Black Civil War Correspondent: His Dispatches from the Virginia Front.* Baton Rouge: Louisiana State University Press, 1989.

Blair, Hugh. *Lectures on Rhetoric and Belles Lettres.* Edited by Linda Ferreira-Buckley and S. Michael Halloran. Carbondale: Southern Illinois University Press, 2005.

Bode, Carl. *The American Lyceum: Town Meeting of the Mind.* New York: Oxford, 1956.

Brandt, Deborah. "Literacy." In Enos, *Encyclopedia of Rhetoric and Composition,* 392–94.

Brewer, John. *The Pleasures of the Imagination: English Culture in the Eighteenth Century.* New York: Farrar Straus Giroux, 1997.

Broaddus, Dorothy C. *Genteel Rhetoric: Writing High Culture in Nineteenth-Century Boston.* Columbia: University of South Carolina Press, 1999.

Brodhead, Richard, ed. "Introduction." *The Journals of Charles Chesnutt.* Durham: Duke University Press, 1993. 1–28.

Brooks, Time. *Lost Sounds: Blacks and the Birth of the Recording Industry 1890–1919.* Champaign: University of Illinois Press, 2004.

Brown, A[ntoinette] L[ouisa]. "Central College." *Frederick Douglass' Paper,* November 19, 1852, Rochester, New York.

Burke, Kenneth. *A Rhetoric of Motives.* Berkeley: University of California Press, 1969.

Campbell, Karlyn Kohrs. *Man Cannot Speak for Her.* New York: Greenwood Press, 1989.

Carretta, Vincent. *Equiano, the African: Biography of a Self-Made Man.* New York: Penguin, 2006.

Casteen, John T., III. "Letter to the University Community on Equal Opportunity in Admissions," September 30, 1999, University of Virginia. <http://www.virginia.edu/president/spch_admission99.html> (accessed October 15, 1999).

Channing, William E. *Self-Culture: An Address Introductory to the Franklin Lectures.* Boston: Dutton and Wentworth, 1838. Reprint, New York: Arno, 1969.

Chenery, William H. *The Fourteenth Regiment Rhode Island Heavy Artillery (Colored) in the War to Preserve the Union, 1861–1865.* Providence, R.I.: Snow and Farnham, 1898.

Chesnutt, Charles W. "The Advantages of a Well-Conducted Literary Society." In McElrath, Leitz, and Crisler, *Essays and Speeches,* 13–24.

———. "Joseph C. Price, Orator and Educator: An Appreciation." In McElrath, Leitz, and Crisler, *Essays and Speeches,* 554–65.

———. *The Journals of Charles Chesnutt.* Edited by Richard Brodhead. Durham: Duke University Press, 1993.

Clark, Gregory, and S. Michael Halloran, ed. "Introduction: Transformations of Public Discourse in Nineteenth-Century America." *Oratorical Culture in Nineteenth-Century America: Transformations in the Theory and Practice of Rhetoric.* Carbondale: Southern Illinois University Press, 1993. 1–26.

Clark, Susan. "Solo Black Performance before the Civil War: Mrs. Stowe, Mrs. Webb, and 'The Christian Slave.'" *New Theatre Quarterly* 13.52 (November 1997): 339–48.

Cmiel, Kenneth. *Democratic Eloquence: The Fight for Popular Speech in Nineteenth-Century America.* New York: William Morrow, 1990.

Conquergood, Dwight. "Rethinking Elocution: The Trope of the Talking Book and Other Figures of Speech." In *Opening Acts: Performance in/as Communication and Cultural Studies,* ed. Judith Hamera. Thousand Oaks, Calif.: Sage, 2005. 141–62.

Cook, John Francis. "Remarks." In Porter, *Early Negro Writing,* 241–48.

Cooper, Patricia A. *Once a Cigar Maker: Men, Women, and Work Culture in American Cigar Factories, 1900–1919.* Champaign: University of Illinois Press, 1987.

Coppin, Fanny Jackson. *Reminiscences of School Life, and Hints on Teaching.* 1913. *Documents of the Old South,* <http://docsouth.unc.edu/neh/jacksonc/jackson.html>.

Cornelius, Janet Duitsman. *Slave Missions and the Black Church in the Antebellum South.* Columbia: University of South Carolina Press, 1999.

Costen, Melva Wilson. *African American Christian Worship.* 2nd ed. Nashville: Abingdon Press, 2007.

Crummell, Alexander. "The Social Principle among a People and Its Bearing on Their Progress and Development." In *Civilization and Black Progress: Selected Writings of Alexander Crummell on the South,* ed. J. R. Oldfield. Charlottesville: University Press of Virginia, 1995. 29–42.

Cushman, Claire. "Women Advocates before the Supreme Court." *Journal of Supreme Court History* 26.1 (March 2001): 67–88.

Daniel, Samuel. *Selections from the Poetical Works of Samuel Daniel.* Edited by John Morris. Bath, England: Charles Clark, 1855.

Dawson, Michael C. "A Black Counterpublic? Economic Earthquakes, Racial Agenda(s), and Black Politics." In *The Black Public Sphere: A Public Culture Book,* ed. The Black Public Sphere Collective. Chicago: University of Chicago Press, 1995. 199–227.

Donawerth, Jane. "Introduction." In Donawerth, *Rhetorical Theory by Women,* xiii–xlii.

———. "Nineteenth-Century United States Conduct Book Rhetoric by Women." *Rhetoric Review* 21.1 (2002): 5–21.

———, ed. *Rhetorical Theory by Women before 1900: An Anthology.* Lanham, Md.: Rowman and Littlefield, 2002.

———. "Textbooks for New Audiences: Women's Revisions of Rhetorical Theory at the Turn of the Century." In Wertheimer, *Listening to Their Voices,* 337–56.

Douglass, Frederick. *Life and Times of Frederick Douglass: Written by Himself.* 1892 rev. ed. New York: Macmillan, 1962.

———. *Narrative of the Life of Frederick Douglass, an American Slave Written by Himself.* 1845. New Haven: Yale University Press, 2001.

Du Bois, W. E. B. "The Damnation of Women." In *Darkwater: Voices from within the Veil.* 1920. Millwood, NY: Kraus-Thomson Organization, 1975. 163–86.

———. *Dusk of Dawn: An Essay toward an Autobiography of a Race Concept.* 1940. New York: Schocken Books, 1968.

———. *The Philadelphia Negro.* 1899. Millwood, N.Y.: Kraus-Thomson, 1994.

———. *The Souls of Black Folk.* 1903. New York: Penguin, 1969.

Edwards, Ishmell Hendrex. "History of Rust College 1866–1967." Ph.D. diss., University of Mississippi, 1993.

Elbert, Sarah, ed. *The American Prejudice against Color: William G. Allen, Mary King, Louisa May Alcott.* Boston: Northeastern University Press, 2002.

———. "Introduction." In Elbert, *American Prejudice against Color,* 1–34.

Eldred, Janet Carey, and Peter Mortensen. *Imagining Rhetoric: Composing Women of the Early United States.* Pittsburgh: University of Pittsburgh Press, 2002.

Ellison, Ralph. *Invisible Man.* New York: New American Library, 1952.

Enos, Theresa, ed. *Encyclopedia of Rhetoric and Composition: Communication from Ancient Times to the Information Age.* New York: Garland, 1996.

Ernest, John. *Liberation Historiography: African American Writers and the Challenge of History, 1794–1861.* Chapel Hill: University of North Carolina Press, 2004.

Fahnestock, Jeanne, and Marie Secor. "Classical Rhetoric: The Art of Argumentation." In *Argument Revisited; Argument Redefined: Negotiating Meaning in the Composition Classroom,* ed. Barbara Emmel, Paula Resch, and Deborah Tenney. Thousand Oaks, Calif.: Sage, 1996. 97–123.

———. "The Stases in Scientific and Literary Argument." *Written Communication* 5.4 (October 1988): 427–43.

Federal Writers' Project. "Florida Slave Narratives: Lee, Randall." Exploring Florida, <http://fcit.usf.edu/FLORIDA/docs/s/slave/slave23.htm> (accessed October 12, 2007).

Ferreira-Buckley, Linda, and S. Michael Halloran. "Editors' Introduction." In Blair, *Lectures on Rhetoric and Belles Lettres,* xv–liv.

Fitzgerald, Michael W. *The Union League Movement in the Deep South: Political and Agricultural Change during Reconstruction.* Baton Rouge: Louisiana State University Press, 1989.

Fleetwood, Christian A. *Diary of Christian A. Fleetwood for 1864.* Holograph manuscript. American Memory. African American Odyssey, Library of Congress Manuscript Division, <http://memory.loc.gov/ammem/index.html>.

Foner, Eric. *A Short History of Reconstruction 1863–1877.* New York: Harper and Row, 1990.

Foner, Phillip, and Robert James Branham, eds. *Lift Every Voice: African American Oratory 1787–1900.* Tuscaloosa: University of Alabama Press, 1998.

Foreman, P. Gabrielle. "'Reading Aright': White Slavery, Black Referents, and the Strategy of Histotextuality in Iola Leroy." *Yale Journal of Criticism* 10 (Fall 1997): 327–54.

Fortune, T. Thomas. "Ida B. Wells, A.M." In *Women of Distinction: Remarkable in Works and Invincible in Character,* ed. L[awson] A. Scruggs. Raleigh, N.C.: privately printed, 1893. 33–39.

Foster, Frances Smith. "A Narrative of the Interesting Origins and (Somewhat) Surprising Developments of African-American Print Culture." *American Literary History* 17.4 (Winter 2005): 714–40.

Franklin, John Hope. *Reconstruction after the Civil War*. 2nd ed. Chicago: University of Chicago Press, 1994.

Franklin, Vincent P., and James D. Anderson, eds. *New Perspectives on Black Educational History*. Boston: G. K. Hall, 1978.

Frazier, S. Elizabeth. "Some Afro-American Women of Mark." *AME Church Review* 8 (1892): 373–86.

Garrison, William Lloyd. "Preface." In Douglass, *Narrative of the Life of Frederick Douglass*, 3–9.

Gere, Anne Ruggles. "Kitchen Tables and Rented Rooms: The Extracurriculum of Composition." *College Composition and Communication* 45 (1994): 75–92.

Glenn, Cheryl. "Rhetorical Education in America (A Broad Stroke Introduction)." In *Rhetorical Education in America*, ed. Cheryl Glenn, Margaret M. Lyday, and Wendy B. Sharer. Tuscaloosa: University of Alabama Press, 2004. vii–xvi.

———. *Rhetoric Retold : Regendering the Tradition from Antiquity through the Renaissance*. Carbondale : Southern Illinois University Press, 1997.

Gold, David. "Nothing Educates Us Like a Shock": The Integrated Rhetoric of Melvin B. Tolson." *College Composition and Communication* 55.2 (2003): 226–53.

Greenbaum, Susan D. *More Than Black: Afro-Cubans in Tampa*. Gainesville: University Press of Florida, 2002.

Griggs, Sutton. *Imperium in Imperio*. 1899. New York: The Modern Library, 2003.

Grimké, Charlotte Forten. *The Journals of Charlotte Forten Grimké*. Edited by Brenda Stevenson. New York: Oxford University Press, 1988.

Hamilton, William. "Address to the New York African Society for Mutual Relief." In Porter, *Early Negro Writing*, 33–41.

Hamilton, William Baskerville. *Holly Springs, Mississippi, to the Year 1878*. Holly Springs, Miss.: Marshall County Historical Society, 1984.

Harper, Frances E. W. "Enlightened Motherhood." In *A Brighter Coming Day: A Frances Ellen Watkins Harper Reader*, ed. Frances Smith Foster. New York: Feminist Press, 1990. 285–92.

———. *Iola Leroy or Shadows Uplifted*. New York: Oxford Press, 1988.

Harris, Elizabeth Johnson. "Life Story, 1867–1923." African-American Women, Digital Scriptorium Projects, Duke University Rare Book, Manuscript, and Special Collections Library, <http://scriptorium.lib.duke.edu/harris/harris-indx.html>.

Heath, Shirley Brice. *Ways with Words: Language, Life, and Work in Communities and Classrooms*. New York: Cambridge University Press, 1994.

Hermann, Janet Sharp. *The Pursuit of a Dream*. New York: Oxford, 1981.

Hill, James, ed. "General Introduction." *The Marcus Garvey and Universal Improvement Association Papers*. Los Angeles: University of California Press, 1983. xxxv–xc.

Historical Sketch of the Salem Lyceum: With a List of Officers and Lectures Since Its Formation in 1830. Salem: Press of the Salem Gazette, 1879.

Holmes, David. "Say What? Rediscovering Hugh Blair and the Racialization of Language, Culture, and Pedagogy in Eighteenth-Century Rhetoric." In *Calling Cards: Theory and Practice in Studies of Race, Gender, and Culture*, ed. Jacqueline Royster and Ann Marie Mann Simpkins. New York: State University of New York Press, 2005. 203–14.

hooks, bell. *Teaching to Transgress: Education as the Practice of Freedom.* New York: Routledge, 1994.

Hopkins, Pauline. *Contending Forces: A Romance Illustrative of Negro Life North and South.* New York: Oxford University Press, 1988.

Houppert, Karen. "Finding Their Voices." *Washington Post Magazine,* August 26 2007, 12–17, 25–29.

Hutton, Frankie. *The Early Black Press, 1827 to 1860.* Westport, Conn.: Greenwood, 1993.

Ione, Carole. *Pride of Family: Four Generations of American Women of Color.* New York: Summit Books, 1991.

Jacobs, Donald M. "William Lloyd Garrison's *Liberator* and Boston's Blacks, 1830–1865." *New England Quarterly* 44.2 (June 1971): 259–77.

Jarratt, Susan C. "Race and Space: The Disposition of 'Classics' in Late Nineteenth-Century University Black Intellectual Life." Unpublished manuscript.

Johnson, D. J. *The Preacher: Special talks to Students of Payne Theological Seminary, Containing Valuable Suggestions to those Seeking Self-improvement as Ministers.* 1894. American Memory. African American Perspectives: Pamphlets from the Daniel A. P. Murray Collection, 1818–1907, <http://memory.loc.gov/cgibin/query/D?murray:5./temp/temp/~ammem_nBnd::> (accessed October 8, 2003).

Johnson, James H. A. "Female Preachers." *AME Church Review* 1 (1884): 102–5.

———. "William Watkins." *AME Church Review* 3 (1886–87): 11–12.

Johnson, James Weldon. *Along This Way: The Autobiography of James Weldon Johnson.* 1933. New York: Viking Press, 1961.

———. *The Autobiography of an Ex-Coloured Man.* 1927. New York: Vintage Books, 1989.

Johnson, Nan. *Gender and Rhetorical Space in American Life, 1866–1910.* Carbondale: Southern Illinois University Press, 2002.

———. *Nineteenth-Century Rhetoric in North America.* Carbondale: Southern Illinois University Press, 1991.

———. "The Popularization of Nineteenth-Century Rhetoric: Elocution and the Private Learner." In *Oratorical Culture in Nineteenth-Century America: Transformations in the Theory and Practice of Rhetoric,* ed. Gregory Clark and S. Michael Halloran. Carbondale: Southern Illinois University Press, 1993. 139–57.

Joyner, Charles. *Down by the Riverside: A South Carolina Slave Community.* Champaign: University of Illinois Press, 1984.

Kates, Susan. "Literacy, Voting Rights, and the Citizenship Schools in the South, 1957–1970." *College Composition and Communication* 57.3 (2006): 479–502.

Kett, Joseph F. *The Pursuit of Knowledge under Difficulties: From Self-Improvement to Adult Education in America, 1750–1990.* Stanford: Stanford University Press, 1994.

Lampe, Gregory P. *Frederick Douglass: Freedom's Voice, 1818–1845.* East Lansing: Michigan State University Press, 1998.

Lemert, Charles, and Esme Bhan. *The Voice of Anna Julia Cooper.* Lanham, Md.: Rowman and Littlefield, 1998.

"Le Moyne Normal School." *American Missionary* 32.4 (April 1878): 114.

Levine, Robert S. *Martin Delany, Frederick Douglass and the Politics of Representative Identity.* Chapel Hill: University of North Carolina Press, 1997.

Levy, Eugene. *James Weldon Johnson: Black Leader, Black Voice.* Chicago: University of Chicago Press, 1973.

Lindhorst, Marie. "Politics in a Box: Sarah Mapps Douglass and the Female Literary Association, 1831–1833." *Pennsylvania History* 65.3 (Summer 1998): 263–78.

Little, Monroe H. "The Extra-Curricular Activities of Black College Students, 1868–1940." *Journal of African-American History* 87 (Winter 2002): 43–55.

Logan, Enid. "Conspirators, Pawns, Patriots and Brothers: Race and Politics in Western Cuba, 1906–1909." *Political Power and Social Theory* 14 (2000): 3–51.

Logan, Shirley Wilson. *"We Are Coming": The Persuasive Discourse of Nineteenth-Century Black Women.* Carbondale: Southern Illinois University Press, 1999.

———. "'When and Where I Enter': Race, Gender, and Composition Studies." In *In Other Words: Feminism and Composition,* ed. Susan C. Jarratt and Lynn Worsham. New York: Modern Language Association, 1998. 45–57.

———, ed. *With Pen and Voice: A Critical Anthology of Nineteenth-Century African-American Women.* Carbondale: Southern Illinois University Press, 1995.

Long, Lisa A. "Charlotte Forten's Civil War Journals and the Quest for 'Genius, Beauty, and Deathless Fame.'" *Legacy* 16.1 (1999): 37–48.

Lunsford, Andrea, ed. *Reclaiming Rhetorica: Women in the Rhetorical Tradition.* Pittsburgh: University of Pittsburgh Press, 1995.

Majors, Monroe A. *Noted Negro Women: Their Triumphs and Activities.* Chicago: Donohue and Henneberry, 1893.

Matory, James Lorand. "Religions, African and Afro-Caribbean, in the United States." Africana.com, <www.Africana.com/Articles/tt496.htm> (accessed June 2001).

McAfee, Ward M. *Religion, Race, and Reconstruction: The Public School in the Politics of the 1870s.* Albany: State University of New York Press, 1998.

McCarthy, Molly. "A Pocketful of Days: Pocket Dairies and Daily Record Keeping among Nineteenth-Century New England Women." *New England Quarterly* 73.2 (June 2000): 274–96.

McClish, Glen. "William G. Allen's 'Orators and Oratory': Inventional Amalgamation, Pathos, and the Characterization of Violence in African-American Abolitionist Rhetoric." *Rhetoric Society Quarterly* 35.1 (Winter 2005): 47–72.

McCrorey, Henry Lawrence. "A Brief History of Johnson C. Smith University." *Quarterly Review of Higher Education among Negroes* 1 (July 1933): 29–36.

McElrath, Joseph, Robert Leitz, and Jesse Crisler, eds. *Essays and Speeches.* Stanford: Stanford University Press, 1999.

McHenry, Elizabeth. *Forgotten Readers: Recovering the Lost History of African American Literary Societies.* Durham: Duke University Press, 2002.

———. "Rereading Literary Legacy: New Considerations of the 19th-Century African-American Reader and Writer." *Callaloo* 22.2 (1999): 477–82.

McMurry, Linda O. *To Keep the Waters Troubled: The Life of Ida B. Wells.* New York: Oxford, 1998.

Mirabal, Nancy Raquel. "Telling Silences and Making Community: Afro-Cubans and African-Americans in Ybor City 1899–1915." In *Between Race and Empire: African-Americans and Cubans before the Cuban Revolution,* ed. Lisa Brock and Digna Castañeda Fuertes. Philadelphia: Temple University Press, 1998. 49–69.

Mitchell, Michelle. *Righteous Propagation: African Americans and the Politics of Racial Destiny after Reconstruction.* Chapel Hill: University of North Carolina Press, 2004.

Montgomery Family Papers. Library of Congress Manuscript Division, Washington, D.C.

Montgomery, Isaiah. "Isaiah T. Montgomery Tells His Own Story." Isaiah Montgomery Subject File, Mississippi Department of History and Archives, <http://www.angelfire.com/folk/gljmr/MontgomeryI.html> (accessed October 2003).

Montgomery, Mary Virginia. Diary manuscripts. In Sterling, *We Are Your Sisters*, 462–72.

Morris, William H. "William Watkins." *AME Church Review* 3 (1886–87): 7.

Moss, Alfred. *The American Negro Academy: Voice of the Talented Tenth*. Baton Rouge: Louisiana State University Press, 1981.

Moss, Beverly J. "A Literacy Event in African American Churches: The Sermon as a Community Text." In *Ethnolinguistic Chicago: Language and Literacy in the City's Neighborhoods*, ed. Marcia Farr. Mahwah, N.J.: Lawrence Erlbaum, 2004. 137–59.

Murray, Heather. *Come, Bright Improvement! The Literary Societies of Nineteenth-Century Ontario*. Toronto: University of Toronto Press, 2002.

National Archives. "The Fight for Equal Rights: Black Soldiers in the Civil War." <http://www.archives.gov/education/lessons/blacks-civil-war/>.

Nell, William C. *The Colored Patriots of the American Revolution, with Sketches of Several Distinguished Colored Persons*. Boston: Wallcut, 1855.

Northrop, Henry Davenport, Joseph R. Gay, and I. Garland Penn. *The College of Life; or, Practical Self-Educator, a Manual of Self-Improvement for the Colored Race*. 1890. Washington, D.C.: National, 1902.

Nunley, Vorris L. "From the Harbor to Da Academic Hood: Hush Harbors and an African American Rhetorical Tradition." In *African American Rhetoric(s): Interdisciplinary Perspectives*, ed. Elaine B. Richardson and Ronald L. Jackson II. Carbondale: Southern Illinois University Press, 2004. 221–41.

O'Meally, Robert. "Slavery's Shadow." Review of *Our Nig*, by Harriet Wilson. *Callaloo* 20 (Winter 1984): 157–58.

Painter, Nell. "Representing Truth: Sojourner Truth's Knowing and Becoming Known." *Journal of American History* 81.2 (September 1994): 461–92.

Perelman, Chaim, and L. Olbrechts-Tyteca. *The New Rhetoric: A Treatise on Argumentation*. Translated by John Wilkinson and Purcell Weaver. Notre Dame: University of Notre Dame Press, 1969.

Perez, Louis A. *On Becoming Cuban: Identity, Nationality, and Culture*. Chapel Hill: University of North Carolina Press, 1999.

Perkins, Linda Marie. "Quaker Beneficence and Black Control: The Institute for Colored Youth 1852–1903." In Franklin and Anderson, *New Perspectives on Black Educational History*, 19–43.

Peterson, Carla L. *"Doers of the Word": African-American Women Speakers and Writers in the North*. New York: Oxford, 1995.

Phillips, Christopher. *Freedom's Port: The African-American Community of Baltimore, 1790–1860*. Champaign: University of Illinois Press, 1997.

Piersen, William D. *Black Yankees: The Development of an Afro-American Subculture in Eighteenth-Century New England*. Amherst: University of Massachusetts Press, 1988.

Porter, Dorothy, ed. *Early Negro Writing 1760–1837*. 1971. Baltimore: Black Classic Press, 1995.

———. "The Organized Educational Activities of Negro Literary Societies, 1828–1846." *Journal of Negro Education* 5.4 (October 1936): 555–76.

Powell, E[dward] P[ayson]. "The Rise and Decline of the New England Lyceum." *New England Magazine* 17.6 (February 1895): 730–37.

Proper, David R. "Lucy Terry Prince: 'Singer of History.'" *Contributions in Black Studies* 9 (1990–92): 187–214.

Quarles, Benjamin. *Black Abolitionists*. New York: Oxford, 1970.

Quillin, Frank. *The Color Line in Ohio: A History of Race Prejudice in a Typical Northern State*. Ann Arbor, Mich.: George Wahr, 1913.

Raboteau, Albert J. *Slave Religion: The "Invisible Institution" in the Antebellum South*. New York: Oxford, 1980.

Ransom, Reverdy C. "Deborah and Jael: Sermon to the I.B.W. Woman's Club," June 6, 1897, MS 85-6, Reverdy C. Ransom Collection. National Afro-American Museum and Cultural Center, Wilberforce, Ohio.

Ray, Angela G. *The Lyceum and Public Culture in the Nineteenth-Century United States*. East Lansing: Michigan State University Press, 2005.

Reynolds, David S. *Walt Whitman's America: A Cultural Biography*. New York: Alfred A. Knopf, 1995.

Rhodes, Jane. *Mary Ann Shadd Cary: The Black Press and Protest in the Nineteenth Century*. Bloomington: Indiana University Press, 1998.

Ripley, C. Peter, ed. *The Black Abolitionist Papers*. 5 vols. Chapel Hill: University of North Carolina Press, 1985–92.

Rollin, Frances. Diary manuscripts. In Sterling, *We Are Your Sisters*, 453–61.

Rose, Jane E. "Conduct Books for Women, 1830–1860: A Rationale for Women's Conduct and Domestic Role in America." In Wertheimer, *Listening to Their Voices*, 37–58.

Royer, Daniel J. "The Process of Literacy as Communal Involvement in the Narratives of Frederick Douglass." *African American Review* 28.3 (Autumn 1994): 363–74.

Royster, Jacqueline Jones. *Traces of a Stream: Literacy and Social Change among African American Women*. Pittsburgh: University of Pittsburgh Press, 2000.

Royster, Jacqueline Jones, and Jean C. Williams. "History in the Spaces Left: African American Presence and Narratives of Composition Studies." *College Composition and Communication* 50.4 (1999): 563–84.

Ryan, Mary P. *Civic Wars: Democracy and Public Life in the American City during the Nineteenth Century*. Berkeley: University of California Press, 1997.

Salzmann, Katharine. "Guide to Resources on Women in the Processed Manuscript Collections of the Moorland-Spingarn Research Center." Moorland-Spingarn Research Center, Howard University, <http://www.founders.howard.edu/moorland-spingarn/Wom.htm> (accessed May 17, 2004).

Savona, David. "The Son of Montecristo: Peripatetic Benjamin Menendez Has Left His Imprint on Nearly Every Cigar-Making Country." *Cigar Aficionado*, March/April 2002, <http://www.cigaraficionado.com/Cigar/CA_Profiles/Cigar_Stars_Profile/0,2547,155,00.html> (accessed February 8, 2007).

Schneider, Stephen. "Freedom Schooling: Stokely Carmichael and Critical Rhetorical Education." *College Composition and Communication* 58.1 (2006): 46–69.

Sernett, Milton C. *Abolition's Axe: Beriah Green, Oneida Institute, and the Black Freedom Struggle*. New York: Syracuse University Press, 1986.

Shortell, Timothy. "The Rhetoric of Black Abolitionism: An Exploratory Analysis of Antislavery Newspapers in New York State." *Social Science History* 28.1 (Spring 2004): 75–109.

Sidbury, James. "Reading, Revelation, and Rebellion: The Textual Communities of Gabriel, Denmark Vesey, and Nat Turner." In *Nat Turner: A Slave Rebellion in History and Memory*, ed. Kenneth S. Greenberg. New York: Oxford University Press, 2003. 119–33.

Simmons, William J. *Men of Mark: Eminent, Progressive and Rising*. Cleveland, Ohio: Geo. M. Rewell, 1887.

Sjöblad, Christina. "From Family Notes to Diary: The Development of a Genre." *Eighteenth-Century Studies* 31.4 (1998): 517–21.

Smith, Amanda. *An Autobiography: The Story of the Lord's Dealings with Mrs. Amanda Smith, the Colored Evangelist*. Chicago: Meyer and Brothers, 1893.

Smith, Gerrit. "Central College of New York." Reprinted in Elbert, *American Prejudice against Color*, 15.

"Speech Acts." In Enos, *Encyclopedia of Rhetoric and Composition*, 690–91.

Spivak, Gayatri. "Can the Subaltern Speak?" In *Marxism and the Interpretation of Culture*, ed. Cary Nelson and Lawrence Grossberg. Champaign: University of Illinois Press, 1987. 271–313.

Stearns, Charles. *The Black Man of the South, and the Rebels; Or, The Characteristics Of The Former, And The Recent Outrages Of The Latter*. New York: American News Company, 1872.

Stepto, Robert B. *From Behind the Veil: A Study of Afro-American Narrative*. Champaign: University of Illinois Press, 1979.

Sterling, Dorothy. *We Are Your Sisters: Black Women in the Nineteenth Century*. New York: Norton, 1984.

Steward, Austin. "Address of the New York State Convention of Colored Citizens, to the People of the State." In *Jim Crow New York: A Documentary History of Race and Citizenship 1777–1877*, ed. David N. Gellman and David Quigley. New York: New York University Press, 2003. 237–48.

Still, William. *The Underground Rail Road*. Philadelphia: Porter and Coates, 1872.

Stuckey, Sterling. *Slave Culture: Nationalist Theory and the Foundations of Black America*. New York: Oxford, 1987.

Swan, Robert. "John Teasman: African-American Educator and the Emergence of Community in Early Black New York City, 1787–1815." *Journal of the Early Republic* 12.3 (Autumn 1992): 331–56.

Swisshelm, Jane Grey. *Crusader and Feminist: Letters of Jane Grey Swisshelm*. Edited by Arthur Larsen. St. Paul: Minnesota Historical Society, 1934.

Tate, Claudia. *Domestic Allegories of Political Desire: The Black Heroine's Text at the Turn of the Century*. New York: Oxford University Press, 1992.

Taylor, Clarence. *The Black Churches of Brooklyn*. New York: Columbia University Press, 1994.

Terborg-Penn, Rosalyn. *African American Women in the Struggle for the Vote, 1850–1920*. Bloomington: Indiana University Press, 1998.

Terrell, Mary Church. *A Colored Woman in a White World*. 1940. Amherst, N.Y.: Humanity Books, 2005.

Ullman, Victor. *Martin R. Delany: The Beginnings of Black Nationalism*. Boston: Beacon Press, 1971.

Ward, Samuel Ringgold. *Autobiography of a Fugitive Negro: His Anti-Slavery Labours in the United States, Canada, and England*. 1855. New York: Arno Press, 1968.

Washington, Mary Helen. Foreword to *The Memphis Diary of Ida B. Wells.* Edited by Miriam DeCosta-Willis. Boston: Beacon, 1995. ix–xvii.

Watkins, William. *The White Architects of Black Education: Ideology and Power in America, 1865–1954.* New York: Teachers College Press, 2001.

Webb, Frank J. *The Garies and Their Friends.* 1857. New York: Arno Press, 1969.

Webster, Daniel. "Adams and Jefferson." In *Daniel Webster, "The Completest Man,"* ed. Kenneth E. Shewmaker. Hanover: University Press of New England, 1990. 104–13.

Wells, Ida B. *Crusade for Justice: The Autobiography of Ida B. Wells.* Edited by Alfreda M. Duster. Chicago: University of Chicago Press, 1970.

———. "Lynch Law in All Its Phases." In Logan, *With Pen and Voice,* 80–99.

———. *The Memphis Diary of Ida B. Wells.* Edited by Miriam DeCosta-Willis. Boston: Beacon, 1995.

Wells, Ida B., Frederick Douglass, I. Garland Penn, and Ferdinand Barnett. *The Reason Why the Colored American is Not in the World's Columbian Exposition.* 1893. Edited by Robert W. Rydell. Champaign: University of Illinois Press, 1999.

Wertheimer, Molly Meijer, ed. *Listening to Their Voices: The Rhetorical Activities of Historical Women.* Columbia: University of South Carolina Press, 1997.

Wheatley, Phillis. From *Poems on Various Subjects, Religious and Moral.* In *Norton Anthology of African American Literature,* ed. Henry Louis Gates and Nellie Y. McKay. 2nd ed. New York: W.W. Norton, 2004. 213–26.

Whipper, William. "Address Delivered before the Colored Reading Society of Philadelphia, for Mental Improvement." In Porter, *Early Negro Writing,* 105–19.

Wilson, Joseph T. *The Black Phalanx: African American Soldiers in the War of Independence, the War of 1812, and the Civil War.* 1890. New York: Da Capo Press, 1994.

Wilson, Keith P. *Campfires of Freedom: The Camp Life of Black Soldiers during the Civil War.* Kent, Ohio: Kent State University Press, 2002.

Winch, Julie. "'You Have Talents—Only Cultivate Them': Philadelphia's Black Female Literary Societies and the Abolitionist Crusade." In *The Abolitionist Sisterhood: Women's Political Culture in Antebellum America,* ed. Jean Fagan Yellin and John C. Van Horne. Ithaca: Cornell University Press, 1994. 101–18.

Woodson, Carter G. *The Mis-education of the Negro.* New York: AMS Press, 1977.

Zaluda, Scott. "Lost Voices of the Harlem Renaissance: Writing Assigned at Howard University, 1919–31." *College Composition and Communication* 50.2 (1998): 232–57.

Zappen, James P. "Bacon, Francis (1561–1626)." In Enos, *Encyclopedia of Rhetoric and Composition,* 61–63.

Index

Shirley Wilson Logan is a professor of English at the University of Maryland, where she teaches courses in the history and practice of rhetoric and composition with an emphasis on nineteenth-century African American texts. Her publications include *With Pen and Voice: A Critical Anthology of Nineteenth-Century African-American Women* (1995), *"We Are Coming": The Persuasive Discourse of Nineteenth-Century Black Women* (1999), and essays in various collections.